The Abingdon Preaching Annual 2022

The Abingdon
Preaching
Annual

2022

Planning Sermons
for Fifty-Two Sundays

Charley Reeb, General Editor

Abingdon Press™

Nashville

THE ABINGDON PREACHING ANNUAL 2022:
PLANNING SERMONS FOR FIFTY-TWO SUNDAYS

Copyright © 2021 by Abingdon Press

ISBN: 978-1-7910-10683

Scripture quotations unless noted otherwise are from the Common English Bible. Copyright © 2011 by the Common English Bible. All rights reserved. Used by permission. www.CommonEnglishBible.com.

Scripture quotations marked (NIV) are taken from the Holy Bible, New International Version®, NIV®. Copyright © 1973, 1978, 1984, 2011 by Biblica, Inc.™ Used by permission of Zondervan. All rights reserved worldwide. www.zondervan.com The "NIV" and "New International Version" are trademarks registered in the United States Patent and Trademark Office by Biblica, Inc.™

Scripture quotations marked (NRSV) are taken from the New Revised Standard Version of the Bible, copyright 1989, Division of Christian Education of the National Council of the Churches of Christ in the United States of America. Used by permission. All rights reserved.

Scripture quotations marked (KJV) are from The Authorized (King James) Version. Rights in the Authorized Version in the United Kingdom are vested in the Crown. Reproduced by permission of the Crown's patentee, Cambridge University Press.

Scripture quotations marked (RSV) are from the Revised Standard Version of the Bible, copyright © 1946, 1952, and 1971 National Council of the Churches of Christ in the United States of America. Used by permission. All rights reserved worldwide. http://nrsvbibles.org/

The excerpt starting on page 168, "The Working Gospel and the Bridge Paradigm," was taken from Frank Thomas, *Surviving a Dangerous Sermon* (Nashville: Abingdon Press, 2020).

The excerpt starting on page 174, "We Preach the Gospel," was taken from George Buttrick, *George Buttrick's Guide to Preaching the Gospel*, edited by Charles N. Davidson Jr. (Nashville: Abingdon Press, 2020).

The excerpt starting on page 180, "Christ: *Deus Dixit*," was taken from Will Willimon, *Preachers Dare* (Nashville: Abingdon Press, 2020).

21 22 23 24 25 26 27 28 29 30—10 9 8 7 6 5 4 3 2 1
MANUFACTURED IN THE UNITED STATES OF AMERICA

Contents

🌿 = *Sunday in Lent*   ◉ = *Sunday of Advent*

ESSAYS FOR SKILL BUILDING

Preface

There are very few vocations that require an insightful and inspiring public address on a regular basis, but parish ministry is certainly one of them. Most parishioners will never know the amount of time and emotional energy needed to preach on a regular basis. "Don't you just get up and talk?" It's also difficult for most laypeople to appreciate the spiritual discipline, creativity, and resourcefulness necessary to offer fresh bread weekly from the pulpit. After all, choirs and praise bands can repeat songs and anthems and liturgists can rely on books of worship. But congregations don't take too kindly to being served leftovers from the pulpit. Preachers, it would seem, are only as good as their last sermon.

I believe this year's edition of *The Abingdon Preaching Annual* will be a useful resource for you as you seek to serve fresh bread to your congregations. I offer this helpful book to you as one who preaches weekly in the trenches of the local church and knows how quickly the well can run dry. I am certain you will find ideas, insights, and illustrations that will lessen the toil of "working up" a sermon each week. My goal as general editor was to acquire commentaries that aided preachers in the practical work of sermon preparation. One can only ruminate for so long on the meaning of a biblical text. Weekly worship is always rapidly approaching and the preacher must land on something to say that is clear, rousing, and relevant. The gifted contributors to this Annual will be reliable guides as you seek to be faithful to the sacred task of preaching.

I am grateful to Connie Stella and her gifted team at Abingdon Press. Putting together this resource takes many capable hands, and they have succeeded yet again.

Charley Reeb
General Editor

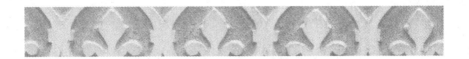

January 2, 2022–Second Sunday after Christmas Day

Jeremiah 31:7-14; Psalm 147:12-20; Ephesians 1:3-14;
John 1:(1-9), 10-18

Will Wold

Preacher to Preacher Prayer

Emmanuel, God with us, may you inspire us through this Christmas season to see where you are interacting in the world. Help us, this season and every season of our lives, to see where the Word becomes flesh. Might these moments inspire the words that we preach and speak to our communities. Amen.

Commentary

Well preacher, you made it. You survived. Advent is officially in the books. The Christmas musicals have been performed. The children have been corralled and dressed up like shepherds and donkeys. The Christmas Eve sermon has been preached and candles have been lifted. Take a deep breath.

Yet, liturgically, we are still in the Christmas season. All of your creative Christmas ideas have been preached, but we continue to celebrate the birth of Christ. What can we say about Jesus's birth that we have not said already?

We arrive at the Gospel of John's first chapter, the prologue. The prologue is a beautiful poem about the Word becoming flesh and making a home among us. There is so much content in this passage that the text almost preaches itself. So, before you, the preacher, read any more of this commentary, read the scripture slowly to yourself. As you read, make notes of what sticks out. Highlight words or phrases that resonate within your heart. Write in the margins what the Spirit is speaking to you. Do that before you move on to the rest of the commentary.

John 1:1-18 is full of images, wordplay, and metaphors. As you are moving from your own notes to crafting a sermon, try not to capture everything at once. If you do, it would be like trying to eat a pound of fudge in one sitting. It is too rich and will overwhelm you and your congregation. Pick one path or image and move deep into that idea. Let the Spirit guide your sermon art to be precise and focused. If you do that, the congregation will be grateful for the morsel you are providing them.

The birth of Christ in the Gospel of John is uniquely different from the other two Gospel birth narratives found in Matthew and Luke. John is not a narrative with shepherds or magi, rather, it is a poem expressing Christ being with God in the beginning.

The Gospel of Matthew begins with the genealogy of Jesus starting with Abraham. Then the author narrates Joseph's experience with the Holy Spirit, the birth of Jesus, King Herod's trouble with the newborn king, and the magi visiting Jesus. In Matthew, the story is locked within that particular time and space—a time where Herod is king and Rome is the dominant empire. There is a temporal understanding of Jesus's birth.

A similar scenario occurs in the Gospel of Luke. Luke narrates the birth of John the Baptist, Mary visiting Elizabeth, Jesus being born when Quirinius governed Syria, and the shepherds visiting Jesus. Again, the birth story of Jesus is locked in the time and space of the world. Luke provides us with a birth story that is found in a particular time period.

The Gospel of John illustrates the birth of Jesus unusually. Instead of a narrative of Jesus being born, John writes of Jesus Christ as the "Word" and being with God in the beginning. John explicitly recognizes Jesus is outside of time and space, but instead was with God when nothing existed. On one hand, this is an artistic expression linking Jesus to Genesis 1. On the other hand, it is a theological expression to have Jesus exist within time and outside of time. The proclamation of John is that Jesus was with God before any existence. Jesus and God are interconnected as the same entity. Jesus is not chained to a temporal understanding, but exists outside of understood time.

Now what this means for the preacher is that the particularities of John illustrate that Christmas is not found only within the month of December. Churches can celebrate Christmas all year round. Everything came into being through the Word and we celebrate the Word, which is Christ, every day. There is no time in which Christ was not, so there is no time that is not Christmas.

How might you celebrate Christmas each day? What would that look like for you and your congregation? How might that shape your understanding of Christ? How might that change your Christmas season this year?

Bringing the Text to Life

When I first started preaching, I encountered a gentle, loving man named Jerry. Jerry was one of those people who never knew a stranger. He had a heart to get to know people and love them. I remember preaching my first Sunday in September and after the service Jerry met me in the receiving line in the back of the church. He introduced himself and his wife, and when he left he told me "Merry Christmas." I thought to myself, "It's September. Does Jerry not know what month we are in?"

The following week when I saw Jerry sitting in the front office volunteering, the first thing out of his mouth was "Merry Christmas, Pastor Will." I must have had a baffled look on my face—it was still September. So, I spoke up and said, "Jerry, it's September and not December. Why are you wishing me a Merry Christmas?"

Jerry then leaned back in his chair with his hands on the back of head as if he were relaxing, and said, "I had a pastor once who told me that when Christ came to the earth is was not just to celebrate one day, but every day. So now, I say Merry Christmas every day as a reminder that Christ is with us every day." I was flabbergasted and had never thought of Christmas that way.

Every time I saw Jerry he wished me a Merry Christmas and I wished it back to him. Four years later, heartbreakingly and ironically, on Christmas Eve, I got a dreadful phone call that Jerry had died of a heart attack. My heart broke and I remembered all of the moments he had wished me Merry Christmas. We had his funeral the following week and the first thing out of my mouth to welcome the congregation were two words, *Merry Christmas.*

Christ coming to be with us is something we remember all year long. In the same way, the Gospel of John reminds us of the "Word becoming flesh and making a home with us."

May you, the preacher, remember that Christmas is available at any time. The Word has become flesh for eternity. During this Christmas season and every season, may you remember the words of Jerry, "Merry Christmas."

January 9, 2022–Baptism of the Lord

Isaiah 43:1-7; Psalm 29; Acts 8:14-17; **Luke 3:15-17, 21-22**

Will Wold

Preacher to Preacher Prayer

God of wonder and inspiration, through baptism, you prepared Jesus for his ministry in the world. In this text, might you inspire us with your Holy Spirit to prepare our hearts and minds for preaching hope into our world. Amen.

Commentary

Preaching the lectionary texts can become difficult to do every year. We often find ourselves scratching the bottom of the sermon barrel after preaching multiple times on the same text. Baptism of the Lord Sunday is no different. We can only orchestrate a renewal of baptism service so many times before it becomes mundane and ordinary. However, what happens in baptism is anything but ordinary. So, what do we do with the Gospel of Luke's narrative of the baptism of Jesus? Are there other ways we can see this text? How can this passage be reimagined with newly baptized eyes?

One of the first questions a preacher must ask is "Am I going to preach on the festival of baptism or am I going to focus on the text itself and see where the Spirit guides me?" Both approaches can serve a purpose for the congregation, but the preacher has to decide which path to take. If the preacher focuses on the festival of baptism, there are many other baptismal texts that one can use (see further Matt 28:19-20; Acts 10; 1 Cor 12:12-14). The preacher might expound upon what baptism is, what it means in our tradition of faith, and how baptism impacts the lives of the congregation.

However, this pericope will focus on the specific Lukan text itself. How might the baptism of the Lord text from Luke open itself up for the preacher, and in turn, how might the preacher be opened to the Spirit of God?

Luke's narrative of the baptism of Jesus is distinctive in comparison to the other Gospel writers in a few ways. First, when John announces that Jesus will baptize the people with Holy Spirit and fire, he uses imagery of a threshing area. Luke writes, "The shovel he [Jesus] uses to sift the wheat from the husks . . . he will clean out his threshing area and bring the wheat into his barn." The threshing area is a space to make crops edible.

Threshing is a process where one releases grains from crops, like wheat and barley. The farmer would tie the stalks together and crush the stalks in order to separate the grain from the stalk.[1] The stalk is then discarded. The grain is the edible part of the plant but contains a covering over the actual fruit. Once the grain is separated, then the process of winnowing begins. Winnowing is the process of throwing the grain into the air and having the wind remove the inedible covering over the grain.[2] In the ancient Near East, you could use your hand to throw the grain into the air or you could use a shovel. In the NIV, the word *shovel* is translated as "winnowing fork." Once winnowing was complete, the grain would be ready for use.

The word in Greek used for wind and spirit is the same word, *pneuma*. The spirit and wind help to separate the usable from the unusable parts of the plant. In the same way, the Spirit helps us to separate the unusable in our lives and our faith, which then prepares us for ministry.

Sometimes this text is preached in an eschatological way, which is to say that Jesus is coming to separate the stalk from the grain in a final judgment. However, what if this text isn't solely about the future, but might be speaking about the present? What hard work needs to be done now with the help of the Spirit to purify us and remove the grain from the stalk? What are the parts of our lives needing threshing and winnowing? How might baptism be a tool of the spirit that gives us new life? How might the wind help us clear the stalks and unnecessary parts of our lives of faith?

Another exceptional part of this text is found in a small detail. Right after Jesus's baptism, Jesus was praying and then heaven opened up. Jesus praying is unique to the entire Gospel of Luke. In Luke 6:12-16, Jesus prays all night before he chooses the twelve disciples. In Luke 9:28-29 before the Transfiguration, Jesus went to the mountain in order to pray and is transfigured while he is praying (the Gospels of Matthew and Mark only state "they were alone" and "he was transformed"). In Luke 23:34, Jesus also prays for those who were crucifying him: "Father, forgive them, for they don't know what they're doing." All of these times of prayer are unique to Luke when compared to other Gospels.

Prayer is powerful both in Luke and in the church. The prayers of Jesus precipitated large movements of the Spirit. Prayer prepares our hearts for how God works within our lives. What does prayer look like for you? How does it shape your relationship with God and others? How are you intentionally praying like Christ? Are there moments where you have seen God move as you have prayed?

Bringing the Text to Life

This time of year is perfect to discuss where God is threshing and winnowing within the congregation's life. Most people attempt a New Year's resolution, so it is timely that this scripture allows for the Spirit to share what stalks we need to thresh and winnow.

What would it look like to buy actual stalks of barley in order to illustrate how threshing and winnowing happens? The preacher would then move to discuss how Christ does this within our lives. Purification can occur through baptism or remembrance of your baptism. The theme of the sermon would be about God calling us into new life and leaving the old life behind.

Other texts the preacher could add into the sermon would be Galatians 3:26-27, where Paul writes, "You are all God's children through faith in Christ Jesus. All of you who were baptized into Christ have clothed yourselves with Christ." The preacher could also discuss John 15:1-2, where Jesus says, "I am the true vine, and my Father is the vineyard keeper. He removes any of my branches that don't produce fruit, and he trims any branch that produces fruit so that it will produce even more fruit." Both of these texts talk about new life given by the Spirit and that the old must be removed.

On the Baptism of the Lord Sunday, may we recognize the Spirit's ability to purify us through the threshing floor and baptism. May we ourselves be prepared for ministry by purifying our own lives of impurities.

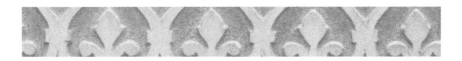

January 16, 2022–Second Sunday after Epiphany

*Isaiah 62:1-5; Psalm 36:5-10; **1 Corinthians 12:1-11**; John 2:1-11*

Chris Jones

Preacher to Preacher Prayer

God, thank you for creating us in your image, for calling us to new life, and for infusing each of us with spiritual gifts. Remind us that these gifts are not for ourselves but for the building up of your church and the advancement of your kingdom on this planet. Please help us to use our spiritual gifts in ways that please and honor you. In the name of Jesus Christ, we pray. Amen.

Commentary

Whoever remarked that modern-day churches would be better off if they patterned themselves after a New Testament congregation clearly never read 1 Corinthians. Corinth was a church with all kinds of issues—from division to sexual immorality to abuse of the Lord's Supper. Like an attorney, Paul skillfully and masterfully addresses these issues as he exhorts the Corinthian Christians. Along the way, he draws attention to the subject of spiritual gifts, a subject of which he fears at least some in his congregation are ignorant. Indeed, he starts off this passage by writing, "Brothers and sisters, I don't want you to be *ignorant* about spiritual gifts" (1 Cor 12:1, emphasis mine).

Why does Paul worry about such ignorance? Because the apostle knows what is at stake if it abounds—the church, and therefore the ministry of Jesus Christ, will suffer. Paul's deepest desire is for the gospel message to go forth and spread into all the world. He wants others to come to know and experience the depth of God's love in Jesus. However, he also knows that for that dream to become a reality, the Corinthians must come to a proper understanding of spiritual gifts.

Spiritual gifts, he argues, have their origin in (surprise, surprise!) the Spirit (1 Cor 12:4-6). This means they're not the product of birth but rebirth. Put simply, spiritual gifts aren't intrinsic to who we are as people. They're not a part of our DNA or genetic makeup. We don't inherit them from our parents. They're not passed down generationally. Instead, they're gifts of the Spirit, gifts that we receive when we give our lives over to God through Jesus Christ. Our conversion to God's goodness and love causes the Holy Spirit to produce certain gifts in us. Further, as Paul reminds us, these gifts are not for us but for the benefit of the church. The hope is that we will use our gifts in conjunction with the gifts of others so that the ministry of Jesus may flourish in the world.

Like any good preacher, Paul doesn't just talk about spiritual gifts in the theoretical. He identifies various examples—words of wisdom, words of knowledge, gifts of faith, and so on. It's an exhausting list but not an exhaustive one. Indeed, Paul goes on to name other gifts in Romans 12:6-8.

While Paul works hard in this passage to expel ignorance concerning spiritual gifts, sadly such ignorance continues today. How many in our congregations are informed of spiritual gifts and their role in the body of Christ? How many of us would be able to identify our own spiritual gifts or the gifts of those around us?

There are a plethora resources out there to help us in this area. (See, for example, the following webpage, which includes a spiritual gifts inventory as well as other information: https://www.umc.org/en/content/spiritual-gifts.) As United Methodists, we pledge to support our congregations in at least five ways—our prayers, our presence, our gifts, our service, and our witness. While we often interpret "gifts" to mean financial giving, what if we expanded our thinking here to include spiritual gifts? (One can make the argument that service includes spiritual gifts.) Too often we hear the expression in our churches, "Some people do everything!" What if instead we flipped that expression around so that it became "everybody does something"?

God's desire is that all of us will play a role in the upbuilding of the church and the advancement of his kingdom. To that end, God has gifted us in various ways. May each of us discover our gifts and use those gifts for the glory of God.

Bringing the Text to Life

My friend Erwin had no idea God had called him to be a pastor. At the time, he wasn't part of a worshipping community. He wasn't even sure what he thought about God! But then one day, he was approached by an older woman whom he had never met. She came up to him and said, "Young man, God is calling you to be a preacher." He thought she was crazy at the time. Now, as a preacher, he looks back on that experience and realizes she had the gift of prophecy—she proclaimed a vision for his life that had yet to be realized.

For as long as I can remember, my mom had the spiritual gift of knowing when and for what to pray. One morning, when I was about twelve, I woke up and found my mom in prayer. She explained that the Spirit led her out of bed at exactly 6:00 a.m. and told her to pray for Joann, who was in her small group. Later that day, my mom went to go run an errand. Meanwhile the phone rang. It was my mom's friend Barbara, who asked if my mom was there. I explained she wasn't and asked if I could take a message. Barbara told me to tell my mom that Joann was in the hospital. Evidently, she had been taken by ambulance at exactly 6:00 a.m., the same moment my mom felt led to pray for her. Who, but the Spirit, could have told my mom to pray for her?

This gift doesn't show up in the 1 Corinthians 12 list. However, one of the spiritual gifts Paul identifies elsewhere (Rom 12) is showing kindness. I'll never forget an act of great kindness that a Christ follower showed me. I had just started serving at my current church. Two weeks into my appointment, my mom was diagnosed with cancer. A month later, she died. Shortly after I came back from her funeral, I was checking the mail at my community mailbox when I ran into my mail carrier whom I had yet to meet. She asked, "Are you Pastor Chris?" I nodded. She then asked, "Is everything OK? You've been getting a lot of cards recently. I was hoping they were birthday cards, but I had a feeling they weren't." I explained to her that they were condolence cards sent to me after my mom died. "That's what I feared," she said. "I want you to know how much I've been praying for you. As a mail carrier, I get an inside window into people's lives. I notice condolence cards, medical bills, overdue credit card statements, and so on. For this reason, I intentionally pray for the people on my route. You've been in my prayers every day." When I walked away from that encounter, I felt a sense of peace. It was an incredible act of kindness demonstrated to me by a perfect stranger, who advanced the ministry of Jesus.

I've never been into NASCAR, but I've always been fascinated by pit crews. Despite the number of people on the ground, pit crew members seem to work in sync to change tires, add fuel, and repair damages. What if Christians, united by their spiritual gifts, worked like a pit crew to advance the ministry of Jesus?

January 23, 2022–Third Sunday after Epiphany

*Nehemiah 8:1-3, 5-6; **Psalm 19**; 1 Corinthians 12:12-31a; Luke 4:14-21*

Chris Jones

Preacher to Preacher Prayer

God, all creation sings of your glory. Your power and might are on display for all to see. Thank you for the marvelous world you spoke into being. This world points to your beauty and magnifies your greatness. Thank you as well for the precepts of scripture, which call attention to your perfect and just ways and reveal your intention for all of us as human beings. Help us to see you in both creation and scripture and to celebrate how you have made yourself known. In the name of Jesus Christ, we pray. Amen.

Commentary

A core conviction of the Christian faith is that human beings don't know anything about God on our own. It's not as if we can go into a laboratory and discover something about God, nor can we think more and, suddenly, our thoughts will lead us to God. Rather, our knowledge of God comes through a single word: *revelation.* God's most definitive revelation of himself happened in Jesus, whom, as John says in the opening of his Gospel, "has made God known" (John 1:18). Elsewhere Paul reminds us that in Jesus "all the fullness of God was pleased to live" (Col 1:19). Still, there are other forms of revelation through which we can come to know and experience God. David beautifully highlights two of these forms here in Psalm 19—creation and scripture.

David devotes the first six verses (almost half) of this psalm to the majesty of creation. In the opening verse, he speaks of heaven "declaring God's glory." Obviously, David is not referencing the spiritual realm of heaven, but rather, the atmosphere above the earth in which the stars and planetary bodies hang like sparkling ornaments on a Christmas tree. In other words, just by looking up in the sky, we see something of God's glory.

All of us can identify with this statement. We've watched a glorious sunrise or sunset. We've visited an area of the country untouched by manufactured light and had our breath taken away by the Milky Way streaking across the dark sky. It's hard to deny God's glory when considering the vastness of creation. Somebody once quipped, "There are no atheists in foxholes." We might also add, "There are no atheists when staring up at the heavens." The reality that God put all this together is nothing less than mind-boggling!

David goes on to write that while creation may not speak like we do (through an audible voice characterized by speech and words), this does not mean creation is silent. Indeed, the various voices of creation can be heard throughout the earth. We hear these voices in babbling brooks and rushing waterfalls, falling leaves and ocean waves. Even the sound of rain speaks of a creator.

In the above verses, David taps into two of our five senses—sight and sound. Then in the latter half of verse 6, he taps into a third sense—touch. He writes how nothing escapes the sun's heat, which of courses includes us who can feel its rays on our bodies. David understands our sensory nature as human beings, and he poetically plays into this nature while drawing attention to God's revelation of himself through creation.

Things take a turn in verse 7 as David describes a second form of revelation that demands our attention—scripture. To be fair, he doesn't use the word *scripture*. However, he does speak of God's instruction, law, regulations, commands, and judgments, all of which are recorded in scripture. David knows that while creation tells us *of* God and even identifies God's glorious nature, scripture gives *specificity* to God. This in turn gives specificity to us, particularly when it comes to how we are to live and behave under God's reign.

The modern tendency is to see scripture in a restrictive way. We tend to assume that the precepts we find in scripture will be joy stealing and suffocating. Consequently, we would prefer not to follow them. However, David speaks of scripture as reviving one's being (v. 7a), gladdening one's heart (v. 8a), and giving light to the eyes (v. 8b). He doesn't see scripture negatively. On the contrary, he grows excited when he considers the inspired words of God. What if we, too, abandoned the assumption that what we discover in scripture will bog us down rather than lift us up? Yes, we must read and interpret scripture responsibly, but we must remember that God's intent is not to bore us or take away our fun but to give us life and joy.

Bringing the Text to Life

Theodore Roosevelt was our nation's twenty-sixth president. He had a larger-than-life personality and a well-documented love of the outdoors, both of which paved the way for the creation of many of our national parks and monuments. It's been said that when he would entertain diplomatic guests at the White House and they were getting ready to retire for the night, President Roosevelt would lead them outside and have them look up in the night sky. They would stare at the vast array of stars in the canopy of space. Then, after a few moments, he would say, "Gentlemen, I believe we are small enough now. Let's go to bed." Despite his big personality, even

Theodore Roosevelt couldn't help feeling small when considering the wonder of Creation (https://www.preachingtoday.com/illustrations/2002/december/14018.html).

Scientists tell us that light travels at a speed of 186,000 miles a second, and our sun is roughly 93 million miles away. These figures mean that when we see the sun, we're not actually seeing the sun as it exists in the *present* but rather eight minutes in the *past*. Actually, all of what we observe in space reflects the past. Further, our universe is constantly expanding. And yet the true wonder is that the God who spoke all this into being calls each one of us by name!

Masterful preacher Fred Craddock tells the story of a young woman who approached him one day. She explained that, during her first year at college, she felt like a failure. She wasn't doing well in her classes, she couldn't get many dates, and she didn't have as much money as the other students did. Then one Sunday afternoon, she decided to end it all by taking her own life. She went to the river near the campus, climbed up on the rail, and was looking into the dark water below. But just before she jumped, she remembered the words of scripture, "Throw all your anxiety onto him, because he cares about you" (1 Pet 5:7). It was at that point that she climbed down from the rail and decided not to take her own life.[3] Those words reminded that young woman that there was a God in heaven who cared for her. Consequently, her life had meaning and purpose. The psalmist was right: the precepts of scripture revive our being and gladden our hearts!

January 30, 2022–Fourth Sunday after Epiphany

Jeremiah 1:4-10; *Psalm 71:1-6; 1 Corinthians 13:1-13; Luke 4:21-30*

Chris Jones

Preacher to Preacher Prayer

God, even as you called Jeremiah and set the prophet apart from before birth, you continue to call women and men to yourself and set them apart for service to your kingdom. By your grace, help us to be obedient to your call, even if that call may not be as glamorous as we imagined. Help us not to make excuses or look to our deficiencies, but rather, remind us of your faithfulness. You call and you equip. Equip us then to carry out the work that you have for us. Send your Spirit upon us as we go forth. In the name of Jesus Christ, we pray. Amen.

Commentary

Jeremiah's call story captivates the reader with language that is poetic and beautiful, moving and inspirational. However, historical circumstances reveal that there is far more to this call story than captivating language.

The year was 627 BC. Centuries earlier, Israel had endured civil unrest, which in turn caused the nation to split into two different kingdoms: the northern kingdom of Israel and the southern kingdom of Judah. Josiah was king over Judah where he had been reigning for the past thirteen years. Although history now recognizes Josiah as an upstanding king who "did what was right in the LORD's eyes" (2 Kgs 22:2), the nation he was tasked with leading was headed for destruction. The nearby nation of Babylon was quickly gaining strength, and God's people—the people God had chosen from all the nations in the world to be his own possession—no longer seemed content with following the One who had made covenant with them. Many of us are familiar with Charles Dickens's *Tale of Two Cities*, which opens with one of the most memorable lines in English literature: "It was the best of times, it was the worst of times."[4] For Judah, it was simply the worst of times. What's more, it was about to get even worse in the ensuing years. It is into *this* context that Jeremiah receives a call.

Jeremiah's call is a true sign of prevenient grace. Prior to his birth, God sets Jeremiah apart to serve as a prophet. More than half a millennium later, Paul would share something similar regarding his own call to be an apostle to the Gentiles: "But God *had set me apart from birth* and called me through his grace" (Gal 1:15, emphasis mine). Through both the prophet and apostle, we learn something of God's call: it is God's idea before it is ever our idea. It is not that we suddenly concoct plans for our lives and then ask God to bless those plans. Rather, God—however God deems fit—reveals those plans and then calls us to embrace them.

In the case of Jeremiah, these plans involved sharing the message of the Lord with a nation that was about to be conquered. This was no small task, especially given that other false prophets were preaching peace and prosperity (Jer 23:9-32; 28:1-17). Consequently, Jeremiah would go on to experience loneliness and despair. History now remembers him as "the weeping prophet." Fredrick Buechner has famously said, "The place God calls you to is the place where your deep gladness and the world's deep hunger meet."[5] I imagine if Jeremiah were here today he would qualify these words. To be sure, the world's hunger will be there, but gladness may not always reign in our hearts as we respond to God's call. Instead of saying, "Send me!" we may cry out, "Why me?"

Like others before him (Moses, for example), Jeremiah comes up with an excuse for why he cannot follow God—his youthfulness. Upon careful examination, however, this excuse may have been masking something deeper. Indeed, while Jeremiah does not admit to feelings of fear, God commands the young prophet not to be afraid (Jer 1:8). Could it be that God detects an underlying sense of fear in Jeremiah that even the prophet is hesitant to admit? If so, how like God to cut straight to the heart of the matter and call out whatever it is that we are feeling inside! We come up with one excuse, but God, who created our inmost being and knows us inside and out (Ps 139:1-18), is familiar with the true source of our apprehension. God goes on to dispel Jeremiah's fear through the same promise issued to Moses at the burning bush (Exod 3:12)—God will be with him. This is the promise to which all of us cling as we faithfully follow God.

Bringing the Text to Life

John Ortberg has pointed out that the command "fear not" is the most frequently cited command in scripture. More than anything else, God tells us not to be afraid. But why does God say these words so often? According to Ortberg, it is not because God is trying to spare us emotional discomfort. Rather, Ortberg believes, it is because fear tends to be the number one reason we are tempted to avoid doing what God wants us to do.[6] Jeremiah was afraid, but God told him not to fear!

We tend to romanticize God's call, but what about those times when God's call causes distress and anxiety? Certainly, every pastor can relate. Not every moment of ministry is a walk in the park. Angry e-mails. Upset congregants. Anonymous "feedback." But God's promise to Jeremiah rings true: even in the difficulty, God is with us.

Jeremiah was technically a child. However, even children have a role to play in God's work. When I was in seminary, I interned at a church that had a partnership with other community churches to support vulnerable children in Kenya. When the youth group of one of the partner churches heard about the work being done in Kenya, they decided to raise money through a carnival. Even the parents and youth pastor didn't take them seriously. In their minds, they pictured a rinky-dink, backyard carnival that would cost more money than it raised. However, this carnival ended up being a huge shindig that defied all expectations. When it was all said and done, the youth—many of whom weren't old enough to drive—raised around $14,000!

Jeremiah talks about God putting words in his mouth. It reminds me of a story President Jimmy Carter has told. In the year he was elected president, Carter was one of the three men scheduled to speak for five minutes at the Southern Baptist Convention. The other two men were Billy Graham and a truck driver. The truck driver was nervous. He had never given a speech before in his life. What's more, he had to immediately follow, of all people, Billy Graham! When he rose to speak, he talked about his ministry at a local bar where he told others about God's love in Jesus and how, as a result, fourteen of his friends became Christian. Carter writes, "The truck driver's speech, of course, was the highlight of the convention. I don't believe anyone who was there will ever forget that five-minute fumbling statement—or remember what I or even Billy Graham had to say."[7]

February 6, 2022–Fifth Sunday after Epiphany

Isaiah 6:1-8, (9-13); *Psalm 138; 1 Corinthians 15:1-11; Luke 5:1-11*

Lori Osborn

Preacher to Preacher Prayer

God who calls, allow me to see your glory and remind me of my calling. Equip me to speak so that others may come to see your glory and know your grace. Give me words that will help your people move from sin and guilt to pardon and action. Amen.

Commentary

Can you imagine how terrifying and awesome this vision must have been for Isaiah? The vastness of God with the hem of his robe filling the temple, winged creatures, the doorframe shaking, loud shouting, smoke, and hot coals in his face all make for one amazing vision. Isaiah has just seen a glimpse of the Lord, and this is a moment of clarity for him as he acknowledges his own sin and the sins of his community. He fears that the glory of God will destroy him, but instead he is purified and experiences God's pardon in a powerful way. This pardon sets him apart to be able to respond when God calls. The remarkable thing is that Isaiah responds enthusiastically before he even hears the message. This is no doubt a transformational moment in Isaiah's life.

This scene reminds us of how holy and "other" God is. Yet God still enlists the help of mortals to do God's work. Isaiah was both convicted and empowered by his experience of God. This experience moved him from a place of sin and guilt to a place of freedom and response. Isaiah saw God's glory, confessed his sins, received God's pardon, and responded to God's call. How can we help our people navigate and relate to Isaiah's call story? How do we help our people take a similar journey from sin and guilt to freedom and response?

I imagine most of us have not experienced such an awe-inspiring vision. Therefore, it is important to help our people find ways to connect with this encounter with the holy. How can we help people identify God's glory today? How is God trying to get *our* attention? Maybe we experience God's glory during corporate worship when we are swept up in a hymn or praise song. Maybe we experience it in a beautiful sunrise or sunset. Maybe God's glory comes to us in a still, small voice in the midst of chaos. The clearer God's presence in the world becomes to us, the clearer we can see ourselves and our sin.

At the very sight of the hem of the robe of God, Isaiah quickly confesses his sin and the sins of his people. It almost seems like it is an immediate response, like he cannot help but pour his heart out to the holy one. How do we help our people understand confession? What opportunities do we give for people to truly pour out their hearts before God? What does corporate and individual confession and repentance look like for us? Do our people secretly believe that God will smite them for their sins? Isaiah's experience reminds us that when we confess our sin and repent, God does not bring condemnation but invitation! God's response is one of pardon, not destruction. This may be an opportunity for you to share some of the things with which you struggle. It can be helpful and freeing to know that "even the pastor" struggles.

After experiencing the pardon of God, Isaiah responds to God's call before he even knows the message! He has experienced God's majesty and is ready to serve. How do we equip our people to respond to God's calling on their lives? Corporate worship, study, and prayer can offer great insight and encouragement. What message does God need for us to share? As individuals? As the church? What is God seeking to say through faithful people today?

The message given to Isaiah was a difficult one. He is to warn the people of God's coming judgment, knowing there is no immediate hope for repentance. They will not understand what he is saying. I wonder if Isaiah wanted to change his response at this point: "On second thought, I'm a bit busy today, God." Maybe so. However, his powerful encounter with God and his pardon from his guilt and shame led him to be faithful to God's calling on his life. What is God is calling you to do or say today?

Bringing the Text to Life

Isaiah seems to respond immediately to God's call. We know this is not always the case! For many of us, the response to God takes a long time. This may be an opportunity to share your call story. How did God get your attention? What was your response? How did God equip you? If your story is anything like mine, it unfolded over a period of time. In fact, it is still unfolding. I need to confess my sin daily and receive a hot coal of pardon daily!

One of my favorite parts of being a pastor is the corporate prayer of confession and the assurance of pardon. Following the corporate prayer and a moment of silence I say, "Hear the good news, Christ died for us while we were yet sinners and that proves God's love toward us, in the name of Jesus Christ, you are forgiven."[1] The *best* part is what follows. The *entire* congregation responds, "In the name of Jesus Christ, You are forgiven."[2] These words are hot coals for my soul. It is both liberation and invitation.

In the Gospel reading for today (Luke 5:1-11) we see Simon Peter offer a similar response to Isaiah when he encounters Jesus. Immediately upon seeing the overflowing nets, impulsive Peter responds, "Leave me, Lord for I'm a sinner!" (Luke 5:8). This is another example of how encountering God helps us see ourselves clearly. Jesus's response is not one of condemnation, but of invitation! Jesus offers an invitation into the profession of fishing for people. The disciples leave *everything* to respond to the call of Jesus. How is God trying to get your attention? Where in your life do you need to experience forgiveness so that you can respond to God's invitation to help with God's holy work?

February 13, 2022–Sixth Sunday after Epiphany

*Jeremiah 17:5-10; Psalm 1; 1 Corinthians 15:12-20; **Luke 6:17-26***

Lori Osborn

Preacher to Preacher Prayer

Loving God, you call us to a radically different way of living in the world. Help me offer a message of hope to those on the margins and a word of challenge to those who have plenty. We long for your reign to come in its entirety. In the meantime, help us live lives that make your reign more of a reality here and now. Amen.

Commentary

Wow, what a way to get people's attention, Jesus! Our scripture begins by telling us that Jesus has grown in popularity because of his power to heal, but I would not want to check his approval rating at the end of this sermon! This message is specifically given to the disciples. The gathered crowds simply overhear their conversation. While these blessings are similar to four of the Beatitudes in Matthew 5, Luke pairs them with four woes, "How terrible for you!" as if to *really* drive the point home. Jesus speaks of the poor and rich, those who hunger and those with plenty, those who weep and those who laugh, and those who are hated and those who are loved. This will no doubt be a difficult message if you are preaching to an affluent congregation!

In order to fully understand this passage we need to place it in the larger context of Luke's message. In Luke's Gospel we see Jesus's deep concern for the marginalized and the poor. It is no secret that Jesus has come to turn the world upside down. This is clearly seen in Mary's song, the Magnificat:

> He has pulled the powerful down from their thrones
> and lifted up the lowly.
> He has filled the hungry with good things
> and sent the rich away empty-handed. (Luke 1:52-53)

Mary knew the heart of Jesus even before he was born! In chapter 4, we see Jesus in the temple quoting from Isaiah:

> The Spirit of the Lord is upon me,
>> because the Lord has anointed me.
> He has sent me to preach good news to the poor. (Luke 4:18)

Sharing examples of this theme may help our congregants understand Jesus's words in our scripture for today.

Luke's Gospel simultaneously highlights the pitfalls of wealth. It is no secret that money can present big challenges to our faith. Peter Eaton says it well: "[Luke] is among the clearest of the New Testament writers on the power that wealth wields to isolate us from God and the rest of the human community . . . but Luke does not consider those with wealth to be beyond salvation."[3] He goes on to cite instances in which people with great material wealth used their resources for good, like Zacchaeus (Luke 19) and Cornelius (Acts 10) to name a few.[4] A hearer should not wallow in despair at these words. Instead, they should consider how they might be able to use their material blessings to bless those whom Jesus blesses: the poor, the hungry, those who weep, and those who are despised.

I am reminded of the quote that is originally attributed to Peter Finely Dunn. He said that the role of the newspaper was "to comfort the afflicted and afflict the comfortable." I'd say this is the role of this scripture as well! Our people will no doubt try to identify themselves in one of these two lists. For those in need, this scripture offers a message of hope that their struggles will not last forever. For those who have plenty, it is a reminder that this world is not all there is. It is a plea to share their resources and blessings with those who are in need. We know that these blessings will be a reality when the kingdom of God is fully realized. Yet Jesus expects his followers to make this kingdom a reality *now*, not just in the future. As followers of Jesus, we are to usher in God's kingdom by blessing others.

This is an opportunity for us to search our hearts. Jesus's messages of caring for the marginalized and turning the world upside down are clear. The question for us becomes, do we *want* to live this way? Are we willing to take the risks that may be present in turning the world "upside down"? Are we willing to make the necessary sacrifices? Do we want a world that is more equitable? Or, are we more comfortable living in a world where the rich and powerful stay on top and those on the margins stay put"? These are difficult questions, but they are necessary in order for us to be true disciples.

Bringing the Text to Life

We cannot expect someone to understand the idea of Jesus as "living water" (John 7:37-39) if they have no access to clean water. We cannot expect people to understand Jesus as the "bread of life" (John 6:25-29) if their bellies are empty. Who in your community needs to be blessed? Who is poor and hungry among you? Who needs a shoulder on which to cry? Who is being excluded and reviled? Are you willing to stand with them? How can you become the blessing Jesus pronounces?

I recommend to you Nadia Bolz-Weber's "Beatitude Benediction." While she references the Sermon on the Mount, I believe the content applies to the blessings and woes in Luke as well. In it she writes, "Maybe Jesus was simply blessing the ones around him that day who didn't otherwise receive blessing, who had come to believe that, for them, blessings would never be in the cards. I mean, come on, doesn't that just *sound* like something Jesus would do? Extravagantly throwing around blessings as if they grew on trees?"[5] She goes on to write beatitudes for those within her community. This may be something for you to consider doing. Obviously Luke's account adds woes, and Jesus is no stranger to calling people out (Matt 21 and Luke 11). What modern-day woes do we need to address from the pulpit? Woe to those who remain silent in the face of oppression. Woe to those who hoard out of a scarcity mindset. Using this literary style may help people feel invited into this different way of living.

February 20, 2022–Seventh Sunday after Epiphany

Genesis 45:3-11, 15; Psalm 37:1-11, 39-40;
*1 Corinthians 15:35-38, 42-50; **Luke 6:27-38***

Lori Osborn

Preacher to Preacher Prayer

Loving God, remind me of your great love and forgiveness so that I might be loving and merciful to others. Help me continue to grow in my understanding of what it means to love you and others. Amen.

Commentary

We know that as Christians we have two main rules: love God and love others as we love ourselves (Matt 2:36-40). When we do these things we fulfill all of the law. It sounds deceivingly easy. Yet this is probably one of the most challenging passages of scripture we have. This scripture will no doubt cause people to shift in their seats. It is uncomfortable and convicting. When we finish reading scripture in worship we say, "The word of God for the people of God, thanks be to God." But are we *really* thankful for this difficult message? Sometimes I just want to grumble the response under my breath! Jesus offers this message to his disciples who are willing to hear. Are we willing to hear? Wouldn't it be much easier if Jesus left this part out?

This scripture immediately follows Luke's account of the blessings and woes. Jesus is speaking to his disciples as the crowds press in around him. In the previous verses we realize that Jesus has come to turn the world upside down. Jesus offers blessings for people who have most likely never been blessed. To all those who have been successful in the world's eyes he says, "How terrible for you" (Luke 6:24). Then, he invites the disciples to participate in his work by offering love and grace to everyone, especially those who do not deserve it. I wonder what the disciples thought as Jesus continued speaking. How many of them tuned out because the message was too hard?

A sermon on this passage must begin by looking inwardly. Christ died for us while we were sinners. Why are we supposed to love our enemies? Because we were enemies of God and God has been gracious with us. In Christ, God has surprised us with mercy, grace, and forgiveness. Therefore, we are called to do the same for others.

Loving our enemies begins when we recognize that God cares as deeply for them as God cares for us. It means recognizing that they are also children of God created in God's image. When we love our enemies, we are loving the image of God within them. We love them not because we think they "deserve" it, but because we have experienced God's love and forgiveness in our own lives and we know the power it holds. How we treat others is a direct reflection of whether or not we have truly received God's grace and love.

We talk a lot about loving God and loving others, but rarely do we talk about loving ourselves. Our scripture includes a version of the golden rule: treat others as you want to be treated. We know that oftentimes people do hurtful things because they are hurting within. It can be hard to know how to treat others well if you have never been treated well. This does not excuse bad behavior, but it makes it even more important for us to surprise others with love and compassion. Our "enemy" may come to know the surprising love of God through us.

I will admit that I have always struggled with this scripture because I imagine how difficult it must be for someone to hear who has been deeply hurt or abused. How does it look to love *that* person who offended you? It may be necessary to share that loving someone does not mean staying with them. Forgiving someone does not mean accepting their behavior. As mentioned before, self-love and care are also part of our two big rules from Jesus.

Love is compelling and transformative. Love breaks down barriers and walls. Jesus loved even until the end. Jesus, even as he was *dying on the cross*, offered forgiveness and love to the thief next to him. As if that wasn't enough, Jesus even loved us *through* the grave, coming back to offer new life for those who condemned him. This is the man we follow. This is the sacrificial love we are called to embody. It is not easy, but it is what will indeed transform the world into the world God intends for it to be.

Who in our lives needs to know the surprising love of Jesus? Who needs to experience grace and forgiveness? Love them. Pray for them. Serve them. Not only will you receive a reward, but you will be transformed in the process.

Bringing the Text to Life

There are so many modern stories of forgiveness and mercy that push us to think and act more like Jesus. I am reminded of the story of how the Amish community responded in the face of a school shooting that resulted in the death of five young girls along with the perpetrator. In a story for NPR, sociologist Donald Kraybill said, "I think the most powerful demonstration of the depth of Amish forgiveness was when members of the Amish community went to the killer's burial service at the cemetery. . . . Several families, Amish families who had buried their own daughters just the day before were in attendance and they hugged the widow, and hugged other members of the killer's family."[6] This story still brings tears to my eyes. These families had no doubt embraced God's love and forgiveness in their own lives and it spilled over to those who also desperately needed it.

There is another story about Megan Phelps-Roper, a young woman who grew up in Westboro Baptist Church. She shares that what convinced her to leave the church was not the loud rejection of her theological positions, but the compassion that she found from individuals on Twitter.[7] What an example of quiet compassion and love transforming the world.

These are both large stories of transformation. Can you think of a time when you received forgiveness when you did not deserve it? How has receiving undeserved love from others helped you come to know God and God's love more fully? While the big stories are amazing, the little ones are transformative as well!

February 27, 2022–
Transfiguration Sunday

Exodus 34:29-35; *Psalm 99; 2 Corinthians 3:12-4:2;
Luke 9:28-36 (37-43a)*

Olu Brown

Preacher to Preacher Prayer

Dear God, as we continue to journey in this new normal and seek to reach the world for Christ, we pray for your direction, guidance, and love. In moments of transfiguration and change, be near to me and the people I lead. Help me discern your will and your way, so that I will remain faithful and hopeful, even in times when I am not sure or certain of the path forward. Like Moses and those who came before me, help me be a guardian of their legacies and leadership. In Christ's name. Amen!

Commentary

Moses's journey, like that of many faith leaders, was fluid and problematic from birth to the day when he assumed his role as a veteran and established leader of the Israelite community on their sojourn to the Promised Land. From the threat on his life at birth, to being raised in Pharaoh's house in Egypt, to standing in the presence of God on Mount Sinai for the second time, Moses's life is a narrative of fluid experiences and problematic circumstances. Exodus 34 is an account of Moses's second attempt to download the Ten Commandments literally from the "cloud." His first attempt didn't end very well after he destroyed the Ten Commandments in Exodus 32 and chastised the people for following foreign gods. While on Mount Sinai for the second time, he experienced a reboot with God and was successful in receiving God's commandments for the people, therefore securing his legacy. As Moses descended from Mount Sinai the second time, he possessed God's glory on his face as he met with the Israelites to share God's law that would be used to help them live according to God's pattern and plan.

This moment on Mount Sinai in Exodus 34 was significant because it was the formal and lasting introduction and publication of what we call the "Ten

Commandments." These were the laws that governed the thoughts, actions, and decisions of the Israelite people thousands of years ago. Today, we typically refer to the Ten Commandments only, but in reality, there were hundreds of commandments that guided and perhaps guardrailed the behavior of the Israelite community. The Ten Commandments still hang in businesses, churches, and homes throughout the world. Moses had no idea that his moment with God would connect him to generations yet to be born.

Society has a tendency to celebrate leaders for their triumphs, but we don't always consider the challenges they face on their journey to victory. In the resource *Leadership Directions from Moses*, the great patriarch had to face challenging decisions throughout his tenure that were summarized within three difficult conversations with self, others, and God.[8] Conversations with leading questions like "Am I enough for the task at hand? Will people believe me if I share the vision God has given me? God, why have you left me alone with these demanding people?" It was not an easy decision for Moses to return to Mount Sinai after a previous leadership failure, but he faced his fears and the difficult conversations, and because of his courage, the world has been blessed with the Ten Commandments, which help guide communities of faith.

As Moses was returning from Mount Sinai to be with the people and share the recently downloaded commandments, "Moses didn't realize that the skin on his face shone brightly because he had been talking with God" (Exod 34:29 CEB). Brueggemann suggests, "We can see enough in this text to know that the person (body, face) of Moses, a new contact between heaven and earth, between Yahweh and Israel, has come about."[9] Surely, this was a new phenomenon in the experience of the Israelites, that one of their own was in the presence of Almighty God. As Moses descended from Mount Sinai and approached the Israelite community, he had to place a veil on his face, and this happened each time Moses descended from Mount Sinai. God's glory could not be hidden and was evident on Moses's face and body.

It is unmanageable to read Exodus 34 and not consider Jesus's moment of transfiguration in Luke 9. Moses experienced his own transfiguration first on Mount Sinai and joined Jesus for his moment of transfiguration hundreds of years later: "As he was praying, the appearance of his face changed and his clothes flashed white like lightning. Two men, Moses and Elijah, were talking with him" (Luke 9:29-30). These two powerful scriptures are held in parallel as Christians around the world reflect on Transfiguration Sunday and grapple with their own moments of change and transfiguration. The change and transfiguration may be a new awareness of self and the call upon our lives to return to ministry. Like Moses and Jesus, we receive a new glow and glory that helps others know that we have been in the presence of God. Transfiguration and change are never easy. If we are not careful, we will be tempted to hold on to God's glory on the mountaintop and delay returning to the lower altitude of ministry. We are empowered by God's glory and word and charged to take it to all the world and trust that what we share will meet the needs of God's people. Like Moses, God doesn't hold our failures against us and gives us an opportunity for a second attempt to get it right.

Bringing the Text to Life

Although Moses didn't get the distribution of the Ten Commandments right the first time, God gave him a second chance and granted a second attempt. On Mount Sinai, he successfully downloaded the Ten Commandments from the cloud and experienced his own moment of transfiguration as his face literally glowed before the Israelites.

I. Moses's Meeting with God

- God was present and available for Moses and God is present and available for each of us.

II. Moses's Return to the People

- His face was glowing, and the people knew he had been in the presence of God and God's presence made a difference.

- Whenever we are in God's presence, there are signs of confirmation, such as peace, love, and joy, which shine a light in the midst of darkness.

III. Moses's Return to God's Glory

- Each time Moses ascended the mountain to meet with God, he experienced God's glory.

- Even after failure, second attempts are possible, and God's glory is always available.

March 2, 2022– Ash Wednesday

*Joel 2:1-2, 12-17 or Isaiah 58:1-12; **Psalm 51:1-17**;*
2 Corinthians 5:20b–6:10

Olu Brown

Preacher to Preacher Prayer

Dear God, give me strength in the midst of my weakness and help me to walk humbly among your people. You are my creator and all that I have belongs to you; I am dust, and when my days on earth end, I will return to dust. I thank you for creating me, loving me, and forgiving me. You are my God, and I am your child. In Christ's name. Amen!

Commentary

It is believed that Psalm 51 is a reflection and commentary of David's repentance after having an affair with Bathsheba and having her husband, Uriah, killed in 2 Samuel 11. This psalm is broken into three major categories: confession, petition, and forgiveness. The emotions within the psalm are palpable, and you can almost hear and feel the brokenhearted and contrite David, after taking accountability for his transgressions and pleading with God for forgiveness and grace. In addition to seeing David's story in Psalm 51, it is also possible to see the Israelites' story of redemption in the psalm as well. "It is appropriate to read Psalm 51 against the narrative background of the golden calf episode of Exodus 32–34 as well as against the background of the story of David and Bathsheba. Both stories are about God's forgiveness of grievous sin."[1] The psalm being about David or the Israelites is secondary to the role the psalm plays as an archetype prayer of confession, petition, and forgiveness. Each of these three categories has been witnessed publicly in places of worship in moments of praise, prayer, and preaching, where an individual or group confesses their sins before God and asks God for forgiveness while committing to turning from his or her sins and finally receiving assurance of forgiveness. David and the Israelites were forgiven of their sins, and they committed to walk in a new light and a new way before God.

Psalm 51, like each of the psalms, shows a personal relationship between the psalmist and God; and although sin occurred, God is not distant, aloof, or uncaring. Even in the psalmist's greatest moments of brokenness, God is present and willing to forgive (vv. 1-2). In current times, it is important for those reading Psalm 51 to know that although the psalm can be a reflection of David's and the Israelites' journeys with God, it is also part of our personal journeys with God as we navigate life and living. This psalm is highlighted on Ash Wednesday as Christians around the world begin Lent, a season of reflection and repentance. Ash Wednesday marks the beginning of Lent when people are reminded that they have been formed from dust and will return to dust. This recalls the Genesis creation story and the understanding that we are God's creation and did not create ourselves. We are also prone to sin and transgression and constantly in need of a forgiving God. The sense of being aware of one's sins and transgressions is a key player during Ash Wednesday experiences that place us at the altar of repentance and not in the hands of an angry God, but a forgiving and gracious God.

Identical to David and the Israelites, when we confess our sins to Almighty God, we are assured of forgiveness and salvation (v. 7), and we have a responsibility to not only live differently but to tell others of the good news of salvation and forgiveness (v. 13). McCann sums up Psalm 51 in an enlightened reflection, "God does not want 'broken' or 'crushed' persons in the sense of 'oppressed' or 'dysfunctional.' Rather, God desires humble, contrite persons who are willing to offer God their whole selves."[2] We should be grateful for the inclusion of Psalm 51 in the Protestant canon as a historic reflection on David and the Israelites' journey with God, but most importantly, for our experiences with God.

Bringing the Text to Life

David and the Israelites experienced times when they disobeyed God and had to confess their sins and turn their hearts toward God again. In these moments of transgression, God's steadfast love never failed, and God was willing and ready to forgive them of all their sins.

I. Confession (vv. 1-6)

- The psalmist confessed his or her sins to Almighty God without reservation and with full accountability.

- When we use the ACTS prayer model, Adoration, Confession, Thanksgiving, and Supplication, we must take note that the second step in the model after Adoration is Confession.

- Confession is an essential part to our relationship with God.

II. Petition (vv. 7-14)

- Once the psalmist confessed, then the psalmist petitioned God for purity, a clean heart, a return to joy, and deliverance from violence.

III. Forgiveness (vv. 15-17)

- The psalmist is assured of God's forgiveness through salvation, and although broken in spirit, is willing to serve God.

- Forgiveness is greater than our transgressions.

March 6, 2022–First Sunday in Lent

Deuteronomy 26:1-11; Psalm 91:1-2, 9-16; Romans 10:8b-13;
Luke 4:1-13

Olu Brown

Preacher to Preacher Prayer

Dear God, I am human, weak and prone to sin and yet you love me and care for me. Thank you for sending Jesus to be my savior and to die on a cross for my sins and the sins of the world. Thank you for sending Jesus to be a witness on earth who endured trials, tribulations, and temptations, and in his suffering taught me how to stand in difficult times. When I am tempted physically, give me strength to overcome. When I am tempted with power, give me humility. When I am tempted with privilege, remind me to value the gifts in others. Thank you God, in Jesus's name. Amen.

Commentary

The temptation of Jesus is positioned between Jesus being baptized at the Jordan River by his relative John the Baptist, where God said, "You are my Son, whom I dearly love; in you I find happiness" (3:22), and the beginning of Jesus's public ministry in Luke 4 and 5. The temptation narrative archives a forty-day experience of Jesus being tempted by the devil and denying himself food. At first glance, forty days may seem an odd number for a fast, but the forty-day narrative is consistent in the biblical text. The Israelites wandered in the wilderness for forty years (Josh 5). Twice, Moses stayed forty nights and forty days on Mount Sinai (Exod 24 and 34). Jonah prophesied to Nineveh for forty days (Jonah 3). Ezekiel remained on his side for forty days (Ezek 4). Themes in the Bible with this duration are not uncommon, so it should not come as a surprise that Jesus participated in a forty-day fast.

The text also gives the name of the tempter: "There he was tempted for forty days by the devil" (Luke 4:2). In addition to being tempted for forty days, he was also fasting from food and was "starving" (v. 2). Having to endure temptation for forty days would be inconceivable, but to add fasting to it is more than the human brain can process and the body can endure. Yet Jesus was able to endure the taunts and tests of the devil while refraining from eating and while being isolated in the "wilderness" (v. 1). The wilderness was more than a place beyond the crowds of ministry; it was a desolate place where Jesus was in a fight with the devil, and thanks be to God, he was victorious. The temptation narrative in Luke illustrates three historic temptations that are significant to society today: physical desires (vv. 3-4), power (vv. 5-8), and privilege (vv. 9-12).

First, Jesus's physical body was tempted to take bread during his fasting experience. During brief or prolonged periods of food fasting, the body craves the food nourishment that it consistently received in the past. For forty days, Jesus was able to deny his body food, and this was a miracle of great magnitude. Fasting is a prevalent spiritual discipline, and today, a person may choose to fast from food, social media, smart phones, and so on. Some believe fasting is a way to gain clarity and discern God's will for their lives.

Second, Jesus was offered power and the opportunity to rule the "kingdoms of the world" (v. 5). When the devil offered Jesus power, the devil did not realize Jesus was being offered something he already possessed. In John's Gospel, it is clear that Jesus was with God in the beginning and therefore had all power before the world was formed. As children of God, we should not be tempted with the inheritance we already possess.

Third, Jesus was encouraged to use his privilege as the Son of the living God and put God to the test. On the Mount of Olives in Luke 22, Jesus faced a similar temptation of privilege. The temptation was an opportunity to use his privilege and call on favoritism to avoid hardship and even death. He did not abuse or misuse his privilege in the wilderness with the devil or on the Mount of Olives with his disciples. As humans, we all have some type of privilege that, if not carefully guarded, we will use to gain an unfair advantage over others or to circumvent certain processes.

In life, the majority of the temptations we will endure will fall in one of the three categories of physical desires, power, and privilege, and it will always be more difficult to overcome these temptations if we are not open to the guidance of the Holy Spirit. Jesus's divinity and humanity meet in Luke 4 because his struggle is not hidden or downplayed, and he gives hope for those of us who face temptations today.

Jesus's moments of temptation teach us that although we can overcome temptation, the very presence of temptation will be a constant reality in our lives. To be human means that we will be tempted from time to time, and we have to constantly be on guard. We also realize that when we overcome temptations that are related to the physical body, power, and privilege, there is no guarantee that we will not be tempted again, and again, and again. Notice the temptation narrative in Luke ends with the following words: "After finishing every temptation, the devil departed from him until the next opportunity" (v. 13). Remember, in the economy of temptation, there will always be a "next opportunity," so stay on guard.

Bringing the Text to Life

Jesus Christ was the Son of the Living God, and though he was able to overcome temptation, he still experienced the temptations that we face today. In life, we will face temptations, and even if our story is not one of victory each time like Jesus's story, we must always be on guard and know that our relationship with God and God's word is more powerful than any temptation that we face in our lives.

I. Physical Temptations (vv. 3-4)

- Jesus fasted from food for forty days, and his body was craving the nourishment that it was being denied.

- Fasting is a spiritual discipline that helps us singularly focus on God and better discern God's will for our lives.

II. Power Temptations (vv. 5-8)

- Although power is desired by most, power in the wrong hands can be destructive.

- As children of God, we have the greatest power on earth, which is God's favor, and we never need to be tempted by the wealth and power of the world.

III. Privilege Temptations (vv. 9-12)

- As human beings, we possess privilege in one form or another. Our privilege may be our health, wealth, where we live, and even our race.

- We always have to be conscious of our privilege and never use it to circumvent a process or to mistreat someone.

March 13, 2022–Second Sunday in Lent

Genesis 15:1-12, 17-18; Psalm 27; Philippians 3:17–4:1;
Luke 13:31-35, or Luke 9:28-36 (37-43a)

Mandy Sloan McDow

Preacher to Preacher Prayer

God of faithfulness and patience: forgive us. We know not what we do. May your mercy
and grace guide us to receive your love, rather than doubt it. Amen.

Commentary

The scripture for today comes early in the book of Genesis, and we already have a novella of stories about death's relentless pursuit of each character upon their introduction. Adam and Eve are expelled from the garden and told they will return to dust; their son Cain (Hebrew for "prosperity") murders their other son Abel ("futility"), and Cain is sent into exile; and Adam and Eve conceive Seth, who is Noah's ancestor by ten generations. God blotted out all life on earth except for Noah and his household, made a covenant with Noah, whose son, Shem, became Abram's ancestor. The new, less wicked generations were compelled to create the Tower of Babel and angered God, who divided their language and scattered them around the earth.

When we finally get to Abram, we are ten generations into a narrative about creation and destruction; it is a story in which almost no party is innocent. We have learned about God's grace and provision, but also that humanity has the capacity to break God's heart and cause God to doubt the decision to create anything at all.[3] In our work as preachers, we are asked to tell the story of how much God loves us, and the opening chapters of Genesis make it clear that God's devotion to humankind and the natural world is hard fought. Love, as we well know, is never easy.

God comes to Abram in a vision, and saying, "Do not be afraid, Abram, I am a shield to you, your exceedingly great reward" (my translation). God shows up to dispel fear, provide safety, and offers divine presence as the gift for Abram's faithfulness. And yet, despite ten generations of faithfulness, Abram finds a way to manipulate the conversation so that his most significant desire is addressed. He immediately clings to the idea of a reward with only one logical consequence: children. Imagine, God revealing God's presence to Abram and saying, "I am your exceedingly great reward," and Abram's response is to ask for more. Abram calls God out for not giving him any offspring, and God reassures him that the heir of his household will not be a servant who was born into servitude, but a child of his own body.

Though it is Sarai who is barren, it is Abram who is stubborn in his insistence that the promise to be the father of many nations cannot apply to him. After all, his immediate response to God's covenant is to "know" his handmaid, Hagar, who becomes the mother of Ishmael. Even if this is Sarai's suggestion, it was Abram who is responsible for pursuing Hagar, using her for her womb, knowing that she would be subject to Sarai's dominance because she was a servant in the household. Not even Abram is free of the evils of doubt.

What do we do with a covenant that is couched in so much uncertainty and the honest acknowledgment of trauma? "Your descendants will live as immigrants in a land that isn't their own, where they will be oppressed slaves for four hundred years" (v. 13) is not the good news of God for the people of God.

Rather, it is God's unflinching honesty that makes the covenant with Abram even more remarkable. Once the expulsion from Eden has occurred, God keeps the promise to increase labor pangs and suffering. God keeps the promise to return humankind to dust. God keeps the promise to Noah not to destroy the earth again. God will keep this promise to Abram to make him the father of descendants who number more than the stars. But God never promises ease. In fact, God assures Abram of the exact opposite and blesses him with the gift of foreshadowing.

Thanks to this, we learn early in our narrative about God's relentless pursuit of humanity that the Promised Land isn't the end. The story doesn't stop there, the credits do not roll. It seems as though the point is not *reaching* the Promised Land, but figuring out how to live there well. At the conclusion of every disagreement, battle, and conflict is a promise that things will be better from now on (we promise!). But Genesis 8:21 states a cold, hard truth: "The ideas of the human mind are evil from their youth." If God has made peace with this truth, then how can we?

The evil of the human heart is our handicap. It is the thing that inclines us to judgment, capitalistic aspiration, selfishness, ridicule, and envy. Our internalized prejudices are based on our anxiety that we might not survive. To cope with this fear, we develop hierarchical systems of power that only serve to oppress. Adam and Eve feared the lack of knowledge, Cain murdered Abel because he was envious, and despite God's ample provision of creation, humankind seems hell-bent on ignoring the command to "be fruitful and multiply," in favor of impotence and hoarding. The only thing that is fruitful in this narrative is doubt.

Death doesn't discriminate between the sinners and the saints, so how do we plan to live this life? Even if we reached the Promised Land, we would not be finished with our job of living well together. Our challenge as preachers is to invite our congregations to deepen their faith without the gift of foresight. God always keeps God's promises, even and *especially* through times of trial.

Bringing the Text to Life

> Death doesn't discriminate between the sinners and the saints,
> it takes, and it takes, and it takes.[4]

Lin-Manuel Miranda's Aaron Burr sings these lines in his biographical anthem, acknowledging the cold truth about death's universal pursuit of life. Birth and death leave no instructions, so it is our custom to seek out meaning and direction wherever we can find it. The organizing principle of humanity is found in the ethics of how we spend our time during the rise and fall of the sun each day. The transactional give-and-take of our effort defines our lives, organizes our time, and preserves our economy. As pastors, it is our duty to preach the good news of God's relentless pursuit of humanity, which has more power than death ever will. Our toiling means that we will have something meaningful to say about ancient texts and old promises.

‹0, 2022–Third
ʌnday in Lent

*Isaiah 55:1-9; Psalm 63:1-8; 1 Corinthians 10:1-13; **Luke 13:1-9***

Charley Reeb

Preacher to Preacher Prayer

Lord, forgive us when we forget to "number our days," as the psalmist reminds us (Ps 90:12). Help us to be ever mindful that the world is hungry for the fruit you call us to produce. Amen.

Commentary

This passage in Luke records one of the rare moments Jesus was confronted with the age-old question: why do people suffer? A crowd has just received word that Pontius Pilate has executed some defiant Galileans and their blood was mixed with their blood sacrifices to God. A common belief among Jews at the time was that sin brings calamity, so it seems the crowd was seeking Jesus to confirm this long-held belief. Were these victims of tragedy worse sinners than the rest of us? Was God punishing them for their sins? Jesus quickly dismissed such thinking.

We may find some comfort from Jesus's dismissal of the idea that our sin brings divine punishment, but it is short-lived. No sooner had Jesus shot down their beliefs about suffering than he used it as an opportunity to call the crowd to repent. He does the same after referencing a tower near the pool of Siloam that fell and killed eighteen people. Jesus doesn't seem too concerned about the crowd's existential struggles. His response conveys that everyone suffers and no one gets out of this world alive, so we better have our affairs in order. What's important to Jesus is not solving theological puzzles but telling his listeners to get right with God. "Unless you change your hearts and lives, you will die just as they did" (Luke 13:5). It is not that questions of suffering are without merit; it is that such inquiries are futile without repentance. For reinforcement, Jesus shared a short, blunt parable about fruitless branches that need to be cut off and thrown out. In the parable there is a hint of God's patience with the unrepentant, but it will not last forever.

As preachers, what are we to do with this troubling text? Jesus wasn't exactly following the pastoral care guidelines we learned in seminary. If we are honest, his response makes us cringe a little. If someone came into our office struggling with questions about God and suffering, we would probably handle it much differently. Chances are we would not say, "Everyone suffers. Get over it. What's important is that judgment is coming and you need to get right with God. Are you saved and, if so, are you walking your talk?"

Jesus's response reminds me of those funerals where the preacher rather boldly stands over the casket and proclaims that tomorrow is not promised to anyone, so be sure you are prepared to "meet your maker." I always walk away from such funerals fuming about the insensitivity of the pastor. Yet here is Jesus taking advantage of a conversation about tragedy by urging the crowd to repent. Maybe those bold funeral preachers are simply following the example of Jesus.

What is challenging about this text is not just how to prepare a sermon about it but how it convicts us as preachers. When was the last time you preached an honest-to-goodness "come to Jesus" sermon? How many of your sermons have called listeners to repent and believe in the gospel? How long has it been since you preached prophetically about the idols in our lives that replace God and prevent us from bearing fruit?

Perhaps finding a sermon in this text is not as difficult as finding the courage to preach it. Honestly, the sermonic message of this passage is as plain as day. We must remind our listeners that out of all the questions of life we grapple with, none are more important than where we stand before God. Do we "live as those who are prepared to die"?[5]

Faithfully preaching on this text will probably not move your congregation to rise up and call you blessed. But one thing is certain. It's a message we all need to hear. We never know when our time will run out. Are we living like it?

Bringing the Text to Life

Although it is the season of Lent, a reference to Charles Dickens's *A Christmas Carol* may drive home a sermon on this text in Luke. It is a story for all seasons. Ebenezer Scrooge repented after receiving stark admonitions about the way he was living his life. Scrooge's first warning came in the form of a haunting visit from his deceased business partner Jacob Marley. The chains Marley laboriously carried for eternity represented all the time he wasted on his own selfish pursuits. Just as poignant were the words of warning he uttered to Scrooge:

> No space of regret can make amends for one's life opportunity misused. . . .
> "Business!" cried the Ghost, wringing its hands again. "Mankind was my business. The common welfare was my business; charity, mercy, forbearance, and benevolence, were, all, my business. The dealings of my trade were but a drop of water in the comprehensive ocean of my business!"

Marley's visit, along with those of the ghosts of past, present, and future, provided Scrooge all the motivation he needed to change his ways. He promised he would live the rest of his life bearing the fruit of kindness. He made good on that promise: "Scrooge was better than his word. He did it all, and infinitely more; and to Tiny Tim, who did not die, he was a second father. He became as good a friend, as good a master, and as good a man, as the good old city knew, or any other good old city, town, or borough, in the good old world."[6]

I recall a friend of mine telling me that when she complained about the unfairness of life, her father wisely said to her, "Newsflash! Life isn't fair. The important question is what are you going to do about it?" Such a response is akin to the old story of someone barking at God about suffering in the world: "Why the poverty? Why the hunger? Why so many neglected children?" God replied, "I was going to ask you the same thing!"

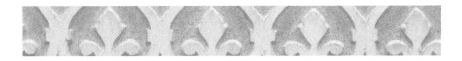

March 27, 2022–Fourth Sunday in Lent

*Joshua 5:9-12; Psalm 32; **2 Corinthians 5:16-21**; Luke 15:1-3, 11b-32*

Magrey R. deVega

Preacher to Preacher Prayer

Gracious God, thank you for surrounding me with your love. Thank you for your grace, revealed in Jesus, that enables me to hear and pursue your calling on my life. Grant me a fresh awareness of Jesus, that I may be a new creation, an ambassador of the gospel, and a minister of reconciliation in the world. Amen.

Commentary

Second Corinthians 5:16-21 contains three vivid metaphors that Paul uses to describe the work and impact of Jesus Christ: (1) *in* Christ, we are a new creation (v. 17); (2) *through* Christ, we have the ministry of reconciliation (v. 18); (3) *for* Christ, we are ambassadors, through which God is making an appeal to the world (v. 20). It is interesting to note how these different prepositions—*in* Christ, *through* Christ, *for* Christ—suggest that all that we are and all we are to do is within the context of the person and work of Jesus.

The famed writer David Foster Wallace once imagined a conversation among fish, one an older fish swimming in one direction, and the two younger fish swimming in the opposite direction. The older fish says, "Morning, boys! How's the water?" To which the younger fish respond, "What is water?"[7] Just as those fish became aware that water was the very source of their life, Paul was reminding the church in Corinth that everything they did was by the grace of God revealed in Jesus Christ. Indeed, the phrase "in Christ" is one of Paul's most favorite and often-used phrases. "For Paul, life 'in Christ' was always a communal matter," writes Marcus Borg and John Dominic Crossan. "This was so, not simply because 'it's important to be part of a church,' but because his purpose, his passion, was to create communities whose life together embodied an alternative to the normalcy of the 'wisdom of this world.'"[8]

So, the preacher might begin unpacking this text by first reminding the congregation of God's constant, pervasive, and loving presence, in which we live as community. Just as water is to fish, so is Jesus both all-encompassing and life-giving for us. Even amid the difficulties and challenges of life, God's grace surrounds us and sustains us, enabling us to fulfill all that God has created and called us to be.

But the background of Paul's second letter to the Corinthians adds an even fuller dimension to the context of God's calling on the church. The work of Jesus not only reminds us of God's presence; it reminds us of God's generosity. Second Corinthians was written as an appeal to the Christians in Corinth to practice financial generosity for the struggling Christians in Jerusalem. It is, in a sense, a fundraising letter, which calls on the Corinthians to give, not out of guilt, but out of gratitude. Because God demonstrated lavish generosity upon us by sharing the gift of Jesus, and because that gift enables us to live as a "new creation," we can therefore be a gift to others.

Paul's reminder of the constant presence and lavish generosity of God in Christ is the basis for our calling to be reconcilers and ambassadors. In Christ, we can become the agents through which God can restore broken humanity back to God's originally intended order.

Bringing the Text to Life

The preacher might choose to explore further Paul's use of "ambassador" as a metaphor for our calling as Christians. Modern-day ambassadors have some basic characteristics and functions we can apply to the spiritual life.

First, ambassadors are not citizens of the countries in which they reside, but citizens of the country they represent. George Shultz, former secretary of state during the Reagan administration, recounted the following story to C-SPAN's Brian Lamb. He kept a large globe in his office, and when newly appointed ambassadors interviewed with him, he would test them. "You have to go over to the globe and prove to me that you can identify your country." Most of the time they would go over, spin the globe, and put their finger on the country to which they were being sent. When Shultz's old friend and former Senate majority leader Mike Mansfield was appointed ambassador to Japan, even he was put to the test. But this time, Ambassador Mansfield spun the globe and put his hand on the United States. He said, "That's my country."

"I've told that story, subsequently, to all the ambassadors going out," Shultz told Lamb. "'Never forget when you're over there in that country, that your country is the United States. You're there to represent us. Take care of our interests and never forget it, and you're representing the best country in the world.'"[9]

We who are ambassadors for Christ may be living in this world, but we are not of this world. We are ambassadors for Christ, which means our primary allegiance and obedience is to the kingdom of God.

Second, ambassadors carry the message of the leader they represent. An ambassador's chief job is simply to be the mouthpiece of the president (in the case of American ambassadors) or the emperor (in the case of ancient Roman ambassadors). As ambassadors for Christ, our only job is to speak the words and desires of Jesus. That means that if we are silent, we are not doing our job. If we aren't communicating

Christ's message of love and hope and justice to people who haven't heard it, regardless of whether or not they will accept it or believe it, then we are not fulfilling our responsibility to Jesus.

Third, ambassadors carry out the mission of the leader. Paul is clear that our job as ambassadors is "the ministry of reconciliation." Our mission is to work toward nothing less than the full reconciliation of the world back to God, and the full redemption of this whole broken creation back to the way that God intends it.

Look for These New Titles from Abingdon Press

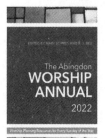

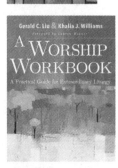

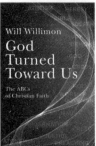

April 3, 2022–Fifth Sunday in Lent

Isaiah 43:16-21; Psalm 126; Philippians 3:4b-14; **John 12:1-8**

Robert W. (Will) Clark

Preacher to Preacher Prayer

Hear us, God, who calls us to love and serve. May we recognize in you one worthy of our extravagant praise. As we walk with you toward Jerusalem, give us ears to hear and wisdom to understand your teachings and the depth of your sacrificial love for us. Amen.

Commentary

This shared meal, hosted by Lazarus and his sisters, takes place only half of a chapter after Jesus commanded Lazarus back to life and only a few verses after temple authorities formalized their plot to kill Jesus. This gathering is only one day before Jesus and his followers enter Jerusalem to shouts of "Hosanna!" Placing this story in context may prove a helpful beginning to your sermon.

Consider a focus on Mary's extravagant acts of devotion: the expensive oil (nearly a year's wages), anointing of Jesus's feet, and drying them with her hair. Why did she go to such extremes and at great expense? How does our worship compare to Mary's passion? There is an opportunity here to challenge the congregation to examine our understanding of who Jesus is, the extent of his sacrifice on our behalf, and what it means to follow him.

In verses 4-6, Judas is presented as a complainer, a thief, a betrayer, and as lacking compassion. Consideration of this lack of compassion is intriguing. If only Judas understood Jesus and his deep care for those considered less fortunate, ostracized, oppressed, and forgotten. Pope Francis expressed similar concerns in his book *Encountering Truth: Meeting God in the Everyday*. He contrasts the worship posture of Mary against the uncaring criticisms of Judas. He writes, "This is the first reference that I have found, in the Gospel, to poverty as an ideology. The ideologue does not know what love is, because he does not know how to give himself."[1] The preacher may investigate how Judas's lack of understanding of Jesus's core teachings and purpose led to the betrayal. Perhaps Judas was so consumed with his own ideas and vision for the future that he failed to comprehend Mary's commitment to, and appreciation of, the present.

When Jesus said, "Leave her alone," he was responding directly to Judas and his selfishly motivated rebuke of Mary's offering. Jesus is also speaking to all who have ever looked down on others who may worship, serve, and practice their faith in a different manner. What Judas harshly labeled a waste of money and a misdirected offering, Jesus deemed a foreshadowing of his death and a worthy anointing (vv. 7-8).

This story sets the stage for Jesus and his followers over the next week. Jesus claims his role as the promised Messiah. Mary prematurely, yet rightly, prepares Jesus for his burial with the pouring of the nard over his feet and by reverently drying them with her hair. Fueled by his lack of character and compassion, Judas will soon betray Jesus to the authorities who are plotting his death (John 11:49-53).

This week's Gospel reading offers a contrast between Mary's sacred expression of worship and Judas's irreverence and deceit. Mary, perhaps unknowingly, prepares the perfect unblemished lamb for sacrifice. Judas is angry and impatient. He attempts to force Jesus into the role of a political and military leader, a role Judas desires, ignoring the role Jesus willingly assumes on our and on Judas's behalf. Jesus is about to do a new thing and his followers did not understand (Isa 43:19).

This is an opportunity to challenge the congregation to explore where we may be placing our own plan above God, church, and families. Are we so in love with Jesus that we fall at his feet in worship? Or are we impatient and in disagreement with the direction our lives are taking or with the decisions made by church leaders? The Gospel lesson for today allows the opportunity to explore an array of emotions. In preaching, we can connect Mary's act of anointing with Jesus's imminent death and burial. We can illuminate the contradictory viewpoints of Mary and Judas as well as Jesus's response: "but you won't always have me" (v. 8). This passage challenges our perspective of the person of Jesus, the depth of his love for us, and our response through praise, worship, and discipleship.

Bringing the Text to Life

As I approach forty years of marriage, I think about lessons learned. How did my wife and I make it this long? Or more appropriately, how did she put up with me all these years? If I could offer one piece of advice to help a marriage (or any important relationship), it would be this: on a regular basis ask yourself this question, "How do they know that I love them?" This is a helpful way to assess our outward expressions of love and appreciation. Over time, some couples find themselves in a rut. Standing back and looking at the words we share, as well as the things we do and don't do, can reveal a pattern of apathy, assumption, and in some cases outright neglect.

In our lesson today from the Gospel of John 12:1-8, we have an example of both extremes. Mary extravagantly expresses her deep devotion and love for Jesus. In contrast, we have Judas Iscariot chastising Mary by publicly complaining and placing his opinion over and above her actions. I wonder how Mary felt upon hearing this proclamation of disapproval from one of Jesus's chosen inner circle? From personal experience, I know what it is like to speak before thinking and having my words hurt or offend another. Did Judas's words make Mary feel inferior, or did they prompt her to question her heartfelt expression of love and care for Jesus?

There is no indication that Mary responded at all. I like to imagine that she was so focused on worshipping Jesus that Judas's words went unnoticed. Well, someone noticed: "Then Jesus said, 'Leave her alone.'" Jesus noticed.

April 10, 2022–Palm Sunday, Sixth Sunday in Lent

Psalm 118:1-2, 19-29; *Luke 19:28-40*

Robert W. (Will) Clark

Preacher to Preacher Prayer

Loving God, may our shouts of hosanna come from our heart and from our understanding of who you are, not who we want you to be. Thank you for loving us. May we be strengthened by your Spirit as we walk with others toward the cross and beyond. Blessed is the King of Peace! Amen.

Commentary

Each of the four Gospels documents the entry into Jerusalem of Jesus and those following him. While John's version is shorter and focuses on the relation to messianic prophesies (Zech 9:9; Ps 118:25), the Synoptics, as the name implies, tell the story similarly, yet not identically. John 12 specifically speaks of "palm branches." Mark and Matthew are more general referring to "branches cut from the fields" and "palm branches off the trees" (Mark 11:8; Matt 21:8). Luke does not mention branches of any kind; instead he points out the spreading of cloaks on the road. All three writers take the time to explain the procurement of transportation for Jesus. Matthew and Mark join John in having the crowd shout "Hosanna!" Luke leaves that familiar cry of *Hoshiya na* (Hebrew phrase meaning "help, save me" or "salvation has come") out of his version.[2]

An interesting preaching focus could revolve around the donkey, or rather, why it is so prominent. Eight of the twelve verses from Luke 19 concern the donkey. The prophetic words of Zechariah 9:9 connect Jesus to the long-awaited messianic figure:

> Look, your king will come to you.
> > He is righteous and victorious.
> > He is humble and riding on an ass,
> > > on a colt, the offspring of a donkey.

In the previous chapter, Jesus attempted to prepare his followers for what was to come: "Jesus took the Twelve aside and said, 'Look, we're going up to Jerusalem, and everything written about the Human One by the prophets will be accomplished'" (Luke 18:31). Beyond the Hebrew prophecies, the fact that Jesus was riding while everyone else was walking would also be understood as a sign of power and authority. This particular donkey colt "has never been ridden" (19:30), implying that the very purpose of this animal's existence was for this moment. This donkey was born to bear the king.[3]

Now what about the human characters in this donkey story? We have Jesus giving the instructions, two unidentified disciples running the errand, and the animal's owner. The two disciples displayed obedience and faith. The rabbi said, "Go find me a ride," and the students found the rabbi a ride. Yet, beyond obedience to Jesus's request, the disciples must have understood the symbolism of this task and the prophetic significance. They were going to find the perfectly suited mount for a king. The words of Zechariah (9:9) and the psalmist (118:25) must have rung in their ears. They were on a royal errand, preparing for the entrance of the king.

The owner of the colt is depicted as one who is obedient to the call of the king. He logically asks, "Why are you untying the colt?" (v. 33). Upon hearing that "its master needs it" (v. 34), the owner offers no response. In this context we can assume that the owner knew exactly who "the master" was, and faithfully contributed to the cause. Perhaps he silently backed into his home, retrieved his cloak, laid it on the ground, and joined in the shouts of, "Blessings on the king who comes in the name of the Lord. Peace in heaven and glory in the highest heavens" (v. 38).

As we celebrate what is referred to as the "triumphant entry," it is helpful to remember the context of Jesus's donkey ride through the Holy City. Preceding these verses is the parable of a king whose people did not want him. The verses following reveal Jesus's sadness as he weeps over Jerusalem and a people who "didn't recognize the time of your gracious visit from God" (v. 44).

Whether the story is told with emphasis on the donkey colt, the owner, the disciples' errand, or the waving of palms alongside a road covered with cloaks, God's love for God's people, and our relationship with God, must be the central themes.

Bringing the Text to Life

Have you ever wondered what happened to the donkey Jesus rode into Jerusalem? Did it make its way back to Bethphage? Did it remain with Jesus and his followers over the next week? Did the donkey have a name? In the scheme of Palm Sunday and the Holy Week events, these seem like trivial questions, and perhaps they are. If we are not careful it is easy to get caught up in the less significant aspects of Jesus's arrival and procession through Jerusalem. The riding on a donkey, the waving of palms, the throwing of cloaks, and the shouting of our hosannas are the better-known symbols of this day. However, our focus should be on the One who gives them importance.

When Jesus instructed two of his disciples to go ahead, find, and untie, "a colt that no one has ever ridden," it was Jesus inviting the disciples to participate in the fulfillment of our Old Testament prophecies. It was Jesus who transformed a young, soon-to-be work animal, into the King-bearing colt. The recognition of Jesus as the "One who comes to save" prompts the citizens of Jerusalem to carpet the road before him with their coats. It is not the traditional dates set aside on our calendars that make this week holy; it is the person of Jesus Christ, the Messiah. The importance of today is more than Jesus entering through a gate on a donkey. Today is about the love of God for us, a love that led Jesus down this road to the cross, a love that led to Jesus's suffering and death on our behalf, and a love that binds Jesus's resurrection to our salvation and eternal life. That is important.

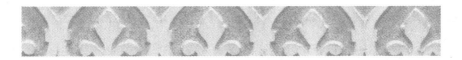

April 14, 2022–Maundy Thursday/Holy Thursday

Exodus 12:1-4 (5-10), 11-14; Psalm 116:1-2, 12-19;
*1 Corinthians 11:23-26; **John 13:1-17, 31b-35***

Robert W. (Will) Clark

Preacher to Preacher Prayer

Our compassionate God, hear our prayers of thanksgiving as we humbly sit at your table.
May we heed your call to serve others following your example of sacrificial love. Hear again
our confessions as we rest in the assurance of the forgiveness you bought for us. Amen.

Commentary

Preparing the congregation to fully experience Holy Week can be challenging. Prior planning by the preacher and worship team will determine the direction and focus of the various worship experiences (palm procession, cantata, living Last Supper, tenebrae . . .). Our task is to communicate with the congregation. In addition to scheduling, it is helpful to provide background regarding why we observe this last week of Jesus's life and how we will do this in a meaningful manner. Communication is contextual (newsletter, email, social media, verbal announcements, etc.). Communicating is essential to relationships and this season is about relationships—the relationship between the Holy Week worship experiences and, more importantly, the relationship between Jesus and his followers.

The Gospel of John tells a different story than Matthew, Mark, and Luke. Whereas the Synoptics agree on a Passover meal setting for this Last Supper, John places Jesus and his disciples at an evening meal before the Festival of Passover (v. 1). The cup and bread are replaced by a towel and a basin (vv. 4-5). In John 13, Jesus offers an object lesson on sacrificial love as he humbly washes his disciple's feet and instructs them to follow his example.

Verse 1 sets the stage for the events of this meal and the Farewell Discourse delivered in the following chapters (vv. 14-17). We now move from anticipating the hour Jesus predicted, to experiencing it.[4] This is a clear shift in the Gospel story as

John tells it. Jesus's earthly ministry is ending and he will return to his father. This will make more sense as the disciples witness Jesus's death, resurrection, and ascension. The NIV, NRSV, and CEB have slightly different takes on the last sentence of verse 1. All three acknowledge that Jesus loved "his own" in the world (v. 1). They differ in the way they interpret what is happening now, at the time of the meal. While the translations specifically address depth or duration, the main point we can take from this opening verse is that something new is happening. This is a transition from preparation for, to participation in, the last days of Jesus on earth.

Verse 2 addresses the source or influence of Judas's betrayal. Contrasting Judas's act with the acts Jesus is about the perform demonstrates the tension between betrayal and commitment, disobedience and obedience. Verse 3 gives us a window into Jesus's mindset. "Jesus knew the Father had given everything into his hands and that he had come from God and was returning to God" (v. 3). When Jesus, as host and leader, assumes the role of a servant, he is modeling his expectation of how the disciples should live their lives going forward and provides the disciples and us a preview of what to expect when the day comes for us to dwell in his father's house.

Peter's initial refusal to accept Jesus's sacrificial act is consistent with the disciples misunderstanding of Jesus as the Messiah. When Peter hears Jesus's words of condition, he realizes that this foot washing is not only an act of radical hospitality, it is an invitation to join Jesus beyond this table. Although Peter is eager to accept, he does not yet understand the persecution and the personal cost of discipleship. This becomes evident in his own impending denial of Jesus, predicted in verse 38.

The depth of Jesus's love for the disciples and how far he is willing to go to prove it are expressed in the second part of our lectionary reading (vv. 31b-35). Jesus explains that his time has come. The disciples are told that Jesus is leaving, and they cannot come with him. Knowing how this must distress them, Jesus offers instruction: "Love each other. Just as I have loved you, so you also must love each other" (v. 34).

This commentary began with a reminder that the Gospel stories we identify as Holy Week are connected in a way that emphasizes relationships. We see how the events of this week are connected, leading us from his approach to Jerusalem, through his last days with his disciples including the Last Supper, through his arrest, persecution, execution, burial, and resurrection. Beyond the temporal events is the valuable teaching of how Jesus connects us to eternity. This relationship that begins in the now is intended to last forever.

A Maundy Thursday message is about the power of Jesus's gesture of humble servant leadership, and it is about the lesson Jesus teaches us about our future with him in his father's house. Our present and future as disciples are summed up in Jesus's instruction to love one another as he loves us.

Bringing the Text to Life

I asked a small sampling of people two questions. The first was "Have you ever had your feet washed by another person?" Specifically thinking about Maundy

Thursday, the second question had two parts, "Would you participate in a foot washing service?" and "If not, do you miss it?"

Considering the potential for spreading harmful viruses (COVID-19) or other contagions, foot washing in the context of a worship experience may be a thing of the past. I miss it. I miss the little things that I previously took for granted. When we locked the doors to the church in March 2020, with no clear end in sight, we had no idea how long it would be before we could gather. We did not know the magnitude or duration of that season of isolation and social distancing. The sudden realization that we would no longer worship together in person hit hard and elicited a variety of emotions.

Then something happened. We experimented with new ways to gather, worship, study, and fellowship. We videoconferenced, prerecorded, livestreamed, and we realized that God in Jesus through the Holy Spirit was with us and had never left.

Jesus instructed his followers to love one another as he loves them (us). The love of Jesus and our expression of it is greater than all that seeks to separate us from that love.

April 15, 2022–Holy Friday/ Good Friday

Isaiah 52:13-53:12; *Psalm 22; Hebrews 10:16-25 or 4:14-16; 5:7-9; John 18:1–19:42*

Allen Johnson

Preacher to Preacher Prayer

Dear Lord, It has already been a long week with Easter Sunday coming. We have preached and prayed. We have waved palm branches and washed feet and now we face "Good" Friday. We pray for strength and guidance. Lift our eyes beyond our context and help us to see this day as part of your plan—a plan from the beginning, one foretold by the prophets through the centuries, your plan for salvation that now comes to fruition on Good Friday. Amen.

Commentary

Good Friday presents to the preacher some rather obvious themes, but you may want to take a chance on a new idea. When our assigned texts are read together, we see how the story of Good Friday was the fulfillment of Old Testament scripture.

As a believer, I cannot help seeing a connection to the Good Friday story in Isaiah 52:13–53:12. It is a beautiful scripture that needs to be read during Holy Week. In fact, in the movie *Jesus of Nazareth* by Franco Zeffirell, the director takes some poetic license and puts the words of the prophet Isaiah on the lips of Nicodemus during the crucifixion scene. While this is not part of the Gospel account, it is a powerful image of Jesus as the suffering servant. Zeffirell uses this scene to show how Nicodemus now understood Christ's words to him, "You must be born anew" in John 3. The connection between the Gospel text and the twenty-second psalm is more direct. John 19:23-24 is a direct quote from Psalm 22:18. Most listeners will also recognize Jesus's cry from the cross, "My God! My God, why have you left me all alone?" (Ps 22:1), which is not in the Gospel of John but is in other Gospel accounts of Good Friday. This psalm is a wonderful complement to our Gospel text as well. In the Gospel lesson itself there are several direct quotations about the fulfillment of prophecy. Beside the focus text there is John 19:36-37: "These things happened to fulfill the scripture, *They won't break any of his bones.* And another scripture says, *They will look at him whom they have pierced.*" In John 19:28 we read, "After this, knowing that everything was already completed, in order to fulfill the scripture, Jesus said, 'I am thirsty.'" These three texts, read together, give us an image of Good Friday that is enriched throughout the centuries by the warning of the prophets and the pastoral call of the Psalms. One is led to believe that God's plan of salvation is now coming to fruition on Good Friday. You might say the dice were loaded.

The preaching point that I am suggesting is that Good Friday was part of God's plan. Christ's suffering was not without purpose. While Christ's crucifixion was an act of injustice, God would use it to transform the world. On Good Friday, when all seemed lost, God makes a way where there appears to be no way. This is where reading the Old Testament scriptures could be helpful. They do not let us trivialize or use a platitude in regard to suffering. It is real and cannot always be understood or explained. But Christ's suffering was part of the plan, God's plan of salvation, and Christ calls us to join him in his suffering. The preacher must invite the listener to join Christ in his suffering by realizing their suffering could be part of God's plan of salvation in their own life. The preacher should help the listener connect their own personal suffering to the larger picture of salvation. Be careful not to say, "God caused it to happen" or even "God let it happen as part of God's will." I have heard it said, "God never causes suffering, but God does not let a good opportunity go to waste." My personal view is that my faith may or may not prevent me from drawing a bad hand or one without any aces, but it does help me to play that hand. In Psalm 139 we read, "Darkness is the same as light to you [God]!" The preacher should be careful to maintain the mystery of Christ's life, suffering, and resurrection.

Bringing the Text to Life

I have heard it said by pastors and rabbis, by religious and secular counselors alike, that the goal of counseling is to help people see their suffering as an opportunity for growth. Moreover, suffering can be an opportunity for self-reflection and going deeper in one's faith and trust in God. In over twenty-seven years of pastoral ministry I can think of no situation where this did not apply. Some folks receive this readily and some may never receive it, but I believe it is true. I may not understand why there is suffering, but I can trust that God knows and understands it and will meet us in the middle of it. Remember our text is on the Good Friday side of the equation, but Easter is soon coming!

In *Man's Search for Meaning*, Viktor Frankl lived through the horrors of a Nazi concentration camp during World War II. Frankl said he survived only by finding meaning within this horrific suffering. He realized he must survive so that someone could tell the world what happened. Frankl's witness is that even in horrific suffering one can find meaning.

Many years ago, I heard a sermon about a man who received a bachelor of science degree in agriculture, and just before his graduation he felt called to be a missionary. The man feared his lack of ministerial training would exclude him from the mission field, so he did not disclose his background in agriculture. The letter in response to his application read that currently the church was sending only foreign missionaries trained in agriculture.

Reading all of the lectionary texts on Good Friday gives me hope that this horrific event we call "good" had been in the hearts and minds of the prophets and psalmist. And it was probably part of the plan "in the beginning." The dice were loaded and it all went down just as God wanted it to. Give your listeners ears to hear the orchestra of heaven.

April 17, 2022–Easter Sunday/ Resurrection of the Lord

*Isaiah 65:17-25; Psalm 118:1-2, 14-24; 1 Corinthians 15:19-26 or Acts 10:34-43; John 20:1-18 or **Luke 24:1-12***

Allen Johnson

Preacher to Preacher Prayer

Spirit of the living God, fall anew on us. May your spirit take this offering of words and thought and bless it with your grace so these, my friends, may experience the living presence of Christ. Amen.

Commentary

Before we consider the larger Easter theme of this text in Luke we must admit that we are immediately confronted with obstacles—the first one being the early hour of the morning, which can truly be an obstacle for some! At that hour, as the women are nearing the tomb, the stone is mentioned. The stone was usually a large bolder or wheel-shaped stone used to seal the tomb, and would have presented a real physical obstacle for anyone. The next obstacle is the absence of the body of Jesus. What has happened to Jesus's body is the subject of volumes and volumes of research and speculation, but for our purposes there was no body mentioned in Luke until the appearance to the disciples on the road to Emmaus. So much time and energy has been spent on what happened to the body of Jesus, but let us not forgot the evangelist's message: "Why are you looking for the living among the dead?" This confusion is further enhanced by the appearance of the "two men." Luke T. Johnson describes them: "Luke does not identify the two witnesses, but wants them to be understood as supernatural figures."[5] Their appearance causes the women to fall facedown on the ground in fear. Johnson also adds, "Luke's two men issue what is in effect a rebuke leading into a reminder," saying, "Remember what he told you while he was still in Galilee, that the Human One must be handed over to sinners, be crucified, and on the third day rise again" (Luke 24:6-7).

The evangelist in just a few verses has raised some real obstacles. I believe it is to make the reader wonder if the message of the resurrection will ever be told. Perhaps this is the old "cliffhanger" technique used in television asking the audience to "tune in next week" to see how things would be resolved. But a turning point seems to happen at verse 8 with "Then they remembered his words." Now the women find a new-found confidence and faith to go and report to the other disciples. Fred Craddock states that "remembering his words is the formula for a new community of believers. . . . Remembering is often the activating of the power of recognition. For this reason alone, it is most important that the teacher and preacher share with the listeners the story of Jesus and the church . . . the times will come when the congregation will remember, and it will make a difference."[6]

What about this day are we asking the listener to remember? "Why do you seek the living among the dead?" Do not look for Christ among the tombs but among the living—among those who have experienced the spirit of the risen Christ. Look first to the women who had gone with Christ all the way, serving his ministry daily: they were at his trial, at the Crucifixion, and now the first to the empty tomb. Then look to the other disciples who experienced Christ on the road to Emmaus. Then look to Paul's conversion on the road to Damascus. Finally, look to those at the ascension and those at the Pentecost. John Wesley's heart was "strangely warmed" at a Bible study at Aldersgate and experiencing the living Christ became a cornerstone of his faith. Wesley said, "Even the demons believe in the Resurrection but they have not experienced it." Mother Teresa had an experience of the risen Christ on a train and received a call to serve the poor of Calcutta. And the countless men, women, youth, and even children who realized the Christian faith was much more than rules and obligations but a relationship with the living Christ.

Bringing the Text to Life

Jesus of Nazareth is a historical person just like Abraham Lincoln. You can love Abe Lincoln and learn about his life through reading history books. Some even impersonate him and can recite his speeches, but you will never meet Abraham Lincoln. His life is now one for the ages. But not so with Jesus the Christ. Many have experienced the presence of the living Christ. Sure, we should learn and study about the historical person and his ministry, but when we experience the grace of his living presence, then faith becomes a relationship over obligation, a living person over cold tombs of religion, a power that has transformed the world. Soon the author of Luke–Acts will tell of the Pentecost and the pouring out of the Holy Spirit, Christ's living presence with us, and the message will go out to all the world.

April 24, 2022–Second Sunday of Easter

*Acts 5:27-32; **Psalm 118:14-29** or 150; Revelation 1:4-8; John 20:19-31*

Allen Johnson

Preacher to Preacher Prayer

Gracious and merciful Lord, help us to give you thanks and praise always and everywhere. We ask that you put thanksgiving in our hearts with every breath and step we take. Teach us to give you thanks through good times and bad for we know not the difference. Enable us to give thanks, for this is the essence of our existence. Amen.

Commentary

If you have ever tried to teach a young child how to say "thank you," then you know there is a mild ritual involved. When our daughter was about two years old, we began teaching her. When she wanted something, we would say "thank you" as we gave the item to her. She slowly learned to respond with "thank you." Then she learned to say it in order to try and get what she wanted! But eventually she learned how to properly say thank you. Later, we would have to repeat this little ritual when she failed to give thanks for something. Our daughter is now an adult but we still remind each other to say thank you. Learning to give thanks requires intention and repetition.

Psalm 118 is a psalm of thanksgiving. It is a ritual of giving thanks to God. One can observe the intention and repetition in verses 1-4, "God's faithful love lasts forever." According to the Interpretation Bible Commentary, Psalm 118 was used as a ritual of thanksgiving as part of worship. It is part of the group of psalms known as "the Egyptian Hallel" used in the joyous annual festivals. The Interpretation Bible says Psalm 118 is in two parts, verses 5-18 and verses 19-28. The first part is a thanksgiving by an individual who has experienced God's deliverance from enemies and the second part, verses 14-28, is a "community performing the ritual of thanks."[7] There is evidence of this in verse 15, "The sounds of joyful songs and deliverance are heard in the tents of the righteous." And in verse 19, "Open the gates of righteousness for me so I can come in and give thanks to the LORD!" This refers to the psalmist's entry into the temple.

A particular preaching point can be found in verses 22-24,

> The stone rejected by the builders
> > is now the main foundation stone!
> This has happened because of the LORD;
> > it is astounding in our sight!
> This is the day the LORD acted;
> > we will rejoice and celebrate in it!

"The saying may be a proverb with a single, simple point, the reversal of what was expected."[8] The thing human beings have discounted and thrown away has now become the most valuable stone in the structure. In verse 5 the psalmist describes being in "tight circumstances" but the Lord delivered them into "wide-open spaces." In verse 12 the psalmist describes being surrounded by bees but "in the LORD's name" they were extinguished like "burning thorns." Verse 17: "I won't die—no, I will live and declare what the LORD has done." In verses 10-11 the psalmist, against all odds, is surrounded by the enemy and there appears no way out, but God makes a way. Even the resources of deliverance are not the usual helpers:

> It's far better to take refuge in the LORD
> > than to trust any human.
> It's far better to take refuge in the LORD
> > than to trust any human leader. (vv. 8-9)

The message of this pericope is a reversal of what is usually expected.

A reversal of fortune or a reversal of what was expected is an easy preaching point in the Easter season. The preacher can go right through Holy Week and illustrate this message again and again. Jesus, the cornerstone, is rejected by the religious leaders but will become the foundation of a new movement. On Good Friday what must seem like the end to many of Christ's followers is really the beginning. The disciples who had left everything to follow him may have believed all was lost on Good Friday only to have it restored on Easter morning. Death turns into resurrection, sadness into joy, suffering into healing, those who think they have lost have really won, and those who thought they had stopped Jesus's ministry were in for a huge surprise. There is a reversal of fortune or a reversal of what was expected throughout Holy Week. Illustrations of a reversal of fortune can be found throughout the Bible: Noah was asked to build a boat on dry land. Abraham and Sarah could only "hope against hope" that they would become the parents of a new nation of people. David was only a youth but was picked over his older brothers to replace King Saul. And who can forget how David killed Goliath not with Saul's armor, but with five smooth stones provided by God. What about Naamam being told to bathe in the muddy waters of the Jordan to cure his leprosy when he knew of much more beautiful waters than the Jordan? It should not take the preacher long to add to this list.

God is a God who honors that which the world rejects—a God who finds value in what the world discounts and casts away—a God who reverses what is expected, bringing light from darkness, life from a dead womb and empty tomb. We have a God who makes a way when there appears to be no way. For this we give thanks.

Bringing the Text to Life

Years ago, I overheard a conversation in a restaurant between an older woman and her younger friend. The older woman told story after story of hardships and sufferings but after each episode she would tell the young woman "in all things give thanks." At first, I thought this was the craziest thing that I had ever heard. Why give thanks for trials and tribulations, for pain and suffering? But it was almost like the older woman could read my thoughts. After each trial she would describe something she learned. After each tribulation came a renewed understanding of God and a deeper trust. Each problem and challenge, which were many, was approached with "praise and thanksgiving." The woman's witness was heavy upon my heart the remainder of the day and well into the night. Finally, as my mind accepted her message, my heart broke and her witness fell into my heart. In all things, all things learn to give thanks and praise. This experience taught me to be intentional in giving thanks for *all* things.

May 1, 2022–Third Sunday of Easter

Acts 9:1-6 (7-20); *Psalm 30; Revelation 5:11-14; John 21:1-19*

Cyndi McDonald

Preacher to Preacher Prayer

God of resurrection and life, it's still Easter. The lilies may be gone, but the stone is still rolled away, the tomb is still empty, and you are still at work breaking down dividing walls and building your church. Help me discern how you are still at work in the world, and how I might be part of your grand story. Amen.

Commentary

Many of our hearers are familiar with the Damascus road story of Saul, who is blinded by a light as he journeys to persecute the early church. Yet Saul is not the only one who hears the voice of the Lord in this story. The tale ends with two miracles. Ananias goes to Saul and lays hands on him, restoring Saul's sight. Just as miraculous as this physical healing is Ananias's name for Saul when he arrives: brother.

Ananias has no reason to help Saul. Indeed, he is well acquainted with Saul (he seems to think he knows more than God does about this foe!). As we often do when there is reason to be fearful, Ananias has paid close attention to news of Saul's activity. Directed to go and help Saul, who has been blinded on the road to Damascus, Ananias wonders whether God understands the situation. It's humorous. Of course God knows what Saul has been up to.

Two clues from the Lord's conversation with Ananias lead to this miraculous change in Ananias's attitude toward Saul. First, Ananias learns that there is more to Saul than he realized. The Lord explains, "I will show him how much he must suffer for the sake of my name" (9:16).

Understanding that Saul will suffer is one reason why Ananias needs to call Saul his brother. There is nothing that Saul can do to rectify the pain he has caused. But understanding Saul as vulnerable is part of this miracle of conciliation. Throughout history, times in which people have been able to see others' suffering has brought healing. More recently, the success of the South African and Canadian Truth and Reconciliation Commissions included the healing that occurred in the sharing of stories of victims and perpetrators.

Second, there is also healing in a shared purpose. When he learns that Saul was chosen to proclaim the name of Jesus to Gentiles, kings, and Israelites, Ananias recognizes a shared mission. The mission of these followers is one of being Jesus's witnesses "in Jerusalem, in all Judea and Samaria, and to the ends of the earth" (Acts 1:8).

Is there a time in the congregational community when people came together with shared purpose? Consider church history. Perhaps a flood, a tornado, a hurricane broke down barriers. Older members may share ministry to one another during the depression. Churches segregated on Sunday morning organized a time of serving together. People from both sides of the poverty tracks came together to feed or provide shelter. Remind the congregation how God used a common purpose to bring good out of a difficult situation.

Bringing the Text to Life

Fred Craddock tells of being stuck in a Canadian snowstorm, in a bus station café. The weather was freezing and the wind bitter; travelers called out, "Close the door!" each time another stranger straggled in. The watered-down soup tasted horrible, but both the soup and the room provided needed warmth. When the manager tried to reject a woman unable to purchase soup, all of the customers got up to leave with her. The manager relented and let her remain. Fred describes sitting at the table, recognizing a new flavor to the soup. Something familiar. "I don't know what was in it, but I do recall when I was eating it, it tasted a little bit like bread and wine. Just a little bit like bread and wine."[1]

Perhaps your community has experienced something similar. Hearing stories, working together, seeing one another in new ways, a meal took on a new flavor, that of bread and wine. Can you reframe this so that your congregation sees their own history as witnessing in Jerusalem, in all of Judea and Samaria, and to the ends of the earth?

If your worship includes a children's sermon, or you have a creative spirit and are willing to poke fun at yourself, consider purchasing inexpensive sunglasses from a dollar store. Use either heart-shaped glasses, or glue a large heart to the nosepiece of a ridiculously sparkly pair. The heart should be large enough so that it blocks most of the view through the lens. Bring these in a box or glasses case.

Set up the story by describing the importance of regular checkups with doctors and eye doctors to make sure that everything is OK. Tell the story of a recent visit to the eye doctor, a Great Physician, who examined your eyes and said that you need new glasses. The good news is that they now have glasses that will help you for the rest of your life. Instead of new glasses every year or two, with these glasses on you will always see as the Great Physician wants you to see. Slowly open a glasses case or other box to show the glasses. Point out that the heart gets in the way and reminds us to look with love. How do we look with love glasses? When I see someone with love, I want what's best for them. I don't need to be jealous of what they have. I can just want what is best for them. When we have known Jesus's love, we begin to look at others with eyes of love. In the story from Acts, we think of Paul as the one who was unable to see and needed Ananias's help. But it turns out Ananias also needed help in seeing Paul. He needed eyes of love to see Paul not as an enemy but as someone who also would suffer in serving God. For a children's sermon, conclude with a prayer: "Dear God, thank you for Jesus, who teaches us to see others with love, the way you see people. Amen."

May 8, 2022–Fourth Sunday of Easter/Mother's Day

Acts 9:36-43; **Psalm 23**; Revelation 7:9-17; John 10:22-30

Cyndi McDonald

Preacher to Preacher Prayer

God, like a mother hen you long to collect your chicks under your wings of protection. On this Mother's Day, we pray for those for whom this is a difficult day. No mother or father is perfect, only you. May the words of my mouth bring hope and healing, pointing to you, and the abundant eternal life you offer. Amen.

Commentary

The metaphor of shepherd is used throughout scripture. Leaders of tribes and even the king are appointed as shepherds to care for their flocks (2 Sam 7:7). Obviously, the beloved Twenty-Third Psalm describes the Lord as a shepherd. In today's passage, Jesus describes his own relationship with those who follow him. The shepherd Jesus offers eternal life within the security of being held in the Father's hand.

Although Jesus describes the inability for others to snatch his flock away, this does not mean that Jesus is offering minimum entrance requirements that a sheep can use to certify that they are safe. Rather, Jesus describes an active relationship. Those who belong to him *listen* to his voice. Listening is an active verb, implying an attentiveness that cuts through distractions and noise.

In describing his own relationship with the Father as being "one," we get a glimpse of what Jesus desires for the flock: unity. Genesis 1:27 describes God creating both male and female, multiple persons, and together they reflect the image of God. Active listening to the shepherd is part of restoration of many persons who will together portray the image of a three-in-one, one-in-three God.

This is an opportunity to describe some of the means of grace that encourage active listening to Jesus. We are surrounded by voices on both extremes of the political spectrum. How can we lead in practices that help our congregation to cut through the noise and listen for the voice of Jesus who desires new life for everyone?

The following prayer practice encourages us to hear the voice of Jesus saying, "Father, forgive them" and calling his followers to love neighbors and even enemies. Consider leading the congregation in the exercise as part of the sermon. The practice can help drown out inner voices that encourage holding on to hurts or resentments.

Begin by stating that we will pray for what is best for another person, what they most need, such as peace or healing or affirmation. After all, when you truly forgive someone, you want what is best for them. First, pray for someone who is easy to pray for, such as a beloved family member or dear friend. After a moment of silence, encourage them to widen the circle, and pray for someone they don't know as well, such as a coworker or neighbor. Again, pray for what is best for them. Widen the circle, and pray for someone with whom you have a difficult relationship. Pray for what God wants for them (not your own resentments or memories). The hardest circle nowadays seems to be that of political enemies. Ask the Republican to pray for a Democrat and vice versa. You could name two recent presidents and direct them to pray for the one they admire least. Jesus forgives enemies, offers love to enemies. Instruct them to listen for resistance to praying for people with whom they disagree. Trust that prayer brings about change, and that interaction with God sometimes changes us, too. This is a means of grace![2]

Bringing the Text to Life

What story do you have of a voice cutting through the noise? As a prank, our two boys changed my cell phone ringer to them yelling, "Mom, your cell phone's ringing!" Without realizing it, they provided a ringtone that would cut through the noise of almost any setting. Sitting in restaurants or offices filled with soft chatter and conversations, the word *Mom* caused the room to hush!

The physical distancing response to the COVID-19 pandemic changed cell phone usage, with dramatic increases in the number of telephone and video calls. Perhaps your church has a story of organizing telephone and text check-ins, either for the congregation as a whole or by those most affected by isolation. Was there an individual who could not go out but was able to use the telephone to call and offer comfort through voice? Perhaps you noticed during the distancing that a phone call to a committee chair that used to take only a few minutes now seems to take three or four times as long. People long to hear voices and don't want to disconnect.

Unfortunately, we are sometimes reluctant to connect in prayer. Some of the finest Christians I know are so humble that they don't feel worthy to pray for themselves, or worthy to pray at all. A helpful children's sermon or illustration is to remind people that God is infinite. Play the following game allowing the congregation to answer (I used to play this with my children when they were in older elementary school). Infinity is more than you can count or even imagine. What is infinity plus one? (Still infinity, more than you can count.) Infinity minus seven hundred? (Still infinity, more than you can count.) How about infinity plus infinity? (Still infinity, more than you can count.) What if you split infinity, divide it by two? (Still infinity, more than you can count.) Divide infinity by a million? (Still infinity.) Divide infinity by 107 billion? (Still infinity, more than you can count.) Point out that 107 billion is about how many people have ever lived on earth. There is an infinity of God for each person who has ever lived. An infinity of God longs for you to reach out to God whether in silence, speaking, or listening, and longs to be present to you. The Father and Jesus are one. Take heart that the shepherd infinitely and lovingly is present to you.

May 15, 2022–Fifth Sunday of Easter

Acts 11:1-18; Psalm 148; Revelation 21:1-6; John 13:31-35

Cyndi McDonald

Preacher to Preacher Prayer

Dear God, sometimes we grow weary of telling the same stories to hearts that seem resistant. Our exhortations to share God's love outside of the core community are not always appreciated. Renew our spirits, that we too will never forget the importance of what we offer with you. Eternal life. Abundant life. Amen.

Commentary

Once again the writer of Acts tells the story of Peter, Cornelius, and the baptism of Gentiles. There's no need to repeat the story; he just finished describing the events (with parts already repeated) in the previous chapter. Why the repetition? Some stories have to be told multiple times in order to be heard. Perhaps your congregation is tired of hearing stories of the need for racial or another form of justice. Don't lose heart. Follow the example of the author of Acts, who also faced opposition to the idea that God's grace through Jesus Christ was for everyone. Keep telling the stories that remind us that there is no limit to God's grace, nor should we stand in God's way.

One approach to the passage is to consider who is outside the bounds of the community. This may not be intentional, but a matter of tradition or the convenience of a subset of the church. During COVID-19, many churches began using technology in new ways. In addition to the usual worship participants, technology invited the participation of those who work on Sundays and those who were shut in. How do we continue to expand the reach of those to whom we offer life?

When my niece Samantha (name changed) turned ten, she asked to invite ten friends to a birthday party. Everyone would bring their overnight bags, but her plan was that after the dinner, cake, and gifts, she would present one guest with a rose. All the other guests would return home. Her mother was shocked and dismayed by the plan (and that Samantha had been sneaking and watching *The Bachelor* on television). It's not only the Gentiles of Peter's time who are told they are not worthy of being included.

I shared my niece's proposed party plans with a member of my congregation at that time, a small rural church in Missouri. The next Sunday, during the last hymn of the worship service, she passed out a flower to everyone in the room, repeating to each person, "Everyone gets a flower." We stood there awkwardly holding hymnals and zinnias as we finished the hymn. Later in the week, I had my first real conversation with a soft-spoken bachelor farmer who usually sat in the back pew, coming late and leaving early to avoid others. He called to say how much the flower meant to him. In his seventy years, no one had ever given him a flower. It was the first of many conversations about grace and the problem of evil. He had questions but never felt welcome to share them.

The writer of Acts tells the story again, step by step, this time adding another nugget. Don't overlook the joy of those who recognized the gift to the Gentiles. God has enabled them to repent—to change their hearts and lives—so that they might have new life.

Almost every time the Christian leaders speak in Acts, there is a call to repentance. But what exactly is repentance? Samantha, in the story above, now has a toddler, who when he knows he is doing wrong, goes to his "time out" chair. Asked whether he is going to do it again, he solemnly shakes his head up and down and says yes. There is no desire for change. It will be a while before he takes to heart the confession in the holy Communion liturgy and requests that God "free us for joyful obedience."[3]

Bringing the Text to Life

In his poem "Adventures in New Testament Greek: Metanoia," Scott Cairns describes a journey of *metanoia*, the Greek word for repentance. In the poem, a slow pilgrim eventually realizes that repentance is more than saying "I'm sorry." Repentance is turning toward and not just away. The poem ends with the slow pilgrim's surprise to learn that "sin is not so bad as it is a waste of time."[4]

What would it look like to realize that hatred is a waste of time? That envy and conceit are a waste of time? To realize that there is no joy in holding on to anger and resentment? The way of Christ is characterized by fruits like love, joy, peace, patience. . . . No wonder that the early church associates changing hearts and lives with new life.

May 22, 2022–Sixth Sunday of Easter

Acts 16:9-15; Psalm 67; Revelation 21:10, 22–22:5;
John 14:23-29 *or 5:1-9*

Cynthia D. Weems

Preacher to Preacher Prayer

O God, help us to be open to new understandings of your mystery even as we seek to help others to understand. Your words are timeless, yet we live and preach in real time. Allow us to preach with confidence and humility. Amen.

Commentary

This passage from John 14 is part of what is known as the "Last Discourse" of Jesus. It is a full chapter of deep thinking and feeling from Jesus with disciples asking questions that prompt responses that are much weightier, surely, than what the disciples were anticipating. One might look back to the end of chapter 13 to set the stage for this long set of Jesus's teachings to come. He has washed the disciples' feet and foretold his betrayal. Then he continues to teach. What does he say at this critical time to his disciples?

First, he focuses on love. There is a fundamental connection between God and humanity through the love of Jesus and the keeping of his words. There are rewards, of sorts, for loving Jesus and keeping his commands. God will reward those who love Jesus. Though there is mention of those who do not love Jesus and do not keep his word, there is no mention of consequence for this. The reward for believers is the image of God coming and "making a home" with those who love Jesus and follow his commands. For those who do not love Jesus and follow his ways there is the absence of such language and images. There is power in that void, that absence. It could be considered a consequence inflicted not by God but by those who choose not to love Jesus and follow his ways. God, the three in one, is a powerful presence in the lives of those who believe. This is an invitation to make choices that will lead to that presence "making a home" with believers and those who seek to follow.

Additionally in this passage, Jesus describes the gift he is leaving humanity as the gift of his peace. This portion of his teaching is significant in that it amplifies the way in which Jesus's life is unlike anything else the world experiences. Jesus gives a gift that is not tangible yet has many tangible results. Jesus gives in a way that is "not as the world gives." Jesus encourages his followers not to be troubled or afraid, though he has foretold the tragedy that is to come. The world expects tragedy to create chaos and brokenness. Jesus gives peace in the midst of tragedy. The disciples have seen Jesus live this kind of peace as they have traveled with him, yet now he is claiming to be offering it as a gift to them, and to all the world.

This is the bridge to John's mention of the Holy Spirit. As Pentecost is nearing, it is helpful to consider assessing this passage in light of what will be amplified on Pentecost Sunday. Here, in John's Gospel, Jesus is foretelling the coming of the Holy Spirit, the Companion, that will continue to guide and teach the people after he is gone from their presence. What a difficult concept to understand, yet a remarkably comforting possibility in light of all the disciples are hearing from Jesus in this Last Discourse. The arrival of a companion to journey with them! Surely the companion they most want is Jesus. Yet, he is teaching them about the triune God, how three in one can and do live together in order to care for all of creation between chaos and eternity.

The Greek word for Spirit, *Paraclete*, means the "one who comes alongside." Indeed, this is a companion they can count on. A common human fear is the fear of being left out, left behind, or left alone. Throughout the Gospels we see examples of the disciples wanting to ensure that they will not be left alone. Jesus makes clear in this passage that not only do the disciples not have to fear abandonment, all of creation will be given the gift of one who will walk with them as a companion. For this reason, there is no need to fear.

Bringing the Text to Life

When I lived through a season of work that required a lot of travel, my young daughter used to go through a routine with me the nights before my departures where we would plan out the next few days, say a prayer, and I would "pinky promise" her to come and give her a kiss when I arrived back home, even if she was asleep. In today's passage, Jesus is laying out a set of promises for life after his departure (or ascension, as the following week will celebrate). He is preparing the disciples, discussing next steps, encouraging them, and making promises for how God will live with and in us.

A preacher could talk about how this relationship between God and humanity plays itself out over and over again as we seek to live faithfully in the presence of the Holy Spirit and with the teachings of Jesus in scripture. What does it mean to live in the peace that Jesus has gifted to us? Are there ways we neglect that peace, or toss it aside, when living in turmoil or anger or chaos is our preference? How might Jesus be challenging us to gift his peace to others through our efforts at reconciliation, justice making, and walking with the most vulnerable? What is the responsibility that comes with the gift of Jesus's peace?

May 29, 2022–Seventh Sunday of Easter/ Ascension Sunday

Acts 1:1-11 *or 16:16-34; Psalm 97; Revelation 22:12-14, 16-17, 20-21; John 17:20-26*

Cynthia D. Weems

Preacher to Preacher Prayer

Lord, as you ascended into heaven you left the disciples overwhelmed with joy. Allow our words to fill your people with that same joy, the joy that comes from knowing you and discovering you anew. Amen.

Commentary

This passage of scripture, the foundation for the celebration of Ascension Sunday, begins with a pivotal piece of information. Acts 1:2 tells us that Jesus was already working in the power of the Holy Spirit as he taught the disciples and prepared them for his ascension. What a powerful image of the triune God of our faith, that the Holy Spirit was guiding the final days of Jesus's ministry as he prepared to depart his earthly existence and give room for the Holy Spirit to be set free into the work of humanity. This displays in vivid detail the presence of God in our world through a son who "came to live among us" and an Advocate who came to walk alongside us.

The short summary offered in this text of what has happened thus far marks critical, material evidence that situates the life of Jesus in the depths of human reality. He mentions Jerusalem as the place the disciples are meant to wait for the coming of the Holy Spirit—Jerusalem, a city with so many memories of joy and pain; Jerusalem, a city of healing and teaching and a city of betrayal and death. He bookends their ministry with a reference to John and the baptism of water and what is to come with baptism through the Holy Spirit. These are images of their journey together, a journey that continues even though it is growing increasingly evident that Jesus's moments on earth are nearing an end. The words of Jesus signify to the disciples that even if there had been any doubt before now, they are the continuation of his ministry on earth. Jesus entered a story that had begun with creation and God's walk with the people of Israel, and he now prepares to exit the earthly story as the Holy Spirit comes to remain with the disciples and the growing number of faithful who will continue the work of God in the world.

The disciples then ask a question that nearly derails the conversation. They want to know about God's plan to restore the kingdom. Jesus's response, if speaking in today's vernacular, would certainly have been something like, "Stay in your lane, friends!" They are focused on things that are not under their purview. Rather, Jesus reiterates that the Holy Spirit will come upon them and they will have one primary job—being his witnesses in surrounding areas and to the end of the earth. This should be plenty to keep them busy!

Interestingly, there is a tension in the passage between what is meant to happen within the disciples themselves and what is meant to be their work in the world. Jesus's attempt to keep them focused acts as a reminder of what they will need internally in order to do the ministry ahead of them. In Ephesians 1:17, Paul writes, "I pray that the God of our Lord Jesus Christ, the Father of glory, will give you a spirit of wisdom and revelation that makes God known to you." Certainly this prayer was first revealed through Jesus's teachings and guidance to the disciples, all of whom would need this spirit of wisdom and revelation from God in order to share the good news of the risen Lord throughout the region and beyond.

The appearance of the two men in white must have startled the disciples. Equally startling would have been the men's admonishment of the disciples for "standing here, looking toward heaven." One might argue, *Where else were the disciples meant to be looking?* Yet, they had been given their marching orders and were clearly not meant to delay. First, Jerusalem. Then, the end of the earth. Ready or not, it is time to heed the words of Jesus and go.

Bringing the Text to Life

The question of *Why are you standing here?* has always stood out to me in this passage. It seems to be a question most Christians are confronted with on a regular basis. When there is so much to be done in the world, why are we just standing here? Often the answer is simply that we do not know what to do.

One idea is to bring a pair or two of shoes to the sanctuary for the preaching moment. One could be a pair of old sneakers, the kind we typically leave at the back door. Another could be flip-flops or sandals. Talk about what the shoes represent—gardening, lawn work, walking, working, even time for play. These shoes aren't typically worn throughout the house but, rather, in the world. Jesus, without the luxury of sneakers, walked into the lives of people and traveled the region living a fully human life in the depths of human heartbreak, pain, and suffering. As Jesus ascended into heaven, the disciples were left on the ground. They were standing there, but that wasn't meant to be the case for long. As the white-robed visitors made clear, the disciples had more journeying to do and their feet would get them where they needed to go and into the lives of people who needed the good news of Jesus.

Focusing on how people use the stories of their lives—where their feet have traveled, how their sneakers have gotten dirty, and what they have learned and shared in these experiences—could be a critical entry point for making the ascension relevant to the faith of those experiencing this message. Evangelists like John Wesley and Francis Asbury, traveling on their horses, and slave runners like Harriet Tubman lived their faith on their feet. How might we be called to do the same and how might the travels of our feet be representative of the stories of our faith and discipleship?

June 5, 2022–Day of Pentecost

Acts 2:1-21 or Genesis 11:1-9; Psalm 104:24-34, 35b; Romans 8:14-17 or Acts 2:1-21; John 14:8-17 (25-27)

Cynthia D. Weems

Preacher to Preacher Prayer

O God, you breathe into our lives the words needed to fill your people. Allow our reflection today to be the Spirit-breathed words of life and hope that you would give to your people on this day. Amen.

Commentary

The celebration of Pentecost in the cycle of a church year is one that should stand out among liturgical holidays. However, by virtue of falling nearly every year at the beginning of summer vacation and given the fact that it is not a favorite Hallmark holiday, Pentecost is often forgotten. It should not be so and the place it holds not only in the historical life of the church but also in the personal stories of believers is one that need be celebrated. Pentecost is both a moment in time that forever shaped the work of God in the world and among creation and it is a renewing moment for Christians to be revisited and celebrated.

Initially, a Hebrew festival called *Shavuot*, Pentecost created a moment in time where Jews from all over the ancient world would be together in one place. This moment proved instrumental for the coming of the promised Holy Spirit. Though earlier passages in Acts and the Gospels would lead one to believe the coming of the Advocate or Companion would happen in a private ceremony with the disciples as the only invited guests, Acts 2 quickly sets the scene for a much larger event. The Holy Spirit arrived and did so with a fiery bang!

At Pentecost, the promised Holy Spirit not only arrived but showed up in a way that created as many questions as it had answered. The disciples now knew what Jesus was talking about when he said the Advocate was on its way and would appear to them in Jerusalem. They could likely discern that the power of this Spirit was, indeed, strong enough to propel them to the end of the earth as Jesus has commanded them. Yet, the way in which this Spirit jumbled words made possible the sharing of proclamations in multiple tongues, and caused confusion among the large number of believers in Jerusalem. This all created a new set of questions about the implications of this Holy Spirit living and moving and working among them.

It is in this place that Christian believers live, isn't it? A place where the Spirit both offers comfort and confidence as well as challenge and wonderment. The arrival of the Holy Spirit continues the experience the disciples had of Jesus himself. He could be both crystal clear and painfully vague. He answered questions and he asked them. He knew the law and traditions and he amplified them too. This Holy Spirit quickly resembles the same Jesus who could be both known and yet remain a mystery. The Holy Spirit's arrival at Pentecost is the arrival of our triune God in a new form and with many of the same characteristics.

The surprise language potpourri that occurs at Pentecost does mystify all who are gathered. It is something that needs to be explained (Peter rises to the challenge), yet even after explanation it is something the church struggles to come to terms with even today. It is the reality that people share much of their lives in verbal ways that require communication among languages. "The end of the earth" meant a cadre of followers who would commit themselves to growing in understanding, empathy, and knowledge of others. The disciples surely did not even have the intellectual knowledge of what the end of the earth really meant! Now, at Pentecost, they were given a taste. And God's response to it was to give them exactly what they would need to share the empowering love of God and good news of salvation to all people. The Holy Spirit came to empower and to enable the people to be witnesses to Jesus's life and teachings. As Pentecost is celebrated in our churches each year, it should be a time of renewal for the ongoing work of receiving the Holy Spirit's empowerment in our lives to do the hard, challenging, and often uncomfortable work of sharing God's message of hope to all people.

Bringing the Text to Life

Considering the importance our global community plays in our daily lives and both the opportunities and challenges it presents to everyday women and men, it would be appropriate for a sermon about Pentecost to lift up the beauty and the difficulty of living in a global world with the presence of linguistic and cultural differences. Pentecost appears to be an uplifting story of bridge building through language. Yet we live in a world where language, skin color, cultural practices, and country of origin often set people apart by causing hostility and suspicion. Pentecost may be a Sunday to lift up the voice of an immigrant in your community, a person who has truly struggled with telling her story in a new language. A story could also be shared of someone who has grown in their understanding of race or language difference and can witness to the Spirit's ability to soften our hearts and open our minds.

The disciples and early believers had a story to tell about their savior. The story needed to be told with words. The Holy Spirit enabled them to do so. Each of us has a story of life and faith. Some stories point to hardship and pain. Others point to joy and accomplishment. Not everyone has the platform to share their stories equally or in a way that allows their stories to be heard. How might the Holy Spirit be empowering the church to make a way for these stories to be told, shared, heard, and better understood? And, might the modern-day work of the Spirit be moving us beyond our reliance on the verbal telling of our stories and toward the living of our stories in diverse communities where mutual respect, love, compassion, and joy are marks of the power of the Holy Spirit to continually reignite our faith and our global community toward the greater purposes of God?

June 12, 2022–Trinity Sunday

Proverbs 8:1-4, 22-31; Psalm 8; Romans 5:1-5; John 16:12-15

Peter Wallace

Preacher to Preacher Prayer

All-loving, all-wise triune God, open my heart to your wisdom, not only for the living of my life, but to equip me to embolden the people who hear my sermon to pursue godly wisdom whenever and wherever they need it. Grant us an abundance of your Spirit's presence so that we may delight in your work in us and through us. In the name of the Father, Son, and Holy Spirit. Amen.

Commentary

During the church year, only on the first Sunday after Pentecost do we focus liturgically on a theological concept. The Trinity is indeed worthy of earnest contemplative study, whether we say *Father, Son, Spirit*; or *Creator, Redeemer, Sustainer*; or *Source, Savior, Sanctifier*; or *Lover, Beloved, Love* (St. Augustine); or *Holy Parent, Divine Child, Breath of God*; or come up with our own descriptive titles.

But you, preacher, must decide if a theology lesson is what your people need to hear this week. Perhaps it is; I have heard many fine sermons attempting to explain this divine relationship that could possibly blow our minds, to help us relate more intimately with each person of the Trinity in the "Divine Dance," as Richard Rohr describes it in his book by that title. Typically throughout its three years, our common lectionary offers texts that simply mention all three persons with no clear thematic relationship between them otherwise, because the Bible itself doesn't spend much time explaining this concept directly.

Unless you have a compelling and novel approach to understanding the Trinity, I encourage you—while observing Trinity Sunday with appropriate hymns and some contextual explanation in your sermon—to explore one of the texts for what it's trying to teach us about our relationship with God, explicitly triune or not. And while the Gospel and Epistle texts offer rich meaning, Proverbs is rarely included in the lectionary, so why not focus on this delightful passage this week?

As part of the Wisdom literature of the Old Testament, the book of Proverbs credits itself as being the work of King Solomon, though it was assembled long after his reign (as a royal *festschrift* perhaps) and compiles a range of writers' work, including other kings. The title is a translation of the Hebrew word *mashal*, "a saying," and most of the content comprises pithy two-line maxims.

Wisdom literature as a whole seeks to find answers to the perplexing questions of life and faith. "Wisdom" speaks of the human pursuit to understand reality from God's point of view. The book of Proverbs attempts to collect the shared community wisdom in order to teach younger generations how to live their best lives as God's children.

Following a section in which young men are encouraged to avoid loose, mysterious women and the deadly paths they haunt (please note that this advice is applicable to all sexes), chapter 8 changes the tone to encourage us instead to follow Wisdom Woman, whom some scholars consider to be a description of the Holy Spirit (hence this text's inclusion in today's lections). The first verses tell us that Wisdom—a godly understanding of and approach to life—intervenes at every path, crossroad, gate, or entrance that demands a decision of us regarding which direction to go: the wise way or the foolish. Wisdom cries out to "all of humanity"—including us. And what does she tell us? A lot, but the lection skips ahead to explore her origins in beautiful poetic form.

God "created" Wisdom at the very beginning. Though that Hebrew term is vague, what is clear is a very intimate relationship. Wisdom was "beside [God] as a *master of crafts*"—another disputed word, which nevertheless tells us that Wisdom is a skilled worker along with God, laboring in such a way that

> I was having fun,
> smiling before him all the time,
> frolicking with his inhabited earth
> and delighting in the human race. (vv. 30-31)

Isn't that a glorious image? God the Creator and Wisdom Woman at work together, reveling in doing what they do best, resulting in complete delight in their work and each other.

How might this encourage us in our lives? Can we mirror this creative activity to make good and wholesome things—holy experiences, meaningful outreach activities, fulfilled lives—that honor the Spirit of God while making us smile? If we aren't truly happy in performing the faithful responsibilities in life, are we really where God wants us to be, doing what God calls us to do? The only way to get there is to follow Wisdom Woman on the path of righteousness and justice (v. 20).

Bringing the Text to Life

Enliven the reality of the Wisdom of God at work in our lives by suggesting events each of us faces when we come to a crossroads and confront a decision to go one direction or another—whether it's calculating business deals honestly and fairly, or responding to a flirty text message, or allowing our pent-up frustrations to explode on some innocent family member. What other examples can you imagine to share?

Then, picture Wisdom Woman beckoning us to the way of righteousness. Think of examples, perhaps involving national figures who thought they could get away with lying, cheating, or even murder until their deeds were laid bare in the glare of public revelation; there are plenty of examples, so use a fresh or local one.

How would you connect Wisdom Woman with the Holy Spirit, whom Jesus promises his disciples in the upper room (John 16:12-15)? Jesus says this is the Spirit of Truth, the one who will guide us into all truth. The Spirit is just as active today in our lives—or can be—as Wisdom was with God the divine parent at creation. And Paul reminds us (Rom 5:1-5) that we have hope "because the love of God has been poured out in our hearts through the Holy Spirit, who has been given to us." So, perhaps this week's texts work well together after all.

June 19, 2022—Second Sunday after Pentecost/ Father's Day

1 Kings 19:1-4 (5-7), 8-15a; *Psalm 42-43; Galatians 3:23-29; Luke 8:26-39*

Peter Wallace

Preacher to Preacher Prayer

Almighty God, whose thin, quiet voice I so often ignore, speak to me in the midst of my wilderness; whisper to me on the mountain of your covenant presence, so that I in response can stop running away and instead obey your call to offer your healing, rescuing word to those who so desperately need to hear it. Amen.

Commentary

Let's jump into the story of the prophet Elijah, an effective spokesperson for God and yet a very human being—just like us! In 1 Kings 19 we enter the story right after Elijah has enraged Queen Jezebel by killing "all Baal's prophets with the sword" after the thrilling contest of the gods in chapter 18. How must Elijah have felt after God humiliated Baal's gang of prophets so utterly? Think of the divine power Elijah witnessed—and the violent death he caused. How might he have felt? (By the way, has a movie of this story ever been produced? Wow!)

But the situation changes rapidly for Elijah as Jezebel sends a messenger with a dispatch that echoes a solemn pledge of the time—it's a clear death threat. Note that King Ahab has apparently been put in his place by his furious wife, Jezebel, who gets all the screen time here, chewing the scenery as she calls for revenge against this problematic prophet. She wants him dead. Naturally, Elijah is terrified.

Without waiting for God to give him any direction for what to do next, Elijah runs for his life to Beer-sheba, which is about as far south as one can go in Israel. He leaves his "assistant" there—perhaps hoping *he* would stop the approaching assassins. Then Elijah goes on another day's journey into the desert—finally stopping under a lonely bush—and gives up. He is exhausted by his exertions and his terror. Begging God for the liberation of death, he falls into the troubled sleep of depression.

A messenger of a different sort than Jezebel's awakens Elijah. Jezebel's messenger brought death; this messenger brings nourishment—life. "Get up," this messenger says with a nudge. "Eat something." And there is sustenance right in front of Elijah, which he enjoys, then falls back asleep. The same thing happens again—presumably Elijah isn't quite ready yet—except this time the messenger adds a reason: "because you have a difficult road ahead of you."

This time Elijah is refreshed enough to take off for Mount Horeb (aka Mount Sinai). It's a forty-day-and-night journey, covering some two hundred miles or more, to the mountain that Moses spent forty days atop (Exod 24:18), the mountain of covenant between Israel and God. Spending the night there in a cave, Elijah hears God ask him, "Why are you here, Elijah?" (How do you imagine God's tone here: Taunting? Compassionate?) Elijah has a self-defensive, self-aggrandizing, self-pitying speech all ready to go, about how passionately he has served God and even so he's about to get killed. It's not fair!

God beckons Elijah out of the cave to stand up, for "the LORD is passing by"— another echo of Moses's experience on Sinai. Then follows in order a violent wind, a rocking earthquake, and a roaring fire. Some scholars attribute such violent activity to Baal, so that God is here distinguishing Godself from the pagan god; but examples can be found of Israel's God acting in wind, earthquake, and fire in other texts, including Kings. Not this time, however. This time God is found in "a sound. Thin. Quiet." The word for "sound" is also translated "voice" in this passage—it's the comforting, compassionate voice of God, a sound that requires intentionality to hear. We must be listening for this "still, small voice" or we'll miss it amidst the cacophony of life.

Elijah responds to this sound in humility, or perhaps humiliation, by wrapping his face in his coat. Then, for the second time in this text, the same event occurs again, as a quiet voice asks, "Why are you here, Elijah?" This time the prophet responds—*with the very same speech as before*. Has he learned nothing from this astonishing encounter with God? Perhaps he just needs time to process it.

But God can't wait. God sends Elijah on another mission to anoint kings and a successor prophet, Elisha. God demands that Elijah put his questions, fears, and self-pity aside, and get to work. That is one bold challenge! No doubt a sequel is coming.

Bringing the Text to Life

I can identify with Elijah in this text—not that any queen has issued a vendetta on my life, that I know of, but I certainly have felt as though an enemy—life—is chasing me, and I try to run as far as I possibly can. I wonder if you ever feel this way. The responsibilities press in on us from all sides. Even when you do what you know God has called you to do in championing the righteousness of God in the midst of a godless culture, next thing you know you are huddled under a little bush, terrified, angry at God over the unfairness of it all. Think about some examples from your life or others' when this situation has been all too real. How did those events resolve?

Do we get so busy justifying ourselves, as Elijah did, that we fail to seek God in all this? It's so easy to do. One thing that encourages me in this text is that, on *two* occasions, God or God's messenger must give Elijah the same message, and even then it's hardly clear that Elijah gets it. This gives me hope, because I too can be terribly dense when it comes to hearing God's word for me, let alone obeying it.

What are some ways this can play out in our lives? What violent distractions can keep our ears shut from God's voice? How can we prepare ourselves to fulfill our calling, to go about doing as God commands, even when we still feel overwhelmed by life's circumstances?

As we see, it takes time and intentionality to hear the "thin, quiet sound" of God's voice. We must get out of our own heads, overcome the distractions of the "wind, earthquakes, and fire" all around us in this world, and *listen*. And then we must obey God's direction to go back to our holy work whether we understand everything or not, whether we are ready or not. Because God will provide.

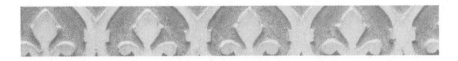

June 26, 2022–Third Sunday after Pentecost

2 Kings 2:1-2, 6-14; Psalm 77:1-2, 11-20; Galatians 5:1, 13-25;
Luke 9:51-62

Peter Wallace

Preacher to Preacher Prayer

Guiding God, shine your light of revelation on the excuses I so easily yet unwittingly make for not taking the next step forward on the way of your mission for me. Help me to follow Jesus no matter what, and give me the courage to invite others to do the same. Amen.

Commentary

Luke 9:51 is a hinge verse of the gospel. At this point Jesus's focus changes from proclaiming God's kingdom to heading for Jerusalem—he "determined" to go, he "*set his face* to go" (NRSV), to the capital city. The verb suggests a "fixedness of purpose."[1]

So his journey from Galilee to Jerusalem begins, a journey that will unfold over ten chapters. Jesus is on a mission from God, determined to fulfill his destiny. His tone is urgent; time is of the essence—not only to travel to Jerusalem and all that awaits him there, but beyond—after he is taken up (in death, resurrection, and ascension)—as his followers spread the good news like a healing virus beyond Jerusalem to Judea and Samaria and to the ends of the earth. This is where all that starts. Jesus must go through Jerusalem, through the cross, to accomplish this mission.

Right away Jesus and his disciples walk through a Samaritan village, where he is roundly rejected. After all, why would they want to listen to someone so determined to go to the capital city of their hostile, despised enemies, the Israelites? Mutual racial animus abounds. Elsewhere Jesus makes a Samaritan a hero (Luke 10:25-37), which would have shocked his Jewish hearers. But not here.

James and John, who always seem to say and do the wrong thing, are angry about the Samaritans' treatment of them (a bigoted response?); they suggest calling down heavenly fire to consume *those people*. They demand God's judgment on these enemies, who traditionally are considered "the other." Here is the one place in the text where Jesus seems to turn his face *away* from Jerusalem and *back* to them: "Jesus turned and spoke sternly to them." We don't know what he said, but there would be no fire. They move on—and Jesus's face is set forward again.

Then come three people along the road to Jerusalem. They have good reasons to wait to join Jesus in his mission to Jerusalem, important matters to tend to first. One offers to go anywhere, but when Jesus explains he has nothing and nowhere to call home, that he's all about moving forward in his life-giving mission, that person is silenced. Next Jesus invites another to follow him; he seems interested but must bury his father (was dad even dead yet?). Jesus shockingly challenges the man to turn his back on his own father and get to work for God's kingdom. Did he? Doubtful. A third claims he will follow Jesus just as soon as he says goodbye to his family. Jesus—his face stubbornly set to Jerusalem—says those who look backward are not fit for God's kingdom.

Jesus isn't kidding around here. This is serious business; he is on his way and he will not be sidetracked by those who may even be well meaning. Discipleship is all that matters.

Elisha got this. In 2 Kings 2:1-2, 6-14, his dedication and determination are overwhelming. In a bittersweet conversation with Elijah, twice Elisha rejects his mentor's imperative to stay behind, saying, "As the LORD lives and as you live, I won't leave you." Elisha, too, sets his face, determined to move forward on the path God had set forth for him. What's more, he requests a double share of Elijah's prophetic spirit—he wants it all. He too is consumed by doing the will of God. He too is *all in* for God's mission. (A rewarding sequel indeed to last week's text.)

Bringing the Text to Life

A travel-themed cable channel once used the tagline, "Be a traveler, not a tourist." In other words, don't be a mere observer of life from a safe distance; no, live it, dive into it, go *all in*. Jesus, it's safe to say, was a traveler—and he calls us to travel with him. He was determined to travel to Jerusalem to fulfill his holy destiny. His face was set, he was steadfast, immovable, relentless. You know people like that; you can't shake them off their course—and they can be very annoying about it. Think of some people you've known who are relentless in their profession, in a hobby, for a cause, or in pursuing a relationship. What drives them?

When James and John suggest calling down fire on their enemies the Samaritans, Jesus sternly rebukes them. Theirs is a response we see a lot wherever we look today, in our political landscape, in the Middle East or other global hotspots, even in our freeway lane when another car cuts us off: "God, please firebomb them." Jesus makes it clear that this is not his way. Only love can burn away our fear and anger. The way of the cross is to love our enemies and pray for those who persecute us.

When confronting the three weak-willed disciples that Luke brings along the road, Jesus can sound harsh. Does he expect us to give up our homes? Walk away from a dead or dying parent, or our family, and leave our comfortable lives behind just to follow him? Is it that important? It must be! Jesus knows we can come up with excuse after excuse to resist his call to fully live our faith. He makes it clear: his priority is his mission, and he calls us to join in it whatever the cost.

Emily C. Heath writes that a farmer explained, "When I start plowing a row in my field I pick out an object in the distance. I keep focusing on it and don't lose track of it. So when I reach the end of the row, it will have been plowed straight." Sounds good, but the problem about Jesus is that he doesn't stand still; he isn't a fencepost that doesn't move. So at the end of your life when you've followed him as far as you can on this side of existence, you won't see a straight line when you look back over your life. My life's plow line is a curvy mess—how about yours? And yet every step brought me to this place now.[2]

Stay focused on Jesus. Every time we look back at what we've left behind, we risk losing sight of the one we are following. And Jesus is a tricky one to follow. He moves fast. He surprises us. He goes to places we don't expect. We encounter pain and difficulty, as he did. That's all the more reason to keep our eyes on the prize and trust him to lead the way. Set your face toward Jesus—and be a traveler, not a tourist.

July 3, 2022–Fourth Sunday after Pentecost

2 Kings 5:1-14; Psalm 30; Galatians 6:(1-6), 7-16; Luke 10:1-11, 16-20

Alex Shanks

Preacher to Preacher Prayer

O God, send us down to the waters of Jordan that we may be washed clean of all our pride. Humble us so we may hear a word from you. Amen.

Commentary

The first verse introduces Naaman with effusive praise: a general, a great man, highly regarded, a victor, and a mighty warrior. The word *but* changes everything and erases all that comes before it. Now he is defined as one with skin disease. This otherwise powerful man is undone by illness. There was no known cure for this skin disease similar to the one in Leviticus 13–14. It is slow moving, debilitating, painful, and socially isolating. The skin disease has marked Naaman as one who is the "other." Our culture constantly labels the "other" by deeming some as less than. One goal of our faith is to liberate people from the less than labels so we might all be children of God.

The healing of Naaman comes from unexpected places. It begins with a recommendation from a young servant girl who has been taken captive. What if she had remained silent? What if no one had listened? Who are the unexpected voices we ignore? Naaman and the king of Aram go about healing in a typical fashion—offering money and a demand for help. In modern equivalency, they had the best health insurance and celebrity status. Naaman arrives at Elisha's humble abode in grand fashion, surrounded by chariots, horses, and an entourage. He was missing the one thing he needed. Naaman needed a mentality that he would stop at nothing in order to be healed and a humility to receive help that no amount of money or fame could provide. Instead his mentality was "I'm better than this." He wanted Elisha to come out. He wanted the healing to be personal. He even preferred the rivers from his own country! Naaman was angry, his sense of status and protocol offended. He was about to miss the simple theological solution in front of him. A man who normally gave orders to others was now on the receiving end of the directives. The healing would cost nothing and only required obedience.

Once again, it is the servants who save the day. With their encouragement and reframing of what is at stake, Naaman finally goes down to the river to be healed. The number of immersions recalls the priestly rituals specified in Leviticus 14. Seven is a symbolic number that evokes perfection, fullness, completion. His skin becomes like that of a young person (the word *na'ar* can also mean servant). What a day of rejoicing that must have been! As the psalmist declares in Psalm 30:11-12:

> You changed my mourning into dancing.
>> You took off my funeral clothes
>>> and dressed me up in joy
>> so that my whole being
>> might sing praises to you and never stop.

The problem of pride and our collective need for humility is clear. The ability of God to heal in ways we do not expect is prevalent throughout scripture. This story pushes us to listen to the "least of these" around us. Money and royal decrees are not needed. Faithfulness activated by humble obedience is all that is required. In 2020, we saw how pride and a focus on personal freedom interfered with the social distancing needed during the COVID-19 pandemic. The health experts offered directives as simple as going down to the river to be washed: stay home, wear a mask, keep your distance, and check your symptoms. Many responded in anger like Naaman, preferring to do it their own way, deciding they knew more than the experts and had a better plan. Healing cannot come when you have to be in control. Jesus mentions this story when he preaches at the synagogue in Nazareth (Luke 4:27). Even then it makes people angry.

When we walk through a time of disease, roles and identities are confused: the powerful become the patient. The rituals of healing are strange to understand. We become dependent on things outside of ourselves. Naaman's eventual healing came not from his own power but from his willingness to believe and respond. Beyond sickness, there is a new horizon, one that may not have previously existed, one forged at the place where vulnerability and trust create new life.

There are limits to healing, some of which we place upon ourselves. Preachers could focus on the discrepancies of power and access to healing resources. Acceptance of healing protocols, even unusual ones, and seeing healing as transformation are additional themes. As we approach July 4 (Independence Day in the US), this story mixes up our borders and boundaries, who is in and who it out. God often throws away the boundaries we erect. Indeed, any boundaries we construct around God's love cannot and will not hold God back.

Bringing the Text to Life

Despite our love of quick fixes and our desire for an "easy" button to solve all of life's problems, we are typically offended when things come off as too easy—especially when we have tried everything and nothing has worked. I don't know how many times I have scoured the shelves in search of something, given up, only to witness my wife find it immediately!

Naaman must have tried other solutions and probably had gone through various stages of grief along the way. Chronic illnesses are long journeys and something not often discussed. Listen to those in your congregation who face chronic illness and how they have found spiritual and emotional health within the ongoing physical trials.

Compare going to the Jordan and dipping seven times to the everyday, routine spiritual disciplines we need in order to find wholeness. Read Pope Francis's "Light of Faith" papal encyclical for some great quotes about faith.

We often depend on our own means and our own privilege to get what we want. Crisis can move us toward humility. The healing of Naaman is a free gift but requires humble obedience. Connect to baptism and how it is a free gift that requires a lifetime of faithfulness. Remembering our baptism enables us to be the recipient of grace that is not contingent on our merit. Although this is not the liturgical season when we typically remember our baptisms, spending some time on our collective knees as we remember our baptisms may be one way to return to the healing waters of our faith. May we be washed fully and completely.

July 10, 2022–Fifth Sunday after Pentecost

Amos 7:7-17; Psalm 82; Colossians 1:1-14; **Luke 10:25-37**

Alex Shanks

Preacher to Preacher Prayer

Merciful God, we want to be people who demonstrate mercy. Give us eyes to see others with compassion. Keep us from crossing to the other side. Amen.

Commentary

Thank God for the one who asks questions. I would assume the lawyer thought he had done a good job caring for his neighbors until Jesus expanded the definition of neighbors. In Leviticus we find a constant refrain to care for the stranger and alien because "I am the LORD your God." Since God created all people, we should be concerned for all people and allow God to tear down the fences of our own tribes.

Attacks along wilderness roads were likely a common threat in those days. No one would have been shocked by the man on the side of the road. The shock is in the response to the people who passed by. Surprisingly, it is the Samaritan who follows the commandment to care. Apparently, the two religious guys, the priest and the Levite, rationalized themselves a pass. Most scholars discount the idea of them trying to maintain ritual purity.

How do people get to the place where their eyes are closed to the other people around them? Actually, it's not that hard to do, is it? Most of us do it with relative ease. The dangerous vulnerability is that we get so good at analyzing and rationalizing, we develop little layers around our hearts. At that point, we give ourselves permission to close our eyes and walk past somebody. Instead of a servant, we become a spectator, a critic, an arm's-length analyzer of all the problems of the world.

The Samaritan did the opposite. He jumped right in and started with what he had. His actions echo Matthew 25:21: "You are a good and faithful servant. You've been faithful over a little. I'll put you in charge of much. Come, celebrate with me." Joy comes from faithfulness in the smallest things. Our inability to solve the whole problem should not keep us from trying. The Samaritan led with his heart.

There's a long and complicated history about how unlikely it would be for a Samaritan to stop to help a Jew. These were people who hated each other for all kinds of reasons, including that they came from very different worlds, racially, socially, and religiously. The key is the phrase "when he saw him." How is it possible to really see somebody else's circumstance? You have to have a new heart that gives you new eyes. As long as we are primarily interested in our own needs, there is no way in the world we will ever be able to see others. All those self-protective filters and assumptions will give us a very distorted view. When we know we belong to God, we receive both the imperative and wonderful freedom to love and serve others—even if that love seems risky or downright dangerous.

What the guy in the ditch needed was some bandages. He didn't need a sermon. He didn't need advice about how to travel safely on dangerous roads. He needed immediate attention to his wounds and a safe place to recuperate. The Samaritan got personally involved. Jesus said that's what it means to live God's way.

The man in the ditch is calling out to us. He reminds us what it feels like to be alone, forsaken, forgotten. Preaching this text could speak to those who feel alone or marginalized. Some scholars see a connection between the Samaritan and Christ through the use of the phrase "he was moved with compassion" and "demonstrated mercy." In most other places in the Gospels these ideas are reserved for the divine. When we imitate the Samaritan, we imitate Jesus.

Jesus changes the question the lawyer asked. It is no longer about who my neighbor is but who showed themselves to be a neighbor. Neighbor is as neighbor does. The "other" ceases to exist as we experience our common humanity. The reader is left to wonder how the lawyer responded. We are called to finish the story ourselves—in the way we love and in the questions we continue to ask around what it means to truly follow God.

Bringing the Text to Life

We are called to put on a new pair of glasses. Life is not a 3D movie—no one is handing out free pairs of glasses at the door. Throughout our lives, we are taught how to see, who to like, and how to classify. We will probably be stubborn to change. I can remember how stubborn I was when I learned that I needed glasses. I fought my mother, telling her that glasses made me look different and people would make fun of me. I avoided glasses until the Department of Motor Vehicles made me wear them in order to drive. We will be similarly tempted to avoid these new glasses.

We often define our neighbors according to those who are like us. By the grace of God may we change how we see the world. As worshippers leave, invite them to ask, "What do I encounter every day that I need to 'see' differently? What model could I emulate that would remind me of God's call on my life to serve?" After Jesus told this story, he said to the expert of the law, "Go and do likewise. . . ." Encourage your congregation to hear those challenging words again.

We all need to choose whether we will be spectators or get in the game. For years, I watched my wife run half-marathons. I liked cheering her on. If there were a category of professional spectator, I could have been the chairperson. We all have our own race to run. A ship may be safer at the dock. A plane may be safer in a hangar, but it was built to fly. We may feel safer up there in the stands, but we were built for the game, created to serve.

The visual image of a sponge is helpful. When you put a sponge in water it becomes waterlogged, permeated, and completely saturated. If you left it in water for two or three days, it would not get any more wet. It's absorbed everything it possibly can until you squeeze it out. Once you squeeze it out, its full absorbency is instantly restored. Sponges work by being filled and then being squeezed out. So do people. We need to be filled up by worship and study and then be squeezed out in service to others. If we don't serve, we become spiritually waterlogged.

July 17, 2022–Sixth Sunday after Pentecost

*Amos 8:1-12; Psalm 52; Colossians 1:15-28; **Luke 10:38-42***

Alex Shanks

Preacher to Preacher Prayer

O Lord, we seek to sit at your feet and listen to you. Remove all our worry and distraction. Do not take your Spirit away from us. Amen.

Commentary

Hospitality is a critical theme in Luke's Gospel. Earlier in Luke 10, Jesus sent out the seventy and told them to expect hospitality from others. Christians are called to extend hospitality. Hospitality and being a neighbor are much higher values than mere tolerance or endurance of difference.

This is a story about choices, and it has a surprise ending. Mary and Martha may be real people, and this may have been an actual conversation, but Jesus undoubtedly intends for these people to symbolize us. It reads like a parable. It is surprising that Martha even lets Jesus in the door. She should be applauded for welcoming him as it probably went against her nature to make an impromptu, spontaneous invitation. There was likely a lot of free-floating anxiety in the kitchen that afternoon as she wasn't ready for a guest.

We can imagine these archetypes of people: The prepared, practical Martha who likes to do things in a certain way. The carefree, relaxed Mary who is more like a wonder-struck child. If you've got two children, you might have one of each of these. Martha can't believe Mary is sitting at the feet of Jesus while she is trying to be the perfect host. She asks Jesus to do something about it. It is interesting that she chose this route rather than talking to Mary herself. Martha seems to break the normal rules of hospitality by embarrassing her sister and asking her guest to get involved in a family dispute. Jesus will not be triangulated. In a voice filled with urgent compassion, Jesus reminds Martha what is important.

Despite these recognizable personality stereotypes, Jesus is not saying to be more like Mary and less like Martha. He is not condemning Martha. We need the diversity of personalities and the different ways of thinking so that God might weave a wonderful rich tapestry of life to do God's kingdom work. We don't need to reject Martha in order to identify with and understand the story. God's grace is rich enough to include multiple expressions. In all her efforts to provide for Jesus, Martha may have missed what Jesus was trying to provide her. She may not have recognized the fact that Jesus is always the host.

The point of the story isn't about personality styles or which sister is better. The point of the story is this: don't miss Jesus. Whatever it takes, whatever you do, make sure you don't miss Jesus. This is not a story about manners or style, it's a story about priorities in life. We know that Jesus is on the way to the cross. Jesus needs to eat and be taken care of but that is not his primary purpose. The kingdom of God is at hand. Jesus came to save the world and Mary is sitting at his feet trying to understand it all.

It is important to recognize that Mary is violating some cultural expectations by sitting with Jesus. Jesus is constantly breaking the constraints of culture and setting people free to a new reality. The church needs to constantly be set free through faithful listening so we can truly love those around us. The preceding story about the Samaritan should be understood together with this story. The Samaritan shows us how to love our neighbor; Mary displays how we love God. Neither would have been likely models of goodness according to the cultural norms, and yet Jesus displays them as images of the kingdom he ushers in. We need to both go and do likewise and sit at the feet of Jesus.

Luke's story is left unfinished. We don't know what happens next. Did the sisters reconcile? Did they get to enjoy the meal Martha prepared? We are invited by Jesus to let go of our distractions. If we aren't careful, all of our activity can leave us devoid of love and joy and resentful of others. Jesus, through both Mary and Martha, points us to a better way. We are invited to give our full attention to Jesus, the one who loves and values each of us as children of God.

Bringing the Text to Life

Normally you don't get praised for taking the bigger piece. The old universal rule of division is that one sibling gets to cut the cake and the other sibling gets to pick the piece they want. A preacher could open with an illustration about taking the bigger piece of cake when divided among siblings and then connect it with Jesus's words to Martha about Mary taking "the better part." This is the bigger piece of cake that can't be taken from you.

The phrase "worried and distracted by many things" could be an invitation for all of us to consider the things that worry and distract us. The word for distracted has the connotation of being pulled or dragged in different directions. Jesus invites all of us to hold on to the better part, the part that nobody can take away from us. This passage implores us to think both/and rather than either/or. We need both action *and* contemplation, work *and* prayer. A preacher could explore more fully what both/and living looks like in a world filled with dichotomies.

In response to all the exhausted, stressed-out people, Dr. Richard Swensen wrote a book entitled *Margin: Restoring Emotional, Physical, Financial, and Time Reserves to Overloaded Lives.* Swensen says that countless people in our culture are suffering from what he calls an uncontrolled societal epidemic: living without margin.[1] Margin, he says, is simply that "space that once existed between ourselves and our limits."[2] It's something you hold "in reserve for contingences or unanticipated situations in your life."[3] With the push in this culture for progress and success, margin has been devoured.[4] We end up feeling a kind of undifferentiated distress or anxiety with unexplained aches and pains. Relationships have suffered because we are badly overloaded.[5] In pointing to Mary, Jesus acknowledges someone who has margin. She had some white space left on her page of life. Mary had enough space to give her the ability to see what matters most and choose it. We all need more margin. Invite worshippers to make a plan for increasing margin in their lives and sharing it with someone else for accountability.

We tend to categorize people as "better" or "worse." What we all need to do is focus on Jesus. Regardless of our giftedness, we should all create "margin" in our lives and our routines in order to follow Jesus.

July 24, 2022—Seventh Sunday after Pentecost

*Hosea 1:2-10 or Psalm 85; Genesis 18:20-32 or **Psalm 138**;*
Colossians 2:6-15 (16-19); Luke 11:1-13

Lisa Degrenia

Preacher to Preacher Prayer

Faithful one, Father-Son-Spirit, you are loyal, you are powerful, you are near. Fill me
with encouragement and inner strength as I prepare and preach. May all who hear come
to value your name and word above all other loves. Help me do the same. Amen.

Commentary

How many times have you prayed for strength? Strength to pass the test. Strength to nail the job interview. Strength to serve and keep on serving. Strength to live another day when your heart is broken, your mom dies, your best friend is arrested for drunk driving again. Strength to learn another new, hard thing because the world has changed.

We want strength for the moment we need it, the moment we need it. We want it to appear like magic, an instant gift, whether or not we've prepared for it.

Strength can come as miracle and gift. But more often it comes because we're prepared. We've studied. We've practiced. We've put in the work. Couples in long-term relationships understand this. Relationships take work. Athletes, dancers, and singers understand this. They can't just walk out their doors and run a marathon or do eight shows a week on Broadway. They put in the work year after year to build stamina and stay strong.

The same is true for inner strength—the strength of soul needed for persevering during hard times, the spiritual stamina needed for joining Jesus in saving the world. Inner strength takes work.

How did we ever buy into the lie that a strong faith would happen without strong intention? In the age of pandemic, cultural Christianity failed us. Inner strength comes from our own experience with God, not by borrowing other people's experiences. Consumer Christianity failed us, too. Inner strength comes from prioritizing and nurturing a healthy relationship with God, not by treating that relationship like a transaction.

In Psalm 138, notice David's depth of commitment to the one true living God. His faith is focused and intentional. His testimony is clear and bold. He gives evidence of his strong commitment to God by giving us a glimpse of his spiritual practices, practices integrated into his way of life year after year. They've become his routine, his "rule of life" as the monastics would say.

The good news is we can have inner strength, too. Just like David, we can be people "after God's own heart." David's spiritual practices are nothing new. Anyone can do them. They're timeless, simple, pandemic proof.

- David practices gratitude, giving thanks to God with all his heart. (v. 1)

- He sings the praises of God and God alone. (v. 1)

- David worships with humility, remembering God's loyalty, love, and faithfulness. (v. 2)

- He honors God's name and God's word as his greatest influence season after season. (v. 2)

When the seasons of need and service come, David calls to God in prayer again (v. 3). David's already strong foundation of faith is further strengthened. The deep trust built over time is built further. The promises of God are claimed again and the prayer is answered. God bestows encouragement and inner strength. David helps us understand the depth of his need and the greatness of God's answer, "You make me live again" (v. 7).

From an unending treasure of grace upon grace, God pours out inner strength. Not given as the world gives. Not found where the world says it will be found. Not seen with obvious outward displays, but hidden in the very depths of our frailty. God pours and floods our practiced faith with the creative strength of resurrection power, strength to strength, life to new life.

This power, this companionship, this indescribable, priceless blessing is waiting for you. Commit to God and nurturing your relationship with God, today. Amen.

Bringing the Text to Life

1. Who or what receives your commitment? A quick check of your bank statement, calendar, and prayer list will reveal the answer.

2. In Psalm 138, the Hebrew word for "strength" is *oz*, a strength bestowed by God. Consider connecting this understanding of strength with the story of the psalmist, David. What is it like to read this psalm hearing David's voice? David made a strong commitment to God and intentionally nurtured their relationship. God bestowed David with might, power, authority, and boldness, which he sometimes used well and sometimes misused.

3. The image of strength as rootedness connects Psalm 138 to Colossians 2:7, "Be rooted and built up in him, be established in faith, and overflow with thanksgiving just as you were taught."

When I was little, our neighborhood was covered in orange trees. We'd climb them and play in their shade. In one season, we'd pick their blossoms. In another season, we'd pick and eat their fruit. There's nothing like opening up an orange and taking a bite, the sweet neon juice running down your chin.

There's an inner strength to orange trees, their root system. They have shallow roots within the first few feet of soil plus tap roots that can reach up to twelve feet deep. The root system anchors the tree when a hurricane blows through. Likewise, through our spiritual practices, we can be anchored to God's inner strength through storms of pain, grief, and uncertainty.

An orange tree's root system also keeps the tree connected to clear, deep sources of water. The same is true for our spiritual practices. As we serve, we need a trustworthy spring of life we can go to again and again. The stamina for service comes from being continually filled with God's inner strength so we can be continually poured out in love and good deeds.

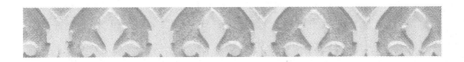

July 31, 2022—Eighth Sunday after Pentecost

Hosea 11:1-11 or *Psalm 107:1-9, 43; Ecclesiastes 1:2, 12-14; 2:18-23 or Psalm 49:1-12; Colossians 3:1-11; Luke 12:13-21*

Lisa Degrenia

Preacher to Preacher Prayer

Tender One, too often I take your love and generosity for granted. Forgive me. Return me to innocence. Like a little child, fill me with wonder at your holy compassion, your unending mercy. Draw me near to the fullness of your presence and grace. You alone are worthy. You alone are my hope, eternal and true. I love you and honor you and need you. Amen.

Commentary

How would you finish this sentence? God is . . .

Was your answer, "God is tender"? It wasn't mine. I started with the table grace I learned as a child, "God is great. God is good." Next came "God is holy, all-powerful." I'd even answered "God is near" and "God is love," but it took a deep look at Hosea 11:1-11 to answer "God is tender."

Images of God as a caring parent are plentiful in the scriptures. Passages include Malachi 2:10, Isaiah 49:15, Isaiah 66:13, and Matthew 7:11. Jesus teaches us to pray, inviting us to call God *Abba*, the affectionate Middle Eastern word toddlers use for father.

Yet, this passage from Hosea 11 reveals an astonishing tenderness to God's being. To be tender is to be gentle, like a caring parent nurturing an infant. God offers each of us this gentleness. Imagine the creator of all that is seen and unseen teaching a little one to walk and that little one is you. See yourself as a toddler, allowing God to lead you patiently, kindly. God bends down to your level, little one, looking on you with love, feeding you. Now standing, lifting you into the air so you're cheek to cheek (vv. 3-4).

Does embracing your littleness with God bring you relief or make you squirm?

As Jesus was blessing little ones, he said, "I assure you that if you don't turn your lives around and become like this little child, you will definitely not enter the kingdom of heaven. Those who humble themselves like this little child will be the greatest in the kingdom of heaven" (Matt 18:3-4).

Max Lucado puts it this way: "Oh, for the attitude of a five-year-old! That simple uncluttered passion for living that can't wait for tomorrow. A philosophy of life that reads, 'Play hard, laugh hard, and leave the worries to your father.' A bottomless well of optimism flooded by a perpetual spring of faith. Is it any wonder Jesus said we must have the heart of a child before we can enter the kingdom of heaven?"[6]

I like the way J. B. Phillips renders Jesus's call to childlikeness: "Jesus called a little child to his side and set him on his feet in the middle of them all. 'Believe me,' he said, 'unless you change your whole outlook and become like little children you will never enter the kingdom of Heaven'" (Matt 18:2-3, Phillips).

Note the phrase "change your whole outlook." No small command. Quit looking at life like an adult and see it through the eyes of a child. Essential counsel for us sober-minded, serious-faced, sour-pussed adults. Necessary advice for us Charles Atlas wannabes who shoulder the world. Good words for those of us who seldom say, "I can't wait until I wake up," and more often state, "I can't wait to go to bed."

Tender means gentle, but it also means easily wounded. We hesitate in accepting our littleness for fear of being needy *and* for fear of being vulnerable. Yet vulnerability is the secret sauce to relationship and new life. Our almighty, omnipotent Lord reveals this in choosing the vulnerability of incarnation. See Jesus vulnerable to mocking, homelessness, and injustice. See Jesus wounded by the whips, thorns, and nails. But also see Jesus nursing at Mary's breast and laughing with his childhood friends. See Jesus tenderhearted, drawing together all kinds of people around food and stories, healing and hope.

Knowing and being known only happens when hearts are wide open to another, not in the distanced acquaintance of strangers. Earlier in Hosea, God declares no one in the land knows God, not even the priests. God isn't talking about the need for more Bible studies and theological reading. God is saying they have no relationship, they don't know each other, they're strangers (Hosea 4:1, 6; 6:6).

How would you describe your relationship with God? God's heart is wide open to you. God wants to know you and to be known, the intimate knowing grown from experience, faithful love, and loyalty.

Indifference, rebellion, and distance break God's heart. In verse 2, hear the cry in God's voice as the people ignore God's call, worshipping instead what will never nurture them nor love them back. Hear God's yearning and frustrations as the people are "bent on turning away" (v. 7). God sees the consequence of placing trust in their fleeting prosperity and fickle political alliances with Egypt and Assyria. Earthly allies will soon be invaders.

In verse 8, watch God's heart break over the idea of breaking the covenant, of losing the people forever to their destructive choices.

How can I give you up, Ephraim?
How can I hand you over, Israel?

How can I make you like Admah?
How can I treat you like Zeboiim?
My heart winces within me;
my compassion grows warm and tender.

Our God is all-powerful, yet vulnerable. Almighty, yet easily wounded. Our choices ripple through our own lives, the lives of others, and all the way to the very heart of God.

Lay aside your self-sufficiency, your unhealthy pride, your need to rule your universe. Lay aside your fickle faith, your doublemindedness, your chasing after falsehood. All you long for is found in accepting your littleness. Open your hands. In joy and wonder, receive.

Bringing the Text to Life

1. Images of God as a parent are troubling and problematic to many, including persons who experienced childhood trauma and neglect. Using scriptural imagination to personally enter into a passage may also be new to some. Proceed with care.

2. I AM (Exod 3:14) reveals who I am

- Loves who I am

- Empowers who I am

- Reminds me who I am

- I am a child of God

Finish the sentence: In Christ, I am no longer . . . I am a child of God.

3. Read Hosea 11:1-11 alongside Jesus's parable of the forgiving father (aka prodigal son, Luke 15:11-32). Both scriptures share the image of God's people as an overconfident, rebellious, pleasure-seeking son. Both scriptures reveal the character of God as a compassionate and merciful parent, whose primary motivation is restoration of relationship.

The beginning of the parable is told from the perspective of the rebellious son. He asks his father for his share of the inheritance, severing their relationship, treating his father as if he were dead. The son travels far from home, wasting the love and generosity of the father by worshipping at the altars of extravagant living. When the inheritance runs dry, the son experiences the consequence of his choices, becoming a starving indentured servant. His circumstance awakens him to repentance, home, and the grace of his father.

All the time the son was away, what is the father thinking and feeling? We know the father kept watch for the son's return and rejoiced in it. We see the father run to the son, the embrace, the kiss, the restoration of the son's place in the family, and the feast. Yet, we can only guess what the father went through emotionally while the son was away. Imagine Hosea 11:1-11 as the forgiving father's emotional rollercoaster of a conversation with himself while the son is away.

4. "The word *prodigal* does not mean 'wayward,' as many believe (based on our tendency to join the brothers in making judgments). It means wastefully or recklessly extravagant, extraordinarily generous, giving 'prodigiously.' The term was meant to refer to the younger son's lavish living—but it's really the father who's prodigal, isn't it? The father extends generous grace and love to both sons when neither of them 'deserve' it."[7]

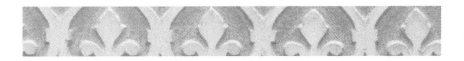

August 7, 2020–Ninth Sunday after Pentecost

*Isaiah 1:1, 10-20 or Psalm 50:1-8, 22-23; Genesis 15:1-6 or Psalm 33:12-22; **Hebrews 11:1-3, 8-16**; Luke 12:32-40*

Lisa Degrenia

Preacher to Preacher Prayer

God of Abraham and Sarah and so many more, your covenant is steadfast, your promises are true. Anchor my hope in what is yet to be. Make the everlasting real. Like the sand, so many brothers. Like the stars, so many sisters. Together heirs of your grace and generosity. Together home with you. Amen.

Commentary

In 2016, Bradford Manning and Bryan Manning left their jobs and started a clothing company. You can shop for their incredibly soft shirts on their website like any other clothing company. Or you can take their Shop Blind Challenge. Pick your price point and they will send you a product sight unseen. Their motto for the challenge: "Trust us, it's worth it."

They started this challenge as a way for others to understand their condition and help raise money to cure it. Both Bradford and Bryan have Stargardt disease, a form of macular degeneration, where you lose your central vision and possibly keep some of your peripheral.

Their company, Two Blind Brothers, employs visually impaired workers and all the profits go to research. Their motivation is simple: they believe with enough funding there will be a cure for blindness within the next ten years (www.twoblindbrothers.com).

What do you believe? What do you strive for, hope for, even though you can't see it yet? Whatever or whoever it is, they have your faith. Faith is belief backed up with action and intention. Faith trusts the promise of God's yet to be.

Perfectionism kills faith. We trade faith for fail-safe. We want guarantees. We want to know all the steps before we take the first one. We want to know the ending before we begin. Why? Because we don't want to fail.

Faith isn't perfect, but it perseveres. Hebrews 11 could be called the Hall of Fame of Faith. By faith Abel . . . by faith Enoch . . . by faith Noah . . . by faith Moses . . . none of them were perfect.

Neither were Abraham and Sarah. By faith they welcomed God's covenant promise of land and unnumbered descendants who would carry God's blessing to the nations (Gen 17). They put their faith into action, leaving their home to emigrate to this strange land. Along the way they also tried to fulfill the covenant in their own strength. They bargained, lied, and laughed at the idea God would still act. After so much time, it was only logical the promised child would be born of a surrogate. Wrong. Their impatience brought great pain, pain we're still living. In time though, they welcomed their son Isaac just as God promised.

God doesn't take back the promise at Abraham and Sarah's first mistake or second or third. God remains steadfast, as does God's invitation. God fulfills even when we fail.

God's "power is made perfect in weakness" (2 Cor 12:9). When we finally surrender to the truth of our weakness, to our primal need for God and others, we open ourselves to the full presence and movement of God in our lives. The weak walls of pride and self-sufficiency crumble so that something new and better may rise from the dust of that death, faith.

Faith is far more about trust than results. It's about trying and trying again. The reaching. The risking. The returning when we blow it by twisting God's work into something it was never meant to be. We're literally practicing our faith. Learning how and putting it in motion.

What are you doing right now that requires faith? What would your testimony say in the Hebrews 11 Hall of Fame? By faith [YOUR NAME] . . .

You know. It's that injustice that keeps you up at night. That need that breaks your heart. That vision for the common good that makes you come alive. Imagine your community when you start building that bridge, righting that wrong, healing that wound in Jesus's name. See folks coming to faith as you step out in yours.

Bringing the Text to Life

1. If you choose to focus on the miraculous pregnancy of Sarah, proceed with extra care. This passage causes great harm to couples struggling with infertility when it is used as a cure, a reason for infertility, or a way to earn God's blessing. "Just pray more. Just have more faith. God will reward you with a child."

2. *La Clairvoyance* (1936) is a self-portrait by Belgian surrealist artist Rene Magritte. The artist is seated in front of a canvas, his pallet in his lap. He looks to the left at the inspiration for his painting, a common egg. Yet on the canvas, at the tip of his brush, is a painting of a bird in flight. With faith and vision, he paints the promise of the egg, making the invisible visible. What would it be like to show the painting,

inviting the congregation to share what they see in the work, as an introduction to your message on faith?

3. "To live in the world without belonging to the world summarizes the essence of the spiritual life. The spiritual life keeps us aware that our true house is not the house of fear, in which the powers of hatred and violence rule, but the house of love, where God resides."[1]

4. "If God's promise of the kingdom of heaven is an empty promise, then a life of seeking justice and showing mercy is a fool's illusion. Only the promised kingdom validates a life of hopeful service. But the promise of the kingdom is sure; therefore, joyful, blessed, happy are those who put their lives on the line, trusting that promise."[2]

August 14, 2022–Tenth Sunday after Pentecost

*Isaiah 5:1-7; Psalm 80:1-2, 8-19; Jeremiah 23:23-29; **Psalm 82**;*
Hebrews 11:29–12:2; Luke 12:49-56

Juan Carlos Huertas

Preacher to Preacher Prayer

Gracious God, there are times when we wonder if you are there, if you listen, if you will respond. We thank you that you welcome our questions, anger, and doubt. Help us in the midst of life to know that you are with us, that you have not forgotten and that in the end you will make all things well again. Through Christ our Lord. Amen.

Commentary

In many of our congregations we might find a natural aversion to questioning God, showing God anger, or expressing doubt. We live in a culture that generally frowns on questioning authority, disorder, and emotional outburst. In our religious spaces we want respect, order, calm, peace, and nice words. At times it seems like our people see their role as protector of God—with God seeming more like the thin-skinned parent, emotionally immature teacher, or an insecure boss. This makes the Psalms extremely difficult to digest but also extremely important to the communities we serve.

The Psalms are key to developing the prayer life of our congregations. As a whole, they provide us with the full spectrum of the human responses to life. They are perfect teachers of healthy emotional responses, even when the responses are not pretty. The psalmist is obviously not afraid to express themselves to God, and neither is the psalmist afraid to put words in God's mouth or to tell us how God spoke to them in times of praise, lament, or desperation. As a whole, the Psalms provide us a faithful blueprint for communal responses for all seasons of life.

Psalm 82 provides us with a compelling yet difficult vision. It begins by acknowledging who God is: God "takes his stand in the divine council." The psalmist is fully aware of who this God is. This God is ruler of all and has the capacity to act, to do something about the struggles in the world. This God is worthy of reverence and respect. It is this God who even judges "among the gods."

And yet, the human one is not afraid to call this God to task. Like in previous psalms, this human is concerned that the wicked seem to be winning the day. The "bad people" are getting away with murder, the guilty ones are going free, the cheaters are prospering. All while the ones who are faithful, the ones who are needy, the ones whom God should be looking after are being ignored! Bad things are happening to good people and good things are happening to bad people. For the psalmist, the world is being turned upside down.

The psalmist is becoming the spokesperson on behalf of those who need God the most. Maybe God will listen to the psalmist? Maybe the psalmist can help refocus God's attention? Doesn't God feel the shake of the earth's foundation? Doesn't God recognize the longing? Maybe humans could do better?

It turns out that God does get it. God does recognize the needs, the hungers, and the struggles. The problem? The people have been seeking the help of false gods. They have been trying to get the help of gods that would never be able to answer, help, assist, or free. God can and will be present but we must recognize who this God is and keep our eyes from wandering. Our penchant for other gods must be resisted.

The Psalms are powerful because they provide us with the language of prayer, the language of life, and the language of the human condition. Our congregations too are tempted to claim that God is not listening, not paying attention, not caring for what God should be caring for. The difference is that often this is done in silence, in their minds, hearts, and spirits.

We need to free our congregations to express the fullness of their emotions doubt, shame, to God. To do so helps us as "curers of souls" to be able to evaluate where our communities are in their lives with God. Is it that God is not listening or that we are praying to a false god? Is it God or our expectations? Is it God or our unwillingness to be agents of God in the world?

Psalm 82 gives us an opportunity to help our congregation open up their imaginations to a new way of praying. We are teaching them to express what they normally keep deep within them, not just as individuals but as a community. If the preacher takes the time, the psalm has the potential to teach the congregation how their life of prayer together can be diagnostic. Psalm 82 can be a barometer of where they are in their life with God. This requires the psalmist's honesty and vulnerability before God. Our congregations can learn to do the same if we open the doors and model it for them.

Bringing the Text to Life

When I teach on the Psalms I often encourage people to write a psalm. What are some key words that you would use? What is in your heart and mind? During a difficult time in your life, what do you wish you would have allowed yourself to tell God? Though difficult for the preacher, this might be an opportunity to model healthy and appropriate vulnerability by writing a short psalm that has come out of a season of struggle, challenge, or growth. Read it alongside this psalm and invite the congregation to think about what words and phrases come to mind for them, then free them to do what you did. If your congregational culture allows, have them share out loud some of the key words that come to mind for them.

August 21, 2022–Eleventh Sunday after Pentecost

*Jeremiah 1:4-10; Psalm 71:1-6; **Isaiah 58:9b-14**; Psalm 103:1-8; Hebrews 12:18-29; Luke 13:10-17*

Juan Carlos Huertas

Preacher to Preacher Prayer

Seeing God, you who have searched us and known us, forgive us. Awaken us to the ways in which we continue to playact our life with you, the ways we continue to go through the motions and do our duty instead of being the people you have called us to be. Help us shake off our hypocrisy and apathy and to pay attention to the ways you are making yourself known in justice and peace. Through Christ our Lord. Amen.

Commentary

The people of Israel were a predictable bunch. The cycles of their life with God are our cycles of life with God. Faithfulness leads to apathy, apathy leads to laziness, laziness leads to unfaithfulness, and unfaithfulness leads to trouble. Trouble then leads to crying out to God, crying out to God leads to whining that God is obviously not hearing, whining leads to the prophet having to remind, call out, and set straight, prophetic words lead to repentance, repentance leads to faithfulness, and the cycle begins again.

In today's text it is obvious that God is frustrated. Like a parent who is exhausted from all the foolishness, God is showing the edges of losing patience. As if their unfaithfulness was not enough, now God's people have resorted to acting like they are faithful to unashamed hypocrisy. This is truly fascinating because it goes from offensive to insulting. Do they even know who this God is? Have we not been in relationship from the beginning of time? What do they think they are doing?

Before we get too judgmental about the people of Israel, we must recognize that this is our pattern too. It is easier to sit in our sanctuaries, sing songs, kneel for Holy Communion, put a few dollars on the plate, and go to lunch feeling satisfied. Our duty fulfilled, we are self-assured that God is impressed with us. We have pushed to the back of our minds what God truly requires because it is life transforming, difficult, and too much to ask.

Today the prophet calls us out! It turns out that it begins with the community itself. Our penchant to make it about us individually will not help. We belong to one another and this time we must hear the disciplining as a community. We must stop pointing fingers at what our fellow community member is doing or not doing, stop our tendency to navel-gaze, stop our harsh words (this includes our engagements in social media), and open our life together to the world around us.

As we begin to pay attention to the hurts, hungers, and hardships in our communities something happens. The pathways for salvation begin to open up and our current circumstances will not seem as bleak. Little by little our souls become refocused and renewed, and as Psalm 30 remind us, our mourning will be turned into joy.

Something else takes place for us as we lift our heads. We begin to see, feel, and experience the presence of God again. We no longer need to playact or manufacture a religious experience. We can stop "going through the motions." In short, we become free. This freedom continues to redeem us as we engage a hungry and broken world. Our recognition of God provides fertile ground that shines a light, making the presence of God known.

As I write this we are in the middle of the 2020 pandemic. Frustrations are mounting that we still cannot worship in person, cannot see one another in person, cannot hug one another, grieve with one another, sing the songs of praise together, gather around font and around table, and cannot mark time in the same space together. Some in our faith communities are finger pointing and speaking evil to one another and their leaders. They claim that "they are being kept from church."

It is true that we cannot do what we are used to doing. This season is forcing us to think about what it means to be the church. We must recognize that attending worship in person does not make us the church, that the building where we gather is not the church, that the Bible study in our parlor is not the church. We, God's people, are the church, wherever we are.

This season of Sabbath is providing us with an opportunity to "take delight in the Lord." This season is opening our eyes to what could become the most transformative season for God's people in my generation. We are being called by Isaiah to stop the finger pointing and the "wicked speech" and to pay attention by providing for a world around us that is hurting, in need of mended fences, livable streets, and running water. Our communities are in need of the salvation of the Lord.

The Lord has spoken indeed!

Bringing the Text to Life

Technology these days allows us to provide our people with visuals that can make our points better than our words could. The pandemic forced many of us to use video as the primary tool to preach, teach, and connect with our people. Take a walk around your neighborhood with your camera. Pay special attention to the broken places (broken fences, buildings, uncared-for yards, pestilence, poverty, etc.), to the areas in a quarter mile, half-mile, mile from your congregation that would benefit from good news. Interview community leaders and ask them what the top three ailments in your community are, and then show that video with the narrative of what the needs are as a way to begin your sermon. Ask: Are we ready to allow God to remove our yoke so that we can become restorers, rebuilders, and redeemers?

August 28, 2022—Twelfth Sunday after Pentecost

Jeremiah 2:4-13; Psalm 81:1, 10-16; Sirach 10:12-18 or
Proverbs 25:6-7; Psalm 112; **Hebrews 13:1-8, 15-16**; *Luke 14:1, 7-14*

Juan Carlos Huertas

Preacher to Preacher Prayer

Eternal God, these have been long days in the patterns of life. As we try to find our way and refocus our efforts, help us not be distracted by all the tasks of life, the things done, and the things undone. Instead, help us stay rooted in what matters most: our relationships with one another, and with you. Through Christ our Lord. Amen.

Commentary

It has already been a very long letter. It has sought to be a reminder for the community that hears it that the work of salvation, new life, and redemption is a work that began long ago. For these early hearers it has been a primer to help them see this Jesus movement as the obvious next phase in their communities' religious journey. Perhaps for the novices this letter is a remedial course on the long and, at times, complex history of Jewish religious practice, with Jesus as the climax of such a narrative. Whichever group was hearing this letter for the first time, it provided a grounding, a connection, and a faithful reminder to keep the faith.

As the letter writer is wrapping up, I can imagine them wondering how they will end this important letter to their fellow followers of Jesus. Like a preacher trying to land a sermon, there are so many ways that it could go. Do they restate the previous twelve chapters? Do they add one final big idea? Or do they use a clever illustration that would help the hearers of this letter remember all that the writer has said?

The writer decides to go in a pastoral direction. The writer reminds the hearers why they follow Jesus. He underscores that the goal has not been for them to be intellectually stimulated, challenged, or to learn something new. In the end, the goal is to be more like Jesus in a world that was constantly pulling them in so many different directions. They are reminded to "keep loving each other like family." This seems easy at first, but we all know how difficult family life can be. Loving each other like family is complicated, to say the least. It requires commitment and sacrificial love. Those who were hearing this for the first time were living in the midst of a changing world. Many were leaving their faith of their religious upbringing and now joining this new Jesus movement. Can you imagine what their families thought about that?

The writer also reminds them of some of the key practices of what it means to follow Jesus: hospitality, caring for prisoners and others of ill repute, faithfulness in the most intimate of relationships, and a proper relationship toward money (and I would say all material possessions).

These practices should not have been foreign to those who heard this letter. If you were a Jew, these were already familiar calls for a faithful God follower. But if you were a pagan, many of these practices would have been totally foreign. In fact, in some cases, such practices would be contrary to what your understanding of "religion" might have been.

These are all practices that require discipline and force us to rely on God's power. Just reading the list that the writer of Hebrews gives us is enough to recognize how powerless we are to live in those ways and yet, as the author reminds us, "the Lord" is our helper.

We also have each other and we have our leaders. For those of us who are preachers the words of the epistle are humbling. If our people are to imitate (mimic, follow our lead, mirror, witness to) our faith, what does that look like? If they do what we are doing now, would they look more like Jesus?

It turns out that our actions, the ways we behave, what we do, who we are, is the "sacrifice" that was so familiar to those who were hearing this letter for the first time. As I read it, I have to acknowledge, and I believe the preacher should also, that it would be easier to offer a dove, bull, or lamb. It would be easier to go through the motions and through the financial expectations of the ancient sacrificial system. The call to make our being the "sacrifice of praise and thanksgiving" requires more of us, more reliance, more faith, more surrender. Doing "good" and "sharing what we have" become the evidence of our relationship with God.

Bringing the Text to Life

The idea that leaders are people to emulate is scary to those of us who lead, but it gives much fodder for sermonizing. I would begin my sermon with this idea of being a mirror. Remember that leaders can be anyone. Leaders are parents, teachers, business owners, civic leaders, you as you shop at the grocery store, and certainly all of us who are pastors. If we are to model this sacrifice of praise and thanksgiving so that others can emulate it, what is the mirror saying? As you stand in front of a mirror, what do you see? If you turn the camera on your phone for a selfie, what do you see? If your day was a video montage, what would you see? It's not often pretty. You might imagine the moments you realized your shirt needed ironing, you had spinach in your teeth, or that your socks were caught on your pant leg. Mirror gazing is scary, but it can be extremely useful.

September 4, 2022– Thirteenth Sunday after Pentecost

Jeremiah 18:1-11; Deuteronomy 30:15-20; Psalm 139:1-6, 13-18;
Philemon 1:1-21; **Luke 14:25-33**

Mandy Sloan McDow

Preacher to Preacher Prayer

Holy and living God, open our ears to hear your invitation into a life of discipleship. Help
us to prepare for the costs, so that we can contribute to building your kingdom. In Jesus's
name. Amen.

Commentary

The cost of discipleship. Most of our Bibles will tip us off to the theme of today's pericope by titling this section *The Cost of Discipleship.* This is helpful because we have now reasonably set our expectations and can begin to prepare a budget. Is the cost of discipleship something we can reasonably afford?

Because you are a preacher preparing a sermon for a congregation, it is safe to assume that your audience is prepared for this expense. But, when it comes to the value of discipleship, I would wager that Jesus's explanation of the profit and loss statement will come as a shock. According to our Lord and savior, Jesus Christ, the cost of discipleship is hating your father and mother, wife and children, brothers and sisters, yes, even life itself.

If our work is to make disciples of Jesus Christ, then this price tag has made that job exponentially more challenging. At best, it means that the only people willing to take up their cross are misanthropic recluses, and it is highly unlikely they would have left their homes to hear Jesus in the first place.

The other reasonable option is that anyone in their right mind would say no. This cost is too high. Who could afford to hate those who are most precious to us, including ourselves?

The very first decision that we have to make in this text is to figure out what Jesus really meant by "hate." The preaching instinct is to translate "hate" (μισεῖ) to mean . . . *literally* anything else. Our desire is to soften it, redeem it, and make it more palatable. I want the Greek root to give me the good news that my children and I don't have to hate each other for the sake of the gospel.

The problem is that there is no softening of the word μισεῖ. It means hate or detest. Period. Specifically, it is used to describe preference for one's riches over the value of God (cf. Luke 16:13). For Jesus to say you must "hate father and mother, spouse and children, and brothers and sisters—yes, even one's own life" (the word here is ψυχὴν, which means spirit or breath) is the worst-case scenario for our discipleship work.

This passage is certainly a stumbling block for us. If the core of the gospel is love, and love incarnate is now telling us that we have to hate the people we love the most, then how do we prepare a balanced budget? I am certain that my limited means will guarantee a deficit. The only conclusion is that the cost of discipleship is simply too high, and I will never be able to afford it.

Lest you think this is a foolish analogy, Jesus places the cost of discipleship into economic terms almost immediately: "If one of you wanted to build a tower, wouldn't you first sit down and calculate the cost, to determine whether you have enough money to complete it?" (v. 28). Once Jesus has our attention, he makes no additional mention of the troubling word μισεῖ. His shift in tone seems to indicate that we're focused on the wrong thing. Perhaps the core of this passage is not about what we hate, but about the value of what we love.

Maybe Jesus is suggesting that we tend to place our value in these titles, and how they become modifiers for our identity. The strong language isn't about the people, themselves. It's about how much we value those titles, and how often we will allow these things to define us more than our relationship to God does. Reverend, doctor, mrs. (there is no masculine equivalent), yours, mine—if those titles ever disappear, it is crushing to our identity. When something that was ours is *not* any longer, whether it's a job, an accolade, a child, a spouse, it takes a lifetime to adjust to our new identity and new reality.

But, is this also the case with our relationship to God? How easy is it for us to make our decisions based on certainty, rather than faith? How often do we prefer to view the world through the lens of pragmatism rather than justice? Through profit rather than equality? If we define ourselves, first, as providers, then we will always seek to provide for ourselves and our dependents. God, in this equation, requires no provision. Therefore, we are disinclined to factor God into the ledger, based on the assumption that God needs nothing from us. Jesus is here to tell us that God has asked for a very significant gift: love. And, it is hard to love someone when we've decided they don't need us. The truth of it is that God loves us so much that God refused to be God without us. And God-in-the-flesh is here to tell us how important this truth is.

Bringing the Text to Life

Preacher, our identity, our value, and our worth is not defined by the relationships we build, in the titles that we hold, or the interpersonal dynamics that we share. Those things are important, certainly! But, the person that you are is *enough*.

Psalm 139 says,

> You are the one who created my innermost parts;
>> you knit me together while I was still in my mother's womb.
> I give thanks to you that I was marvelously set apart.
>> Your works are wonderful—I know that very well.

God knows every hair on your head, and the seed of who you were in infancy has bloomed into the person you are now. That includes the blessing of life, and work, and relationships, and enemies, and friends along the way. But those things certainly don't define us. And if ever they keep us from our earnest and sincere approach to God, then perhaps Jesus is saying our priorities have been inverted.

If Jesus showed up right now and said, "Follow me, and I will make you fishers of people! We're going to places you've never been; trust me," I would have to think twice and make a lot of phone calls.

Remember that you belong to God. The creator who designed you will never abandon you, even when the cost of discipleship is so high that you can't pay it.

Let us take this particular passage that stops us in our tracks, and instead of hearing it as a barrier to our discipleship, let's hear it as the perpetual welcome. Even if the answer is "not yet," Jesus's invitation to discipleship never goes away.

September 11, 2022–
Fourteenth Sunday after
Pentecost

Jeremiah 4:11-12, 22-28; Exodus 32:7-14; Psalm 14; Psalm 51:1-10;
1 Timothy 1:12-17; Luke 15:1-10

Mandy Sloan McDow

Preacher to Preacher Prayer

God of might, God of love, God of grace, we have sinned. We have fallen short of your glory. Have mercy upon us. Amen.

Commentary

Destruction as creation. Jeremiah is a prophet whose story begins with a love song to his creation. Perhaps you've used the words "Before I created you in the womb I knew you; before you were born I set you apart" (Jer 1:5).

These are holy and humbling words. They are also a battle cry.

As these words are being written, prophets and protestors are raging in the streets as a pandemic cripples the world's physical and economic health. It is impossible to separate Jeremiah's text from the current reality, as we hear the cries of modern-day prophets who raise their voices for justice, equality, and the dismantling of systemic racism, the virus that has plagued our nation for too long.

Lest we think that prophetic work is finite, Jeremiah preached the message of repentance to the Israelites for forty years, and ended his career in Egyptian exile.

Being consecrated to this work is not a blessing.

Jeremiah's call to prophecy came in the thirteenth year of King Josiah, around 627 BCE, and he accompanied the Israelites seeking exile in Egypt. His prophetic career paralleled a time of political and religious unrest. Seeing that the chosen people of God were placing a higher importance on the "form" of worship rather than a change of heart to embrace God's commandments, Jeremiah's call was to preach repentance. The Israelites, however, had lost their faith in God's eternal promise to protect and care for them, and they had acquiesced to the Babylonian Empire in order to avoid destruction.

Jeremiah's prophetic work was centered on persuading the Israelites to abandon their false religion (worship of the temple) and to return to God again. If our work as preachers is to tell the great story of God's love for humanity, then we would be remiss to shy away from the anger God expresses through the prophet Jeremiah.

Walter Brueggemann suggests that prophetic discourse "is not a prediction. It is not an act of theology that seeks to scare into repentance. It is, rather, a rhetorical attempt to engage this numbed, unaware community in an imaginative embrace of what is happening . . . because . . . evil finally must be answered for."[1]

The evil that must be answered is *idolatry*. Jerusalem had fallen in love with itself and out of love with God. Their worship practices had become a form of idolatry. It would be misguided for us to direct our preaching to worship wars, because this isn't a parallel to traditional versus modern styles. The issue at hand wasn't *how* they were worshipping in exile, it was *why*.

As people, we will shake our fists at the heavens to demand an answer to our prayers with furious immediacy. Distress places us in a pressure cooker of urgency, and our pleas to an infinite God often seem unacknowledged by the creator of all time and space.

The problem with our prayers is that they prioritize us and our experience, without accounting for the mutual relationship we have with God. When we center ourselves in our own love story, we decentralize our partner. Jeremiah's prophecy is the language of a brokenhearted God. If the litany of creation in Genesis is a love story, then the litany of destruction in Jeremiah is God's devastated response to Israel's rejection.

Every love story has two sides. If we want to soften or ignore Jeremiah's word to the Israelites because what he says is so hard to hear, then we will miss the reason for God's outrage. In verse 11, חַ רוּחַ (ṣaḥ rū·aḥ), a "dazzling/dry wind," is what fuels Jeremiah's voice. We know from Genesis 1:1 that the Spirit (רוּחַ) of God, which breathes over primordial nothingness, has the capacity to create *everything* out of nothing. But, this wind, this Spirit, is one of equal force for destruction. This wind is too full and strong for comfort. This Spirit is one that flows from the outrage of a betrayed lover.

Jeremiah's oracles of judgment are painful to hear, because we want God to speak to us in words of comfort. But, perhaps today, your congregation needs to set aside their comfort for the sake of truth. Perhaps someone's life, dignity, and story matters more than the placated feelings of the stakeholders and critics.

Preaching prophetically is not a blessing. But it is what bends the moral arc of the universe toward justice. Our task as preachers is to engage our audience, and to move them toward meaningful action of loving God and our neighbor. Perhaps today is the day they need to be shocked into awareness of how to decentralize themselves from the love story God is writing with them, and prioritize the partnership to which God is calling them.

Bringing the Text to Life

This text parallels the creation narrative in Genesis 1 to demonstrate a very challenging reality: God does not worship creation. In verses 23-28, God is willing to sacrifice God's own handiwork, pointing out that not even mountains, living creatures, the fruitfulness of the land, and the cities were more sacred than God's relationship with God's own people. The catastrophe of destruction is foretold in poetry and verse, with lyric memory of the creation and all that could be lost.

Akin to the lost sheep in this week's Gospel reading (Luke 15:1-10), God will search until the lost are found. What the Israelites don't realize is that they were never lost. Their second exile was wilderness for them, but along a path that God had created before the foundation of time.

In the midst of the COVID-19 pandemic, we have witnessed how our lives have been deconstructed. Unemployment is at a record high, the US economy is in a recession, and more than two hundred thousand lives have been lost at the time of this writing. As the pandemic numbers peaked, demonstrations and protests in support of Black Lives Matter broke out worldwide. The earth is crying out for mercy, justice, and peace. But, the prophets are crying out,

> They treat the wound of my people
>   as if it were nothing:
> "All is well, all is well," they insist,
>   when in fact nothing is well. (Jer 6:14)

Perhaps you led your congregation through the most traumatic event of the twenty-first century, and now are in the process of picking up the pieces that remain. Jeremiah's words of destruction do not sound hopeful. The description of God's fury is the least comforting thing to us as we examine all that we've lost.

But, perhaps, God intends to use destruction as creation. Perhaps what was torn down were the idols we created to white supremacy, inequality in health care access, and capitalism. Once these idols have been destroyed, then we can return to God and rest in the world that was created for us with loving and equitable intent.

If we consider that God is unwilling to worship creation, then we can examine the things that we unintentionally worship. The serpent in the garden of Eden tempted Adam and Eve with knowledge, which was an invitation to define themselves outside of God. The things that we use to define us and our priorities (our jobs, our kids' sports schedules, even the traditions of the church) will lead us to seek out definitions of our life outside of God's claim on us.

This passage challenges us to examine the things in our life that cause us great discomfort, and to take account of the ways that we have turned from God. The Israelites provoked God's fury and jealousy over and over, and yet, God remained faithful. The depth of God's fury is an indication of the depth of God's love. We have the opportunity now to rebuild a life, a world, and a church that centers God's call to do justice, love mercy, and walk humbly.

September 18, 2022–Fifteenth Sunday after Pentecost

Jeremiah 8:18-9:1; Amos 8:4-7; Psalm 79:1-9; 113; 1 Timothy 2:1-7;
Luke 16:1-13

Mandy Sloan McDow

Preacher to Preacher Prayer

Holy and abundant God, give us the wisdom to value what will help build your kingdom on earth. Amen.

Commentary

What do you value? I am deeply and immediately offended by Jesus's accusation that worldly people are more clever than people who belong to the light. Scholars have often translated the word φρονίμως (*phronimōs*) as "shrewd" or "wise," and in this form, it only occurs once in the entirety of the Greek New Testament. Jesus has chosen his word carefully. Perhaps you, like me, have aspired to being clever. But, in this text, it appears as though cleverness is not an aspirational goal. If this is the case, then how are we to interpret this: "I tell you, use worldly wealth to make friends for yourselves so that when it's gone, you will be welcomed into the eternal homes." This feels antithetical to the rest of Jesus's teachings. Except, I trust the author of the story knows more than I do. I assume Jesus is telling this parable because it contains *truth*.

When we earn wealth—by any means, dishonest or otherwise—then we are bound up in the system that produced our wealth. The economic drivers of our lives are not unilaterally funded. A company, institution, or business can seek to earn its profits from honest measures. But their capital and resources are generated externally, from vendors, clients, and consumers. It is almost impossible to ensure that the money that is exchanged wasn't acquired by dishonest means. The push to boycott businesses for accepting funding from organizations with whom we fundamentally disagree is one step we take to distribute our own wealth wisely. But, this doesn't address the unintended consequences of how we *earn* our wealth in the first place. How many of us have preached comfortable sermons, so as to avoid uncomfortable conversations? Jesus knows that even the most generous giver at the synagogue is almost always the most opinionated.

Our money talks, and it tells us in clear terms what we value. All wealth is bound up into an inescapable system of oppression. Even when we try to make one positive decision, we are making a host of unintended bad ones. Our problem is that we have a limited understanding of the repercussions of our actions. It is God alone who can see the long-term view. For Jesus to praise the shrewdness of the dishonest manager must mean something about his eternal life. There is another factor at play in this parable.

If the text is not about cleverness or wisdom, then it must be about something else: the value of freedom. The parable's message is about debt and freedom from it. Everyone in the passage is beholden to something: The debtors are beholden to the manager. The manager is beholden to his employer. His employer is beholden to his wealth. Perhaps the point of this parable isn't about what binds us, but about what *frees* us: "You cannot serve God and wealth." Jesus calls us to liberate ourselves from the capitalistic forces that have bound us, not to God, but to economics.

If this text is about liberation, then how do we teach our congregations about freedom? Jesus says you cannot serve two masters, for the enslaved will "be loyal to one and have contempt for the other." This identifies that we will always have a master whom we serve, and we can choose for that master to be God, who created the universe and everything in it for good, or for it to be the allure of wealth. It is too hard for most white Americans to realize that we made mammon our master, and then enslaved African people as a commodity in our efforts to serve it.

If freedom is the goal for humanity, then what does it mean to be truly liberated? Quite simply, *liberation is the freedom to choose, and the ability to live out that choice.*

If one feels called to pursue a life that requires an education, liberation means she is free to choose this path *and* has access to the resources to accomplish it. True liberation means that the systems of oppression would no longer stand in the way. It means that sexism, homophobia, systemic racism, ableism, economic injustice, and all of the invisible threads of subjugation we have woven into the fabric of our society, intentionally or not, would no longer be a barrier to pursuing a vital and healthy life.

The dishonest manager used his cleverness to free both his clients and himself from their burden of debt. In doing so, he took the yoke of mammon off their necks and cast it aside in favor of reconciled relationship.

Bringing the Text to Life

"Whoever is faithful with little is also faithful with much, and the one who is dishonest with little is also dishonest with much." This is a challenging word, but it is asking the hearers to consider, *What do you value?* If we value liberation and freedom (for all), then our lives should be a reflection of this truth.

There is a conceptual gap between equality and liberation. Equality describes what is fair. The unintended consequence of equality is that everyone gets the same thing, even if it's not really what each person needs.

Equity makes more sense. It's not *fair*. But it is *just*. Everyone doesn't get the same thing, but they do get what they need to achieve the same result. The dishonest manager didn't erase everyone's debts equally, but he made a difference in the life of each person.

The image of liberation is radical, because it shows the well-intended inefficiency of equality and equity. These measures aren't necessary when the fence is removed altogether.

Perhaps we've been asking the wrong question. Instead of asking, "How do we implement measures for equity?" we should be asking, "What could we change so that we no longer need measures for equity?"

Preacher, I believe that Jesus is asking us to *tear down the fence*. We have made an idol of the fence, and allowed our lives to be oriented around its maintenance. This is what wealth does. It creates a barrier between us and what is right. We become servants to the master, which tricks us into thinking we are clever, when we have never considered what it would mean to be truly liberated.

There is grace in this parable, because Jesus didn't exempt the dishonest manager from the possibility of eternal life. This is important, because grace isn't fair. It isn't even *equitable*. But it is true. The same grace extended to the unjust manager is extended to all of us. In Christ, there is no fence. In Christ, we can all be free.

September 25, 2022– Sixteenth Sunday after Pentecost

*Jeremiah 32:1-3a, 6-15; Psalm 91:1-5, 14-16; **1 Timothy 6:6-19**; Luke 16:19-31*

Sky McCraken

Preacher to Preacher Prayer

Gracious God, we so often find ourselves not being enough or having enough, and it is harder still to convince those we shepherd of the same. Help us to be content with what we have, and ask you for what we need rather than what we want, reminding us all the while that we are—at best—trustees of what you give us. May that be enough, and may we be found rich in our faith and generosity. In Jesus's name. Amen.

Commentary

The author is giving instruction and advice to a young leader, "Timothy, my child." He is not only fond of Timothy; he wants him to do well. All of 1 Timothy is full of solid leadership advice, pitfalls to avoid, and warnings about fickleness among those he will encounter. This particular passage addresses the trappings of the seductions of life, not just for Timothy to avoid but instructions on how to lead others on avoiding them as well.

Verses 6-8 are foundational to the rest of the text: the staples of food and clothes on your back are enough, and even those you can't take with you after your death. Being rich with God begins with knowing that you already have "enough." This underlying principle is the grounding from which all seductions can be avoided, but the author warns Timothy that this will be a lifelong fight: without a working plan of piety and discipline, other passions can quickly take over. Today's consumerist society could have us list many passions that can quickly overtake us, but the love of money for the sake of money and profit is the crux of the author's concern.

Verses 11-16 are written like a rubric: articulated in these verses is a command for Timothy to order his life to "pursue righteousness, holy living, faithfulness, love, endurance, and gentleness. Compete in the good fight of faith." They are also a confession of faith. The author is trying to not only set Timothy up for success, but to help him early on with the disciplines that will help him remain unfettered by that which could hamper his ministry: debt, high standards of living, and egoism.

Preaching from this text will require some pastoral awareness and sensitivity, because the temptation is to say, "Avoid loving money! Avoid extravagance! Follow Dave Ramsey's advice: pay cash for a used car and only borrow money for a house!" The temptation is also high to romanticize ancient or modern monastic communities where people live simply and contribute to one another. The reality is that many of the people in our pews are faced with more indebtedness than they ever imagined, and our lawyers, physicians, even pastors are weighted down with student loan debt that may take a lifetime to pay off. While verse 10 laments that "some have wandered away from the faith and have impaled themselves with a lot of pain because they made money their goal," there are many in our congregations who find themselves in desperation because they have been impaled with massive amounts of debt, for which they need massive amounts of money to overcome. So they are not only driven to make money their goal but also have the goal of not being foreclosed upon.

The key to approaching this text is not guilt, but balance. Money and wealth are not evils, but rather tools. "Much will be demanded from everyone who has been given much, and from the one who has been entrusted with much, even more will be asked" (Luke 12:48). If we start with the premise that food and clothing are enough, we are all rich. That helps us start from a positive that, at the very least, (1) we all have enough, (2) we are given enough to be generous, and (3) this motivates us in attitude and action to how we approach our life with others *and* our own life situation.

I have learned just as much about the evils of the love of money and the blessings of being "rich" from both the poor and the wealthy. I learned quickly the strategy of being pastor of an urban church and carrying little cash in my pocket, because even the poor can succumb to the temptations that money could bring. I have also learned, by my own experiences of the poor, the modest, and the wealthy, that one need not be limited to an automatic tithing formula to be a blessing to God and to others.

Bringing the Text to Life

Bette was a faithful—and interesting—congregant of the church I serve. She lived in low-income housing, had health and mobility challenges, and could sometimes try my patience. At the same time, she would occasionally bring me small trinkets she made, one being a cross that she made out of clothespins. Nancy, one of our church members who helped settle her very meager estate, gave witness at her funeral. She had found a spiral notebook that was Bette's ledger, including her contributions to the church. Bette had very little, but in comparison to what she had, she was a very generous giver to the church. "I wept when I realized how generous this woman was, and how little she kept for herself," Nancy said.

Morris was a curmudgeon whose heart was bigger than his scowl and his pocketbook. He had built up a very successful family business by being shrewd and an excellent steward. He was generous to his church, and generous to his community. He paid for a lot of funerals and college tuitions of his employees and their children. He could have driven any automobile he wanted but instead drove old vehicles until they fell apart. He believed that the church and those who had been "entrusted with much" should actually do as Jesus commanded: to love and care for one another.

October 2, 2022– Seventeenth Sunday after Pentecost

*Lamentations 1:1-6; 3:19-26 or **Psalm 137**; 2 Timothy 1:1-14; Luke 17:5-10*

Sky McCraken

Preacher to Preacher Prayer

O God, sometimes we just don't know what to say to you or ask of you. We hear of unspeakable things happening, we read news that is unsettling, and we watch those we love tear each other apart on social media. We hurt, we grieve, we hurt some more, and we want to lash out. Help us temper our urge to fight and bite with a measure of grief and grace, and grant us the forgiveness to be kind to ourselves after we vent to you and ask you to crush our enemy, instead of loving them. Through Jesus Christ our Lord. Amen.

Commentary

This is a psalm in a category all to itself: some scholars have even referred to it as a cursing psalm. More than just a lament, it could even be called a communal "psalm of vengeance." Though not an admirable quality, there is certainly nothing new in the concept of "never forget." The destruction of Jerusalem was not far from the memory of the psalmist, who cried out not just for God to restore things, but to exact—even demand—revenge upon their enemies:

> Jerusalem! If I forget you,
> > let my strong hand wither! . . .
> LORD, remember what the Edomites did
> > on Jerusalem's dark day.

In the psalmist's mind, it would have been traitorous to forgive and forget such a thing!

The cycle of (a) lament, (b) loyalty out of national memory, and (c) hatred of enemies is a predictable one and all too common. We see similar patterns in Psalms 6, 31, and 79, where not only the lament is named, but petition is made that God deal with their enemy in the worst way possible.

National memory and hatred of enemies are not particular to Judaism, but in the context of the psalm there are reasons to lament. "But how could we possibly sing the LORD's song on foreign soil?" is not just a feeling of being away from home, but the frustration and feelings of unworthiness in singing to God in a land considered unclean, possibly eating food that might be unclean, adding to the frustration and indignity of being mocked by their tormentors to sing their holiest of songs. The "Rip it down, rip it down! All the way to its foundations!" shows the angst of the psalmist born out of indignity and rage.

The last two verses of the psalm bear out that rage:

> Daughter Babylon, you destroyer,
>> a blessing on the one who pays you back
>> the very deed you did to us.

This completes the cycle of lament-memory-hatred, with the most bitter of phrases we read in Holy Writ: "A blessing on the one who seizes your children and smashes them against the rock." A rough task is in store for any cantor or lector on this Sunday. "This is the Word of God, for the People of God. Thanks be to God." Really?

There are certainly themes of forgiveness, love of enemy, and the danger of bitterness poisoning our hearts that the preacher *could* address, but it would be wise to allow for the psalm to be what it is: a lament. To live a life full of bitterness is to squander our life. But to deny feelings of rage, loss, and harm done to us is equally detrimental to the health of our body and soul. We are not always a people who lament well, even and especially to God. Yet, we find much lament in the scriptures (even a whole book of Lamentations), which point to something beyond vocalizing honest feelings and practicing good mental health. Lamenting helps us practice our faith and tell the truth.

Bringing the Text to Life

I recall the early morning that my mother died. She was only sixty-three years old but suffering from COPD. Unknown to me, she had also been anorexic and depressed much of her adult life, although she never received any therapy or mental health treatment. She was a kind woman, but not particularly warm or affectionate. When she died, my brother leaned over to me and said, "Read or pray something." I had no words of my own, so I read a prayer from a pocket book of worship. I could not put into words or emotion any of my feelings.

I learned later about all of her physical and mental challenges. Medically, she should have never been able to conceive any children. All of these things began to answer the questions I had been asking myself all of my life. It also deepened my anger and despair about things never encountered, things that were now lost. While I had felt cheated in life, I now began to feel cheated by death. The rage began to surface. I went to a retreat a month later and attended a service of healing—and I began to lament. Sometimes it came in tears, sometimes in wailing. I was angry. My grief and my fears were real and I did not hold them back. I gave God a piece of my mind, and yet God did not smite me. I wasn't quite healed, but I had been faithful in my honesty. Now, I could begin the hard work of healing and receiving mercy.

This is not an easy text to preach from, and the preparation and delivery of a sermon from this text is a challenge. The act of lamentation is not encouraged in our society, and in many ways the church is to blame for that. However, very few in our congregations have been immune from the same feelings expressed by the psalmist. We have endured a lot of pain and suffering as individuals, families, communities, nations, and as a world. Our crying out to God is a vital part of our healing and redemption. This text gives the preacher an opportunity to model it for others.

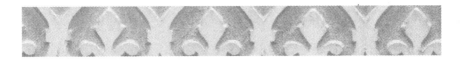

October 9, 2022–Eighteenth Sunday after Pentecost

*Jeremiah 20:1, 4-7; Psalm 66:1-12; 2 Timothy 2:8-15; **Luke 17:11-19***

Sky McCraken

Preacher to Preacher Prayer

Lord, we too often reduce the greatest miracles in our midst to an afterthought, not realizing that we take them for granted. Help us to see the lepers in life, and help us help them to see their healing to completion. In the name of Jesus. Amen.

Commentary

Anyone who studies Luke's Gospel and does any depth of work in word studies and historical context will quickly be overwhelmed, and this passage is no exception. While some scholars suggest delving into geography with Jerusalem mentioned as a destination (this passage marks the third occurrence), what genre of literature it fits, why Jesus criticized the nine who didn't come back (after all, they *did* do what he asked them to do), and so on, I side with the late Fred Craddock. He suggests moving past these textual-historical difficulties and seeing this passage as a two-part story: verses 11-14, a healing story, and verses 15-19, the salvation of a foreigner.[1]

Healing is a loaded term in Christian circles. More recent Protestant books of worship have included services of healing in them, but it still conjures up images of a televangelist exclaiming, "Throw away those crutches and *walk*!" The Greek word is *sozo*, which translates as "healing," "wholeness," and "salvation." For those involved, the healing was not just from their physical affliction, but also brought wholeness to their lives that made them acceptable in the community and society. It was a liberation of health and body. When Jesus says, "Your faith has healed you," then comes the healing of the soul—salvation.

It is important not to pass over the cry for mercy. In biblical times, one with the stigma of leprosy was banished from family and society, and their desperation for belonging was high if their will to live remained. The preacher would do well to note that many might have not raised their voices, either from feeling futility to utter despair. When one has been cast out by society, friends, even family, despair is an easy temptation to embrace. Sometimes, we may have to be proactive and inviting in our search of those who need healing.

Craddock notes that nowhere did Jesus "cancel out" the law in this passage, but neither was the foreigner excluded from the healing. The takeaway is that there is no specific chosen race: we are *all* chosen. When seen this way, the gratitude of the Samaritan is made clear: after praising God loudly, "he fell on his face at Jesus's feet and thanked him. He was a Samaritan." This is a good word for us as well, for we are living in a tribal culture, as well as a land of "nones" and "dones" where a faith tradition is concerned. The "blemish" they may feel is that they aren't churched people, and their despair may be from wounds they carry inflicted by the church.[2]

Perhaps Jesus's rebuke is a reminder that we should not take God's grace and mercy as a given without being thankful, even if we *are* a chosen people. To those of that time, the singling out of the Samaritan reminds us that not only does God bless them, but so should we. The "Get up and go. Your faith has healed you" instills upon the foreigner *and* the reader that we do not keep this act of God's mercy to ourselves, or reserve it for the few.

Bringing the Text to Life

When I graduated from seminary, the HIV/AIDS epidemic and its impact on the world was in full swing. Reported cases were in the hundreds of thousands. Magic Johnson was diagnosed as HIV positive, and singer Freddie Mercury had died from AIDS complications. Had it not been for the death of Rock Hudson and people urging for research and a cure a few years previous to this, we could have easily treated AIDS patients as we once did lepers: banished apart from society.

As it was, being diagnosed as HIV positive or suffering from AIDS was still a terrible stigma. I went to the hospital to visit a church member at the request of his mother, and while I was told that he was suffering from advanced pneumonia, the reality was that he was dying from the late stages of AIDS. As we talked, he told me this and talked about how difficult it had been to suffer in silence and alone. When I got up to leave, I took his hand and prayed with him—a short prayer as I remember. He grasped me with both hands and tearfully said, "Thank you." That was the first day I realized that I had met a leper, someone who had been told he was "unclean."

At that same church, a year or so later, Russ, our music director, was stricken with cancer. He had fought the battle with cancer before, but it had come back with a vengeance. The new *United Methodist Book of Worship* had just been released, and it included a Service of Healing. The senior pastor and I conferred about having a healing service for Russ, and Russ embraced the idea, but we knew that it would be irresponsible to do something "new" without some serious education and discussion, given the "loadedness" of the word *healing*.

We had the service in the church parlor instead of the sanctuary, thinking it would be a small crowd. As we started and explained the service, the church parlor was full and people spilled out into the hallway. Some were there out of curiosity, some were there for Russ, and all of us were praying that our gathering, as well as asking for God's mercy and grace, might be poured out as we laid hands on Russ.

A few months passed. Russ had a short reprieve, but was soon back in the hospital. I went to visit, where his doctor was present. I told him that I was sorry that healing hadn't happened. Russ was quick to correct me: "Oh, I *have* been healed. I know it's all okay." And he smiled—perhaps for my benefit—but his sincerity was clear. His faith had healed him.

October 16, 2022– Nineteenth Sunday after Pentecost

Genesis 32:22-31; Psalm 121; 2 Timothy 3:14–4:5; Luke 18:1-8

Jason Micheli

Preacher to Preacher Prayer

Almighty God, more so than others, we preachers are addicted to the glory story. We wrestle with your profligate grace that needs only our need. Use this heel grabber and this annoying widow, we pray, to spare us from the comforts of merit and demerit. Amen.

Commentary

I like Jacob. I like Jacob even though it's not clear from the biblical witness why I'm supposed to like Jacob. In a culture that prizes the eldest son, Jacob isn't. In a religion whose exemplar, Abram, leaves everything behind to follow by faith when God calls, Jacob doesn't.

I like Jacob, but in a tradition where names mean everything, convey everything, foreshadow everything, it's not clear from the name, "Jacob," that we're meant to root for this character.

When he was yet unborn, Jacob, who later wrestles God in the dark along the riverbank, for nine months wrestled his twin brother in the dark waters of his mother's womb. And when she gives birth to them, Esau first, the younger comes out clutching at the leg of the elder, as if to say, "Me first." So, Rebekah names him Jacob. In movies and television, Jake is always the name of the hunky, altruistic hero. But, in Hebrew Jacob means heel grabber, hustler, overreacher, supplanter, scoundrel, trickster, liar, and a cheat. In a religion where names signify and portend everything, it's not clear that I'm meant to but, nevertheless, I like Jacob.

No doubt, dear preacher, you know already that scripture gives us plenty of reasons to dislike Jacob. God had even spoken to him in a dream—gave him a vision of a ladder traveled by angels. When Jacob awoke from the dream and marked the spot with an altar stone and prayed to God, Jacob didn't pray for forgiveness. He didn't confess his sin. He didn't express any remorse or give any hint of a troubled conscience. Instead, Jacob prayed with fingers crossed and one eye opened, a prayer that was really more of a deal: "If you stand by me God, if you protect me on this journey, God, if you keep me in food and clothing, and bring me back in one piece to *my* house and land, *then* you will be my God." God revealed Godself to Jacob. And, afterward, Jacob is still the same Jacob—the same sinner—Jacob was before. Like a lot of us (most of us?), Jacob's encounter with God leaves Jacob completely unchanged.

Jacob's a liar, a cheat, and a thief. Jacob's got a wandering eye and a fickle heart. Jacob's got shallow scruples and fleet feet. Jacob's always ready to run away from his problems.

Jacob's not a Bible hero. He's not holy. He's a heel. Still, I can't help it. I like Jacob. You might not. You might not *like* Jacob. You might not *be* like Jacob. Maybe you're batting perfect when it comes to the commandments, preacher. Congrats, but how about your listeners?

How many of your listeners have never lied to their mother or father, or their husband or wife? How many of them have never sat idly by as a sibling or a friend, or a neighbor wanders out of their life, gets into trouble and then beyond their reach? Odds are likely close to zero percent. Have any of them ever betrayed someone they should've honored and obeyed? Have any ever returned a good deed with a petty one, or turned to God only when they needed the Lord?

I'd bet the house, yes.

But, that's not why I like Jacob.

No, I like Jacob because Jacob is not the sort of guy who would ever send a Hallmark card that says, "God never gives you more than you can handle." I like Jacob, because Jacob, whom God leaves lame and limping and bruised, knows that the good news is *not* "God never gives you more than you can handle." I like Jacob, because Jacob knows that God is not to be found up at the top of that ladder God showed him, and Jacob knows that the good news—the gospel—is not that God is there at the top of that ladder to meet us if we but climb our way up to him.

Jacob has the scars to prove it. The ladder was not for us to journey up to God. The ladder was for God to come down to us. God, Jacob learns, is like a judge who's willing to condescend to the appearance of a bad judge in order to relent to a widow's annoying pleading. Jacob has the scars to prove it. The good news is that God meets us in the very midst of that which we cannot handle.

Martin Luther said that, from Adam onward, you and I are addicted to the "glory story"; that is, we're hardwired by sin to imagine that God is far off in heaven, up in glory, doling out rewards for every faithful step we take up toward him and doling out chastisements for our every slip-up along the way. The "glory story" prompts all kinds of unhelpful questions and painful clichés, because it gets the direction of the gospel story backward. The gospel story, the story of the cross, is not the story of our journey up to God, but God's journey down to us. And the story of the cross isn't a story that starts with Jesus. Rather, the God who comes to us in the crucified Christ is the God who has always condescended. Indeed, that's why the first Christians believed it was the preincarnate Christ Jacob wrestles here in the dark of the night. This angel in the darkness is the Second Adam (Jesus) who has the authority to (re) name God's creatures.

Bringing the Text to Life

Chris Arnade is a photojournalist who recently published a book titled *Dignity*. Arnade used to be atheist. The book started out as an essay he wrote for *The Guardian* titled, "The People Who Challenged My Atheism Most Were Drug Addicts and Prostitutes." Arnade was an unbelieving, French-cuffed financier on Wall Street. When the market crashed in 2008 and he lost his job, he began traveling through urban America, interviewing homeless addicts and prostitutes and squatters and taking their pictures. "I had always counted myself an atheist," Arnade writes,

> I picked on the Bible, a tome cobbled together over hundreds of years that provides so many inconsistencies. . . . When I first walked into the Bronx, photographing homeless addicts, I assumed I would find the same cynicism I had toward faith. If anyone seemed the perfect candidate for atheism it was the addicts who see daily how unfair, unjust, and evil the world can be. None of them are. Rather, they are some of the strongest believers I have met.[3]

Arnade writes about a forty-something woman named Takeesha. She talked to him for an hour standing against a wall at the Corpus Christi Monastery in the South Bronx. When she was thirteen, Takeesha's mother, who was a prostitute, put her out to work the streets with her, which she's done for the last thirty years. Takeesha has a framed print of the Last Supper that she takes with her—a movable feast—wherever she goes to sleep for the night. She's hung the image of it above her in abandoned buildings and in sewage-filled basements and leaned it against a tent pole under an interstate overpass. She's taken it with her to turn tricks.

On the streets, with their daily battles and constant proximity to death, Arnade discovered that his atheism was made possible by his privilege. People like himself, Arnade realized, often don't believe in God because, with their cash and comfort, they don't need to believe in God. Which is but another way of saying God only meets us in our need. The cure for atheism, in other words, is found not at the top of the ladder, but at the bottom.

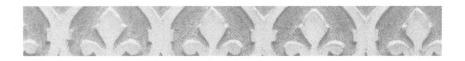

October 23, 2022—Twentieth Sunday after Pentecost

Jeremiah 14:7-10, 19-22; Psalm 84:1-7; 2 Timothy 4:6-8, 16-18;
Luke 18:9-14

Jason Micheli

Preacher to Preacher Prayer

Lord Jesus Christ, we love to count what you are no longer counting, our sins as well as our faithful works. Help your preachers with this parable, Lord Jesus, for our hearts have a desperate need to believe its exact opposite. Amen.

Commentary

Two men went up to the temple to pray, Jesus dishes, the first a Methodist preacher—a professional Christian—the second a lobbyist for Washington's latest tax cut for the wealthy. The latter, not the former, went back down to his McMansion justified, Jesus says, dropping the mic.

You can change out the identifying careers of Jesus's two characters. It doesn't much matter. Everyone in the world is either one or the other of these two characters. Some people are absolutely convinced that with all their good deeds they've drawn the winning hand at the game of justification. Others have discovered, often by the painful process of becoming least, lost, and, for all intents and purposes, dead, that the only thing they have to offer God is a total lack of any claim.

What makes this parable as slippery for us as it was to Jesus's first hearers is that the roles of self-righteous prig and authentic, vulnerable sinner refuse to be reified. If you've been a preacher longer than a month of Sundays, then you've already likely discovered how you can't rely upon the constancy of the publican's self-awareness. Under a different set of circumstances, it could just as easily be the Pharisee, not the publican, who has collided with the folly of attempting to put themselves right with God. Come next Sunday it could just as easily be the tax collector Ubering home while congratulating himself that he really gets how God's grace works, unlike that holy-rolling bookkeeper who makes himself the subject of all his prayers and gets caught red-handed in his holier-than-thou hypocrisy. We've all fallen short of the glory of God, but I guess that doesn't stop us from measuring distances. We're always, if not simultaneously then from one Sunday to the next, at once, sinners and saints. We leave church tax collectors enjoying our forgiveness, yet as soon as we get into the fellowship hall or log into Facebook we're back to being law-enforcing Pharisees.

They're two different characters in the parable, but they're both in us. That's why (this might sound obvious to some of you preachers, but I promise you it's not self-evident to many of your listeners) the gospel is for Christians. The gospel is *even* for Christians. We tend to think of the gospel (the promise that while you were yet hostile to God, Christ died for your sins and was raised for your justification) as though it's for non-Christians. Street-corner evangelists stand on street corners, not in church parking lots. We tend to think of the gospel of grace as a doorway through which we pass to get into the household of God, so that we can then get on with the real business of living like Christ and doing as Christ for our neighbors. But thinking of the gospel as prologue to the Christian life? Nothing could be more unbiblical.

The Bible teaches that Christ comes to dwell in our hearts by what exactly? By faith. And the Bible teaches that the faith by which Christ gives himself to us comes to us how? Not by doing. By hearing. Christ gives himself to us by faith that comes to us by hearing the word. The promise of grace. The gospel word.

The gospel, Martin Luther taught, gives Christ himself to us the way a wedding vow gives a bride her groom. The gospel, therefore, is for Christians. The gospel is for Christians because the gospel that gives you Christ is the same gospel that grows Christ in you. The way to grow in grace is to cling to the promise of it, to return to it over and again. Living a grace-filled life is like learning a song by heart—this song about Jesus Christ called the gospel.

Because we don't ever stop being a tax collector one Sunday and a Pharisee the next, we don't ever stop, we don't ever advance past, we don't ever level up beyond needing to hear the gospel. This good word, the gospel of Christ—just as Jesus said— it's the living water without which first we get thirsty, and then we get exhausted, before finally our faith dries up, and we die in our sins. The gospel word that gives Christ to you is the bread of life that keeps on feeding Christ to you. That's what Jesus means by calling himself manna. The gospel is the bread of life, and we're always one meal away from starving. And, without that meal, without the gospel, we have nothing to offer our neighbor, we have nothing to offer the poor and the oppressed, we have nothing to offer them other than what the world already offers them and how the world offers it.

Which is to say, thank God. God has not made us like other people. God has made us Christians. We are different from other people. We are the particular people God has put into the world who've been set free by the gospel to admit that we're just like other people. We're publicans and Pharisees all. We're worse than our worst enemy thinks of us, yet we're loved to the grave and back. Thank God, we're not like other people. We're different in that we have this gospel that frees to confess that we're no different. And that difference—a people set free to know and own that we're no different than other people—is the difference Christ makes in a world of us versus them.

Bringing the Text to Life

My first church put on a Christmas pageant one Advent season. There were no teenage girls in the congregation to be cast. So Mary was played by a grown woman who was married to a man more than twice her age. She'd married him only after splitting up his previous marriage. The holy Mother of God was being portrayed by a homewrecker.

"Mike" was an insurance adjustor with salt-and-pepper hair and dark eyes. He led a Bible study on Wednesday mornings that met at the diner. He delivered Meals on Wheels. He chaired the church council. He supervised the coat closet. He mentored kids caught in the juvenile justice system. He was the little church's most generous donor. And he was more than little officious in his righteousness.

Mike never liked me all that much. Mike sat down, fixed his reading glasses at the end of his nose, opened his program and began mumbling names under his breath: *Mary played by . . .* His voice was barely above a whisper but it was thick with contempt. "Of all the nerve . . . ," he said, and then he rolled up his program and he poked me with it. Just when the angel Gabriel was delivering his news to Mary, Mike whispered into my ear, "You think this is appropriate? You really believe she's the best person to represent the story of Christ?"

"Appropriate?" I replied, "No, I don't think it's appropriate, but, yes, I do think she's the best person for the job. She knows her need more than any of us do."

And, just to show how slippery this parable is today, I confess I'm the one who went home that day thinking I understood the gospel of grace better than that Pharisee.

October 30, 2022—Twenty-First Sunday after Pentecost

Habakkuk 1:1–2:4; Psalm 119:137-144; 2 Thessalonians 1:1-4, 11-12;
Luke 19:1-10

Jason Micheli

Preacher to Preacher Prayer

Gracious God, give us patience for the people our friendship with you obligates us to befriend. Give us wisdom to discern the dishonest wealth from which you would save us. And give us faith to exemplify already your kingdom that is not yet. Amen.

Commentary

"Today, salvation has come to this household," Jesus announces to the crowd about this little man peeking through branches because he was so loathed no one would let him to the front of the line. Notice, Jesus refers to himself as salvation. That Jesus himself is the personification of salvation means we cannot, as we so often attempt, separate the person and the work of Christ. Therefore, following Jesus—being caught up in his narrative in the manner Zacchaeus is so caught up—*is* salvation. Of course, that the person and work of Christ cannot be separated in a manner that spiritualizes our account of salvation and reduces Christ our Lord to the secretary of afterlife affairs should not come as a surprise to anyone who has read the complete narrative Luke has written.

As early as Luke 4, for his first sermon, echoing his mother Mary's song, Jesus unveiled his gospel in terms of the jubilee. A fifth component to the jubilee commandment in Leviticus 25 is that every fiftieth year all property that had been lost through hardships or lawsuits or debts would be redistributed to its original owners. Obviously it strikes many today as seditious even to mention the word *redistribution* in church. It sounds like a political term. And it is political, just not in the way people would expect.

In Jesus's day, to be a wealthy Jew in a land occupied by Roman invaders meant that in all likelihood your wealth was ill-gotten. Odds were that a wealthy Jew in

Jesus's day was a collaborator, colluding against his people with the Roman invaders. This is why tax collectors were despised in first-century Israel. Caesar hired Jews to collect excessive taxes from their fellow Jews—taxes that went to pay for the Roman army occupying their land and crucifying those who protested—and Rome encouraged those tax collectors to raise the rate and skim off the top for their own gain. Imagine the US army hiring Iraqis to collect taxes from fellow Iraqis to pay for American military personnel. You can imagine how popular that would be in Iraq. So when the rich young man approaches Jesus, in Luke's Gospel (18:18-30), asking about supposedly spiritual matters (eternal life), we should be suspicious immediately about how he's earned his wealth. And we shouldn't be surprised that Jesus turns his spiritual yearning into a question about riches.

Jesus's instruction to him, "Sell everything you own and distribute the money to the poor. . . . And come, follow me," should be heard as an echo of the jubilee command. He's telling the rich man that for salvation to be made available to him, he must give back to the poor the wealth he has taken from them, and then come and follow him who has become poor so that we might all become righteous.

The rich man refuses, walking away weeping. In the very next chapter, Jesus encounters Zacchaeus, a tax collector. Zacchaeus and the rich young man are meant to contrast with each other.

Luke describes Zacchaeus as a little man but you can be sure he was a big shot, making a fortune off the backs of his oppressed fellow citizens. Zacchaeus, though, is transformed by the grace shown to him by Christ. Though despised, Jesus wants to eat at his house for dinner. Such unexpected grace prompts Zacchaeus to return his ill-gotten wealth to the poor, a response that provokes Jesus to declare, "Today salvation has come to this household."

What's this mean?

Are we to indict ourselves for the wealth we have and enjoy? Are we to give everything away, examine what we have that's been gained by another's disadvantage or just feel guilty and pray for forgiveness? Maybe none of the above.

We're meant to realize that if Jesus's gospel isn't simply an otherworldly, spiritual message but a message about rectifying (that, after all, is the best definition of the word usually translated "justify") the wrongs in our present world and living graciously toward the poor, then whatever salvation means it has to mean more than our soul's escape from this world. Jubilee, the rich young man, Zacchaeus—they all remind us that salvation is about more than going to heaven after we die. Salvation isn't only a not yet in the future. It has arrived already in the flesh in Jesus Christ, and it is here and now whenever we as the church embody his kingdom.

Bringing the Text to Life

The singer-songwriter Brett Dennen has a song titled "Ain't No Reason" in which he laments the fact that he has slavery stitched into the fabric of his clothes. I thought of this song when, as a missionary, I toured a slum in Cambodia and happened upon the sweatshop where the very clothes I was wearing at the time had been made. The refrain in Dennen's song goes, "I can't explain why we live this way / We do it every day."[4]

Our salvation, Jesus announces to Zacchaeus, has to include our willingness to put our wealth into the practice of compassion. It's always important for Christians like us to recall that this would not have been a surprising message to a Jew, that is, a son of Abraham. Salvation is realizing, like Zacchaeus, that oftentimes our wealth stands in the way of what God wants to do in the world and with us. Salvation is participating with our whole selves—our hearts, souls, hands, feet, and *riches*—in what God is doing through Jesus Christ.

Jesus preemptively invites himself to supper before Zacchaeus, the publican, can find a change of heart or figure out how to sound more like a Pharisee. This is grace, free grace.

But grace, we learn with Zacchaeus, sets us free to give our everything to his service.

Does some of our wealth come from unjust systems?

Of course, maybe even a lot of it.

And part of any Christian's discipleship is discerning those complexities and choosing to exemplify an alternative way we believe Christ's death and resurrection is made possible in the world.

This is why mission and service work, I believe, is as much a means of grace for the doer as it is for the receiver. Part of what mission does is to lead you to places you never would have gone were it not for Jesus inviting himself into your life, and to introduce you to people you never would have met were it not for him.

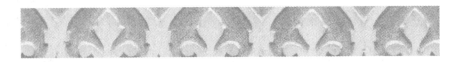

November 1, 2022–All Saints Day

Daniel 7:1-3, 15-18; Psalm 149; **Ephesians 1:11-23**; Luke 6:20-31

Jennifer Stiles Williams

Preacher to Preacher Prayer

Powerful God who has adopted us into the family through the gift of Jesus Christ, we long to be saints in training. Too often we live reacting to the days and events, without a proactive map that leaves a legacy behind. Help us to be intentional as we receive the inheritance of being called your children and your church. Help us to recognize the power and responsibility of what it means to be saints in the world representing your power. Amen.

Commentary

Most funerals follow the same format in the Christian tradition. There is a eulogy or naming moment, spoken by one or more who knew the deceased, sharing about their inspiring life. The eulogies are often followed by a witness to the resurrection, recognizing that the departed saint has now received their inheritance of eternal life through Jesus Christ. The deceased motivates those who mourn to live into the gift of eternity offered now and to continue the legacy of the departed saint. Death is a time to look back and recognize what life's purpose has been and how their life will live on through others.

But when did a eulogy become something only said for those who have died? In its earliest form, a eulogy was meant as a speech of praise or affirmation for the work of someone *living*. It was an opportunity to offer accolades for a life well lived and achievement of purpose and distinction. The word comes from the Latin *eulogia*, which means to praise. The writer of Ephesians, longing to meet with the Gentile followers in Ephesus, begins with an introduction offering high praise. It reads much like a eulogy, offering the people of the community acclamation for their faith in Christ Jesus, lived out in the actions of loving God and loving others. As the writer of Ephesians reaches out to this community they have yet to meet, the writer seeks to let them know their actions and lives of faith precede them. Who they have been proved who they are, faithfully serving Jesus the Christ. They are living as "holy ones" who embrace the inheritance of life abundant they have received, and are making their existence known by the way they love and serve God *and* God's people. The writer, in effusing admiration, reminds them as Gentiles that they were a part of God's plan of salvation from the beginning, called to continue the legacy of work and gospel of Jesus Christ. This is their life work as saints *now*.

All Saints Sunday is the day we honor those in the body of Christ who have died in the past year. We celebrate the glorious saints of light who have received their inheritance of eternal life. We read names, ring bells, light candles, and commemorate their lives among us. But could it be the work of this holy day is not to just look back at the lives of the departed, but learn how to look to our lives in the present and the sainthood we live in now?

In many ways, the eulogizing that the letter to the Ephesians professes toward its audience encourages us to begin writing our eulogies today. To consider what it is we want to be said about us as we claim our crown of eternal sainthood, and to use this as a way to write our stories as individuals and as a community of faith *now*. What does it mean to receive the fullness of the inheritance of Jesus Christ and the "overwhelming greatness of God's power"? What does it mean to do whatever it takes to live holy justice and grace-filled lives as saints right now? How does the church begin to help disciples write their own eulogies and create legacies that prove their faithfulness and trust in the power of God?

Each of us is an immortal saint, holy one. By this definition and theological understanding, how we map out our life and purpose seems to hold much more significance and responsibility than we often allow it. As a member of the church, I am called to follow in the footsteps of such a legacy—to be a member of a body where our deeds, our integrity, and our love of God and others are recognized by the world. I want to be a part of such a legacy; I want to contribute my actions, my devotion to such work. How does the preacher encourage and recognize the work of the saints, not only who have passed, but who are sitting right before them?

Bringing the Text to Life

What if congregants were invited to actually consider their own eulogies? What would be the praise they would want to hear about decisions they have made, the actions they have taken? Does our eulogy glorify the power of God and the inheritance of Jesus Christ or ourselves? How do we help create life maps that help people grow toward such aspirations? But also how is the larger congregation writing a legacy of praise based on God's vision and mission as well? How can the worship experience help members understand their stewardship of the eulogy or praise of God's church as a "holy one" in that congregation? What if all saints above and saints among the pews are celebrated, consecrated, and reminded of their power and responsibility on this holy day?

November 6, 2022– Twenty-Second Sunday after Pentecost

Haggai 1:15b-2:9; *Job 19:23-27a; Psalm 17;*
2 Thessalonians 2:1-5, 13-17; Luke 20:27-38

Jennifer Stiles Williams

Preacher to Preacher Prayer

God of yesterday, today, and tomorrow, you call us to rebuild and trust you in the process. Rebuild churches, rebuild lives, rebuild bridges between us and those who have lost hope in their own exile. Give us prophetic vision to sense what those who have gone before us felt: connectedness, belonging, purpose, and most importantly, your presence. May this vision move us to begin the work of building the kingdom of God with you, for those who will come after us. Amen.

Commentary

Haggai is the first of the last three prophets to the Israelites after exile. The remaining believers have been brought back to Jerusalem and given permission to rebuild the temple. But how do you rebuild something you only know from memories and stories of the generation before? How do you rebuild something when life is in ruins and it feels as if you have been abandoned?

How many congregations struggle to move forward with new vision and new ministry when it feels they have been abandoned? Pastors have come and gone. Neighborhoods and demographics change. Communities experience economic turnover and blight. While the generations before oversaw the fastest growth of churches in modern times, the megachurch of the 1980s and 1990s has begun to wane as boomers retire early. Gen Xers are trying to move into pastorates just as pandemics, race riots, #MeToo movements, and the younger generations demand change. Churches that had maintained their large numbers have been forced to socially distance their congregations while relearning the power of small groups. The postmodern generations of millenials and Gen Z mistrust institutional religion, which they have labeled as judgmental and out of touch. It feels as if the "temples" of church as we know it are starting to fall apart at the seams.

We have experienced exile in our midst. The physical buildings have not been destroyed as the temple had been in Jerusalem, but the former glory of large congregations and attractional ministry is shattered. People look to the past and for something to blame—which would often be found on the lips of the prophets. The prophets would trumpet the words of repentance to a people whose sin was turning away from God.

Haggai, who was a mouthpiece of God for only three months, takes a different approach. Haggai speaks words of encouragement. Going to the leaders of the time, he calls forth the memory of those who had witnessed the "glory" days, in order to help them dream again of what could be. "Who among you is left who saw this house in its former glory? How does it look to you now?" (2:3). Haggai knows they remember not just the physical temple, but the feeling of being there for worship and community. The recalled emotions were not about the building, as splendid as it was. They were the memories of stories and experiences of the generation before, and their feelings of connectedness, belonging, holiness . . . and ultimately their experience with God.

"Work," Haggai says. Do the work to rebuild and trust that, as you do, those feelings will return. Community, connectedness, belonging, holiness . . . and a personal experience with God. Those sacred emotions will come when the followers of Christ trust God enough to do the work. When a congregation comes around a vision or goal of ministry and commit themselves to it together, the Holy Spirit ignites something that connects them to a sense of purpose and belonging.

How many sports movies have we seen where the coach brings the team to an old stadium to give them uplifting encouragement? The coach tells them the story of the glory days, inciting in them hope that if they work hard and trust one another they will find victory. Or what about the countless stories of teachers who inspired their students to find their purpose for tomorrow as they gaze over the yearbooks and mementos of yesterday? What of the stories of a community that comes together after devastation to rebuild when it seems all hope is lost? Humanity loves these stories. There is something within the human spirit that rallies around the memories of yesterday, not because they were perfect days, but because they inspire in us a sense of purpose and meaning that we continue to search for. All of those feelings of connection and belonging come to life when congregations and individuals are willing to do the work, to trust that God is going to make something of our willingness. All this with the hope that others will also feel this way tomorrow.

Too often prophetic words come with the indictment of wrongdoing. But what if the prophet is just encouraging people to *remember*? Not to remember what they were doing, or how it came about, but instead remembering what they *felt*, what was different, who they were as people. Haggai wasn't just helping them recall the splendor of the temple, but the trust the Israelites had in building it, giving to it, and worshipping in it. It was about the trust they had in *God*, and the experience they had with God and with one another when it was there. That is something worth working toward rebuilding, not for the sake of walls, but for the sake of connecting people to a relationship with God and the church.

Buildings are most likely not what need to be rebuilt in most places today. What is needed is a rebuilding of visionary ministry to connect congregations inside those buildings to the world outside the walls. A word of encouragement from someone like Haggai could help build a new expression of faith that allows people to find meaning and purpose. The Spirit is waiting to inspire and connect congregations willing to trust God enough to do the work of building new sacred spaces of relationships for faith formation and belonging. When the church trusts the prophet enough to work and trust the one who gives the silver and gold, there will be splendor in what is created—lives changed, communities transformed, neighborhoods rebuilt, this the work of the temple God will prosper.

Bringing the Text to Life

The Appreciative Inquiry vision model for business and nonprofits moves the organization through a four-step process of discovering gifts and assets of the organization, dreaming about how those gifts can meet the needs or demands of the community, and then designing a destiny to fulfill those dreams based on strengths. The desired outcome is to build a vision and strategy based on the gifts and assets of the organization. The first step is to discover the gifts of the organization. Asking a congregation to answer "what brought you to this church?" and "why do you stay?" is an exercise that Haggai would have probably employed. Buildings, programs, or ministries may have attracted someone, but what keeps people connecting and investing their lives in a church is something intangible. It's the feelings of connectedness, belonging, and ultimately their experiences with God that holds them in a place to covenant in partnership. How can the preaching moment help elicit those responses to reinvigorate a stewardship of commitment in those we serve.

November 13, 2022–Twenty-Third Sunday after Pentecost

Isaiah 65:17-25; *Malachi 4:1-2a; Psalm 98; 2 Thessalonians 3:6-13; Luke 21:5-19*

Jennifer Stiles Williams

Preacher to Preacher Prayer

Gracious creator God, we yearn for the prophet's vision of a new day to come to pass. We long and hunger for the vision of your kingdom to come among us, bringing heaven to earth. Let us hear with hope what you promise us, painting a picture of your kingdom come, and willing in each of us the strength to work toward your vision in all we do. Give us the courage and strength to examine the ways we hold on to things you would cast off as former things, so we can begin to see glimpses of your new creation. Amen.

Commentary

The year 2020 was one we will never forget. A pandemic shut the world down. Black men were murdered in the streets in front of our eyes. As we protested racism and injustice, we found ourselves feeling like Israelites in exile. The cry of "how long, O Lord" arises from people of faith wondering when God will do something miraculous, to come save us from ourselves.

With hope weighed down by anguish and fear, we looked to the Isaiah promise of a New Jerusalem. We are desperate for God's kingdom to come, on earth as it is in heaven. Visions of the new city of Zion seemed so far from reach. We were hungry for the day when the lion and lamb will lie down in peace, when work will not be in vain, when crying and weeping will be replaced with joy and gladness. The prophet speaks in Second Isaiah to give hope to those Israelites in exile, reminding people lost in brokenness and desolation to remember the faithfulness of the God who brought them out of Egypt and promised to dwell with them, beloved. Isaiah promises in this powerful vision of a New Jerusalem to eradicate the sin of the people, alleviating the curse of toil and labor from their sacred story of origin. Visions of a city of equity, gladness, joy, and justice give them hope to hold on to and return to them a God they can trust.

The images from the protests following the death of George Floyd showed us a nation hungry to eradicate racism and usher in equality. We were awestruck by the pictures of black children holding signs emblazoned with "I Matter" in black marker, and the video of fierce little Wynta-Amor Rogers, walking with steadfast urgency, shouting "no justice, no peace!" Little children, strong and resolute, leading us with a hunger for the world God envisioned and Isaiah prophesied to come alive among us.

The prophet paints a glorious picture of what God will do: create a new heaven and new earth. Out of the chaos of our world, God will create something *new*. The groaning pains of earth and humanity, the destruction that began in the garden, will be eradicated. All things will be made new.

While preachers can also easily paint a picture of the yearning for a New Jerusalem, the trouble is to define what needs to be refashioned. Can we hold on to the heart of what is important while shedding the legacy they have created? How do we, as Christians, maintain the integrity of our love, while letting go of the systems we have held so dear? Can we name what makes them so hard to let go of in the first place?

I received an email during 2020 as the church released strategic plans to slowly and safely open campuses. For some the phases were too quick, as many congregants worried that any gatherings on campus would cause a spike in COVID-19 cases. For others, the phases were too slow, and meant the leaders were living in fear of the inevitable. One person wrote an email imploring the importance of kneeling at the rail weekly during the Lord's Prayer. In their eyes, online worship was just not the same, and they could not be spiritually fed without coming each week to kneel in an act of pious, *proper* worship. In my response, I shared the same grief at the loss of what felt like our holy space. I lamented with the writer that things were not the same and would not be for the foreseeable future. I then shared the work of Susan J. Wright, from the book *Foundations of Christian Worship*, who wrote that kneeling rails at the Communion table were established in medieval Europe. At the time, the place of worship was also the place of commerce. Apparently, what was, for the writer of the e-mail, a holy and sanctified tradition of *true* worship was actually used originally as picket fences to keep the dogs away from the Communion bread.[1]

Kneeling at the Communion rail may seem small, but it is part of a larger body of practices that have shaped the Christian faith. Common acts of ritual worship are important; but when they become so sacrosanct that they override the processes of keeping vulnerable people safe, one has to wonder what *else* is holding us back from the New Jerusalem coming to pass. Could the "former things" be our definitions of marriage, statues commemorating the Civil War, binary checkboxes on forms of gender conformity? What will we be surprised to see has been forgotten as God ushers in a new kingdom of love?

Could the former things we hold so dearly be the sins of idolatry and pride that keep us at arm's length from God and community? It is the prophetic call of the sermon moment not only to *paint the picture* of the longing we have for this new kingdom but also to claim and start the process by which disciples begin to let go. Naming that which God would put in the categories of "former things" is to recognize that our vise-like grip on them are obstacles to God's kingdom here and now. It is in the process of letting go that we learn to receive glimpses of God's faithfulness for what is to come.

Bringing the Text to Life

Owlah services are usually offered on New Year's Eve. *Owlah* is the Hebrew word for burnt offering. This process is a liturgical means of letting go of past regret, hurt, harm, shame by offering those experiences as burned offerings to end the year and begin a new year with openness.

The church is coming to the end of the Christian year. Before moving into the cultural season of thanksgiving and also before the beginning of a new year, could there be a time for a claiming of the "former things" as we allow God to heal and help us let go of the things we hold so dear that we miss the kingdom? What would it mean to allow prayer time to write those things down and begin the process of healing and receiving a vision of the New Jerusalem to come, by offering them as a burnt offering in the fires of the Holy Spirit?

November 20, 2022– Twenty-Fourth Sunday after Pentecost/Reign of Christ

*Jeremiah 23:1-6 or **Psalm 46**; Luke 1:68-79; Colossians 1:11-20; Luke 23:33-43*

Magrey R. deVega

Preacher to Preacher Prayer

Gracious God, speak into the whirlwind of my life, and into the storms within me and around me. Silence all voices but your own, that I may hear you with clarity, and receive the comfort and conviction to meet the demands of this moment. Thank you for being my refuge and my strength. Amen.

Commentary

Psalm 46 is a veritable soundtrack for anxious times. The first six verses crank up the volume with vivid descriptions of how noisy our lives can be: the earth changes, the mountains shake and tremble, the waters roar and foam, the nations are in an uproar, and the kingdoms totter.

Then, like many of the Psalms, there is a rather sudden pivot. Often in the Psalms, this quick shift of tone is from despair to hope, or helplessness to trust. What is unique about the pivot in Psalm 46 is the change in speaker, from the voice of humans to the voice of God. It shifts from being a declaration *about* God to an invitation to *hear* from God directly.

It is found in verse 10: "Be still, and know that I am God!" (NRSV). It summons of the psalmist a choice: What are we to do in response to what God has said? Now that God has broken into the noise and spoken a command of silence, how then shall we live?

We discover two options in how to handle the text, each with different ways of understanding what God is saying. Does this verse command us to be silent, or does it command us to work with God in doing the silencing?

The first option has been a popular one over the years, making Psalm 46:10 one of the most often-quoted verses in the Psalms, as many have drawn comfort and serenity from it. We imagine that amid the roar of the world's noise, God calls us to stillness and quiet, a "peace that passes all understanding," as Paul suggests to the Philippians.

Silence and solitude have been prominent spiritual practices throughout the history of the church. And Psalm 46:10 would remind us that true spiritual stillness does not begin with our own initiative, nor is it manufactured by our own efforts. It comes from a "knowledge of God."

But there is a second option, a different way of understanding that verse, which unlocks a deeper level of meaning and an even more powerful application.

The New Revised Standard Version and New International Version translate the verse in the well-known "Be still, and know that I am God," based largely on the old King James Version. But the Jewish Study Bible, known as the "Tanakh Translation," is based on the original Hebrew and translates the scripture with much stronger language: "Desist, and learn that I am God!" Tom Long, in his book *The Witness of Preaching,* says the tone here is "like a command to stop doing something destructive and prideful."[2]

Then, in the Common English Bible, this verse is translated from the Hebrew with even more force: "That's enough! Now know that I am God!" Yes, there may be times when one needs the soothing, comforting translation of Psalm 46:10. But sometimes, we need the strong and forceful version, with the kind of tone that Jesus must have used when he silenced the roar of the storm, or ordered the demons to leave, or rebuked the moneychangers.

Ultimately, the preacher might choose which of these routes to take by exegeting the congregation, along with the text. Does the congregation most need to hear a word about practicing Sabbath and solitude, and creating space for more stillness in their lives? Or do they need to hear a word of how God is working through us to silence the noise of injustice and brokenness, and how we can participate in that silencing with confidence and conviction?

Bringing the Text to Life

Should the preacher choose the route of saying that Psalm 46:10 encourages us to be still and silent, a helpful illustration comes from Rob Bell. In his *Nooma* video titled "Noise," he describes Bernie Krause, a noted "soundscape artist," who produces albums of sounds found in nature. Krause said that in 1968, in order to get one hour of natural sound (no cars, planes, machines of any kind), it took about fifteen hours of recording time. To get that same hour of natural sound today requires over two thousand hours of recording time. We are bombarded by sound.[3]

Not only are we surrounded by manufactured sound around us, we are immersed in the noises within us. The preacher might ask, "If it were possible to make a soundscape recording of your mind and your soul at this moment, how long would it take to record an hour of mental and emotional quiet? Perhaps it would take longer than two thousand hours." We hear the constant drone of deadlines. We sense the thunderous booms of anxieties, the heavy pulsing of pressures, agendas, and ambitions.

Should the preacher choose the route of explaining Psalm 46:10 with a more forceful sense of desisting and silencing the noises of oppression and justice, they might ask the question, "What is in your life right now to which God can help you say, 'That's enough! Now know who is God'?" This may be followed by a list of examples, each followed by the exclamatory, "That's enough!" which may invite of the congregation a spoken response. For instance,

To the feelings of loss and despair that you may be facing, God can help you say, "That's enough!"

To the anger that we feel at the institutional racism and systemic oppression against marginalized persons, God can help us say, "That's enough!"

To the injustice of a society filled with economic disparity and unequal access to affordable health care and housing, God can help us say, "That's enough!"

And to the sense that we are all alone to face these feelings all by ourselves, God says to us, directly and emphatically, "That's enough!"

"Now know that I am God!"

November 24, 2022– Thanksgiving Day

*Deuteronomy 26:1-11; **Psalm 100**; Philippians 4:4-9; John 6:25-35*

Magrey R. deVega

Preacher to Preacher Prayer

Loving God and giver of all good and perfect gifts, draw me close to you in gratitude for the blessings I enjoy and too often fail to acknowledge. Remind me of the privilege it is to serve you, and for the faithfulness you demonstrate time and again to help me fulfill my calling. May you lead all your people into a spirit of greater thanksgiving to you, for the living of these days. Amen.

Commentary

Psalm 100 calls us to make this day one of praise and thanksgiving. In reading it, one can't help imagining what it must have been like for the Israelites, shouting and cheering as they ascended the hill toward Jerusalem, with the mighty gates of the city looming larger in their sights.

The psalm says, "Enter his gates with thanks, enter his courtyards with praise." Of the many Hebrew words for praise, the one in verse 4 is *halal*, from which we get the word "hallelujah." It is the most vivid, most expressive word for praise in the Hebrew vocabulary. It doesn't just mean "praise," it means "raving and cheering in such a bold, public way, that you don't care how other people see you." One translator even suggests that it means, "making a fool of yourself," and not caring what others think when they see you.[4]

The preacher might ask the congregation when the last time was that they worshipped God in that way. We can imagine such a response in a sports stadium, a live theater, or a rock concert. But we can admit that we don't typically associate that kind of enthusiasm with worshipping God, especially when we do not feel like it.

But it is not impossible. We remember that Psalm 100 does not tell us to make a joyful noise to the Lord only when we feel the urge to do so. It does not tell us to worship the Lord with gladness only when we are gathered in a sanctuary on Sundays, or only when we are having a good day. The call to praise is constant, including—and especially—when we don't feel like it.

The good news is that Psalm 100 not only tells us that praise and thanksgiving are important, it also shows us how to do it. Verse 4 gives us some practical guidance on how to praise God:

> Enter his gates with thanks,
> > enter his courtyards with praise! Thank him!
> > Bless his name!

The verse makes a very subtle but important distinction between praise and thanksgiving. We often lump them together, and they are both important. Just as a song is made up of both lyric and melody, you can't have praise without thanksgiving, and vice versa.

But here is the important distinction: thanksgiving focuses on what God has given you, and praise focuses on who God is. Thanksgiving is about the gift. Praise is about the giver. Thanksgiving shows gratitude for the gift itself; praise is gratitude for the character of the giver.

True, it might be easier to practice thanksgiving—to count your blessings, to remember the good things that God has given you. But that is just the place to start. It is just the "outer gate," the starting line, not the finish line. Eventually, we must move from entering the gates of thanksgiving to moving into the courts of praise.

Because if it were just about thanksgiving, then that would be a mighty egotistical way to worship. It would make it about us. We'd basically be saying, "Thanks, God, for what you've done for me. Thank you for what you've given me. Thank you for this worship service that does everything I need it to do for me." But it is not about us, because thanksgiving is just the first step. It's just the "outer gates."

The critical next step is praise. It's acknowledging God's goodness and God's power and God's love, regardless of our situations, regardless of whether we feel blessed or not. Praise simply means "God, I am in awe of you. Just being in your presence is breathtaking. And regardless of what is happening in me and around me, there is no better place to be but in your presence."

Bringing the Text to Life

In her book *In God's Presence: Theological Reflections on Prayer,* theologian Marjorie Suchocki said it this way: "Our gratitude for the gifts of God leads to gratitude for the knowledge of God, which leads simply to gratitude to God." This offers a helpful and succinct way of describing the singular movement of thanksgiving and praise that Psalm 100 calls us to take.[5]

The hymn "Be Thou My Vision" is also helpful in recalibrating our spirit away from an egotistical fixation on the self and moving us toward praise and thanksgiving of God. It begins with the beautiful and poignant line "Be thou my vision, O Lord of my heart. Naught be all else to me, save that thou art."

If one were to rework the Old Irish syntax of that first line and translate it into more contemporary language, the hymn would basically say, "God, I want to see everything through your eyes. Nothing else matters but you. You are the best I have, both day and night. When I am awake and when I am asleep, you are the light."

Finally, this quote by C. S. Lewis illustrates these points well: "I believe in Christianity as I believe that the sun has risen, not only because I see it but because by it, I see everything else."[6]

A sermon on Psalm 100 is a meaningful and appropriate way to observe Thanksgiving Day. It calls us to praise God by asking God to be our vision. Not just so we can give thanks for what we can see, but for the means by which we can see it.

November 27, 2022–Fir... Sunday of Advent

*Isaiah 2:1-5; Psalm 122; Romans 13:11-14; **Matthew 24:36-44***

Charley Reeb

Preacher to Preacher Prayer

O Lord, as we begin a new church year, help us to be ready for anything you have in mind. Amen.

Commentary

The Gospel lesson from Matthew for the first Sunday of Advent doesn't evoke the warm sentiments of the season. In fact, some preachers will avoid this text because they believe it is misplaced. "Isn't this text about the second coming of Christ? Why does the lectionary include it as the Gospel lesson for the First Sunday of Advent?" It is a good question and might not be a bad place to begin your sermon.

I'll admit this warning in Matthew is a bit off-putting. Your listeners may shift in their seats and scratch their heads. This is a stark warning from Jesus to "keep watch" and stay alert because he could come out of nowhere. Don't be caught unprepared. Fair enough, but are we ever truly prepared when Jesus shows up?

Advent reminds us that our Lord is not very predictable. Imagine God had gathered all the best advertisers, marketers, and campaign managers and said, "Okay, I am planning my grand entrance into the world. What do you think of this? I begin as a baby born from the womb of a teenaged peasant girl. I spend my first days in a feeding trough. I grow up poor. My first sermon is so offensive that I almost get thrown off a cliff by my own people. I hang out with outcasts and drunks. Oh, I also insult the religious establishment. Finally, I get arrested, tortured, and killed. What do you think?" Who would have ever guessed?

Most didn't have a clue what God was up to in Jesus. The religious leaders who were looking for a Messiah wanted him dead. The political authorities felt he was a nuisance and washed their hands of him. The masses saw him as a great orator who performed a few tricks but tired of him when he kept speaking the truth. Even the

..es fell asleep before he was betrayed. Later, his followers turned their backs on .. Ironically, in Mark, it was a Roman centurion, after observing Jesus dying on the ..oss, who said, "Truly this was the Son of God" (Mark 15:39). How come no one ..lse noticed?

Let's face it. Most of us would not have recognized Christ either. We would have been unprepared for his entrance into the world. God's plan for overcoming evil, sin, and death would've never appeared on our radar. This is precisely why I believe the lectionary includes this text for the First Sunday of Advent. It reminds us that Jesus rarely shows up in a way we expect. Most of us aren't very good at predicting or anticipating how God operates and God does not expect us to be. "But nobody knows when that day or hour will come," says Jesus in verse 36. The unpredictability of God reminds us that God is God and we are not.

If indeed God's ways are "higher" than our ways (Isaiah 55:9), then we should accept that God often moves in ways worlds apart from our frame of reference. Our job is not to guess or presume but to be ready for anything God might have in mind. Jesus said as much: "Therefore, you also should *be prepared*, because the Human One will come at a time you don't know" (verse 44). Our willingness to embrace the unpredictability of God opens the door to the power and plan of God. God may reach out to us in ways we never imagined. Never in a million years will we anticipate it. But when we look back we will realize it was something we could have never dreamed up. It was the creative work of God and God alone.

So, instead of focusing on the sense of expectation in Advent, perhaps your sermon should remind folks of how often God works in unexpected ways. Maybe your message is that Advent is less about waiting on God and more about keeping our minds and hearts open for the baffling ways God chooses to show up. Isn't that the real wonder of Christmas? "Keep watch!"

Bringing the Text to Life

I remember having a conversation with an older man sitting next to me on a plane. He asked what I did for a living. When I told him I was a preacher, his face sunk. "I believe I was supposed to be a preacher," he replied. "Oh really? What happened?" I asked. He mentioned having the desire to attend seminary after college but other things always got in the way. "I stayed home to invest in a toxic relationship. I kept a job that was easy and paid well. I also spent a bunch of money on trips trying to relive my college days." He paused a moment to reflect and then concluded, "I didn't realize it at the time, but when I look back it's clear that God was trying to get my attention. I guess I was too preoccupied with life. I am sad when I think about it. I wonder what else I've missed."

Jesus said, "Therefore, stay alert! You don't know what day the Lord is coming."

December 4, 2022–S
Sunday of Advent

Isaiah 11:1-10; Psalm 72:1-7, 18-19; Romans 15:4-13;
Matthew 3:1-12

Charley Reeb

Preacher to Preacher Prayer

Dear Lord, give us courage to preach the gospel with boldness. Your relentless act of love through the incarnation demands a response. May our preaching give listeners the opportunity to respond to your gift of grace. Amen.

Commentary

This week's Gospel lesson makes it clear that to arrive at Christmas we must first go through John the Baptist. It is no easy task because John doesn't mince words. The Lord is coming and we had better repent. Now there's a message you don't often hear from pulpits during Advent! We are usually told to slow down and simplify Christmas. "Remember that Jesus is the reason for the season." That is standard Advent sermon fare, and truthfully, the message we prefer to hear (and preach!). But John has a different Advent message for us: "Produce fruit that shows you have changed your hearts and lives" (v. 8) or perish. He says that a "fire that can't be put out" is waiting for those who don't heed his warning (v. 12).

I don't believe someone like John the Baptist would last very long preaching in the mainline church. Imagine it is Christmas Eve. The sanctuary is packed. Children are restless and giddy about Santa coming to town. Everyone is in the Christmas spirit. Carols are sung. The Christmas story is read. The children's choir has presented their adorable anthem. The preacher then enters the pulpit and doesn't offer one of those sermons with three sentimental points and a poem. Instead, the preacher proclaims, "The Lord is coming, so if you know what is good for you, come down this aisle tonight and repent of your sin. I've got a big barrel of water down here and will baptize you on the spot. If you're serious about receiving Jesus then you must repent baptized." Do you think all those Christmas Eve visitors would ever return at church?

Say what you will about John the Baptist, at least he is clear about where he stands. There is no hemming and hawing with this prophet. In our world filled with shades of gray and lazy relativity, this week's text boldly draws a line and demands that we choose a side. For John, there is right or wrong, good or evil, and those who are for God and against God. There is no wiggle room. We, on the other hand, like to consider all sides. We have a habit of qualifying everything with "Well, it could be this, but it might be this. . . . Everyone has a different viewpoint. Everyone has their own frame of reference." But John's message of repentance forces us to recognize that when it comes to Jesus Christ we can't sit on the fence. A decision must be made. We must choose who and what we are going to follow. We can't be everything and nothing and still call ourselves Christ followers. Life is filled with a lot of gray, but this text reminds us that some matters are very clear. The question no one can avoid is "What will you do with Christ?"

So, what is a preacher to do with John the Baptist and this text? We could take the edge off and say something like, "Make room for Christ in your Christmas this year. 'Prepare the way for the Lord'" (v. 3). But we know that is not being true to John's message. We could also choose to preach on another scripture text, but if you're still reading this commentary perhaps the Holy Spirit will not let you walk away from this one. The only faithful option is to convey John's message of repentance. How do we do that? I am not advocating that we get up in the pulpit and beat up on our listeners for their sins. We have plenty ourselves! What I am suggesting is that we must demand a response. Our responsibility is to present a clear message of the gospel and give our listeners the opportunity to decide for themselves what they will do with Jesus. After all, if Christ doesn't empower us to turn from sin, do we really have a genuine message to preach? Christmas is either an empty holiday remembering the birth of a historical figure or it's an event that brings new life. If Christ doesn't transform us then what is all the fuss about?

Bringing the Text to Life

I remember my high school geography teacher. He was a very kind man. Never gave us homework. He would show movies and let us leave class early for lunch. Occasionally, he would read Trivial Pursuit questions about geography. People loved him. Who wouldn't? There was a waiting list to get into his class. But you know what? When I graduated I couldn't tell you where Wisconsin was on a map. I didn't learn a thing about geography.

Then there was my English teacher. She was a pain in the neck. She was relentless. Tons of homework. Always a paper to write. She would return my papers drenched with red ink. She was never satisfied with my work. For her, there was a right way and wrong way to do things. After the final day of her class I felt like I had been paroled. But you know what? I still remember and use the lessons she taught me when I sit down to write a sermon. I'm a better writer and preacher because she was so tough on me.

John the Baptist may be tough and relentless, but we are better Christians and preachers for it.

I will never forget playing golf with a man I was paired with while on vacation. He told me he stopped going to church. When I asked him why, I thought he would give me the usual excuses: "They made me feel guilty about everything"; "The preacher offended me"; "The church was filled with a bunch of hypocrites." I was taken back when he replied, "The preacher never said anything I couldn't get from a TED Talk or self-help book. I thought you preachers were supposed to be different."

December 11, 2022–Third Sunday of Advent

Isaiah 35:1-10; *Psalm 146:5-10 or Luke 1:46b-55; James 5:7-10; Matthew 11:2-11*

Sue Haupert-Johnson

Preacher to Preacher Prayer

Dear Lord, help us proclaim the vision of Isaiah that will deliver our people from wilderness to home, from terror to joy, from brokenness to wholeness. In Jesus's name we pray. Amen.

Commentary

Going home to God. Good Advent preaching requires us to preach both the first and the second coming of Jesus the Christ. Fortunately, the lectionary offers us tremendous selections, often from Isaiah, that catapult us into the fantastic imagery of the cosmic and the eschatological. We, the people of God, need to hear a word of hope and reclaim this vision that has sustained the people of God through the ages: God is at work setting all of creation right, God will return and take full charge of everything, and God promises us restoration and *joy*! On this Third Sunday of Advent, when we light the Advent candle of Joy, Isaiah 35:1-10 reminds us that the Lord's return will "overwhelm" us with happiness and joy. Proclaim joy to your people!

Isaiah speaks to an exiled Israel, a people who have been forcibly removed from their homeland and are now living in a strange land, where their religion and customs are not the norm. For forty years they will live in captivity, lamenting and longing for the day when they will return home. Isaiah's vision, however, goes far beyond merely describing physical release and traveling back to the homeland. Isaiah's vision describes homecoming in a different way: going home to God.

In Isaiah's vision, going home to God is far better than going home to any place we can imagine in this world. Going home to God is so remarkable that Isaiah must use images so that we can create mental pictures to begin to comprehend its full wonder. Let's explore how Isaiah communicates, and try to adapt his communication skills into our sermon preparation.

Isaiah first emphasizes that all of creation will blossom and rejoice in anticipation of God's reunion with us. He has described separation from God through the bleak images of chapter 34: streams turned to pitch, dust into sulfur, smoke, waste, chaos, emptiness. Thorns, weeds, and brambles grow. Jackals, ostriches, wildcats, hyenas, snakes, and vultures populate the land.

But in chapter 35 all of creation senses that God is about something new. The desert and dry land become glad, and the wilderness rejoices and blossoms like the crocus (v. 1). They burst into bloom and rejoice with joy and singing (v. 4). Waters spring up in the desert, and streams in the wilderness (v. 6). Burning sands become pools and thirsty ground turns into fountains of water (v. 7). The ugly habitat for jackals turns into pasture (v. 8).

Having described the renewal of creation that heralds a new order, Isaiah points to another sign of the new order: God's people experience unexpected support, health, and wholeness. He tells of a new sense of peace to those who are terrified: weak hands are strengthened, unsteady knees are supported, and words of encouragement and comfort come to those who are panicking: "Be strong! Don't fear!" (vv. 3-4). They are assured that God is coming to make things right and save them (v. 4)! They know that they will see the Lord's glory, the splendor of God (v. 2).

Isaiah gives us more signs of the coming reunion: the blind will see, the deaf will hear, the lame will leap like deer, the tongue of the speechless will sing (vv. 5-6)! This renewal of creation and its people sets the stage for the appearance of God's highway, The Holy Way (v. 8). God's people will travel home to God, overwhelmed with happiness and joy (v. 10). They cannot lose their way on this highway; no lions or predators will threaten them. Best of all, grief and groaning will flee away, and they will return to God and enter Zion (the promised holy city, the new creation) singing, "with everlasting joy upon their heads" (v. 10). The redeemed and ransomed of God will be home (v. 10).

Bringing the Text to Life

1. Even as a child I loved time-lapse photography. I remember vividly a movie that showed flowers in the desert springing forth in radiant beauty. Lush blossoms appeared out of the dust. These video images in worship could set the stage nicely. Another effective visual is to start worship with empty planters or containers with dust and brambles. They could "bloom" as the service unfolds, culminating with beautiful flowers and shrubs covering the chancel area. I have also used this imagery throughout the Sundays of Advent, starting very simply with little light and building gradually until Christmas Eve, which is full of light, beautiful images, and floral decor.

2. Isaiah refers to the most beautiful places of his day when describing the blooming of the desert wilderness: the glory of Lebanon and the splendor of Carmel and Sharon (v. 2). What familiar beautiful areas could capture the imaginations of your people? Are there particularly gorgeous places nearby or known throughout

your region? Why not incorporate pictures of these places into your worship? Also, how can you contrast these with the dark, ominous images of our day: COVID-19 wards, refugee camps, angry riots, mass incarceration? Death and despair are as prevalent now as in Isaiah's day. A word of joy proclaiming God's presence and ultimate deliverance is desperately needed.

3. Throughout scripture, God's presence brings wholeness and healing. You might explore the wonder of immediate healing: a cochlear implant allows a child to hear, a woman formerly blind has sight restored, a man near death is given new life through an organ transplant. Also note that when John the Baptist's disciples go to see if Jesus is really the expected one, Jesus says, "Go, report to John what you have seen and heard. *Those who were blind are able to see*. Those who were crippled now walk. People with skin diseases are cleansed. *Those who were deaf now hear. Those who were dead are raised up. And good news is preached to the poor*" (Luke 7:22). Is it any surprise that Isaiah describes such things as indicators of God's saving work?

4. Isaiah explores two ways that God delivers: redemption (to buy back someone who is enslaved or in debt) and ransom (to set free from political captivity, to buy back a person from an obligation). Focus on God's salvific activity. To what are we enslaved? What are the political and economic effects of our enslavement? What does God need to make right in our systems, communities, homes, and hearts?

5. Marketing gurus bombard us with beautiful images of "home" during the holiday season. Perfect homes, perfect families, perfect relationships. For most of us, as much as we long for home, it never seems quite right. Are we cosmically homesick to go "home to God"? Are we really longing for Zion, the city of God, where we will be overwhelmed with happiness and joy? I am amazed at how many songs dream of home. I've long wanted to have aCommunion service with songs about home in the background. One oldie but goodie is Kenny Loggins's "Celebrate Me Home": "Play me one more song that I'll always remember. . . . Sing me home."[1] Please sing your people home to God this Advent. Let the celebration begin!

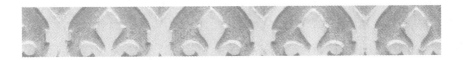

December 18, 2022–Fourth Sunday of Advent

*Isaiah 7:10-16; Psalm 80:1-7, 17-19; Romans 1:1-7; **Matthew 1:18-25***

Sue Haupert-Johnson

Preacher to Preacher Prayer

Gracious God, we rejoice at the birth of your son, Emmanuel, "God with us." We are grateful that when you come, you bring grace even in our disgrace. Your loving presence transforms us more than any punishment or embarrassment ever could. Help us to be like you and bring grace to those whom the world disgraces. In Jesus's name. Amen.

Commentary

Grace in disgrace. On this Fourth Sunday of Advent, Joseph takes center stage. He stands at the heart of Matthew's birth narrative. But let's face it, Joseph never gets the attention he's due. He always just kind of hangs out in nativity sets. There are no great Joseph biblical quotes—in fact, Joseph doesn't say anything! Joseph is certainly one of the unsung heroes of the Bible. So, this week let's sing his praises!

We enter the scene in Matthew 1 after Joseph is engaged (or betrothed, for King James lovers) to Mary. Neither of these words really describe well the Jewish understanding of marriage, which was not at all romantic or dreamy. Their engagement "party" consisted of Joseph going over to Mary's parents' house, signing the contract, and paying the bride price to her parents. Certainly not a Hallmark Channel movie or social media celebration! Mary would continue to live with her parents for months or even a couple of years until the marriage ceremony sealed the deal, and she would move to Joseph's place.

Things get dicey when Mary turns up pregnant. Matthew tells us she became pregnant by the Holy Spirit (v. 18), but that explanation probably won't carry a lot of weight with Joseph, Mary's parents, the religious leaders, and the gossipy neighbors. Matthew also tells us that Joseph is a "righteous" man (v. 19), so we would expect him, when confronted with this complication, to uphold the Jewish law and seek the course of action most pleasing to God.

Unfortunately, Jewish law provided that a virgin engaged to be married who becomes pregnant by another man shall be stoned to death by the men of her town (Deut 22:23-27). Joseph, not wanting to humiliate Mary (and presumably wanting her to live), chose his other option under the law, annulment of the marriage contract. He "decided to call off the engagement quietly" (v. 19). According to Jewish law, going through with the marriage was unthinkable, no matter how great his regard for Mary. Pleasing God by living in strict compliance with the law was of far greater importance to righteous Joseph than any thought of pleasing himself or pleasing Mary.

While he is still thinking about calling off the engagement, an angel comes to Joseph in a dream and tells him to go ahead with the marriage (v. 20). The angel confirms that Mary is indeed pregnant by the Holy Spirit (!). The angel tells Joseph to name the child Jesus (from Hebrew as in *Joshua*, meaning "God helps" or "God saves"), because "he will save his people from their sins" (v. 21).

The angel extends to Mary and Joseph grace not afforded or available under the law. God's story unfolds in an unexpected and marvelous way. Mary avoids disgrace and embarrassment in her community. Joseph opens himself to a strange new possibility and a revered place in the gospel narrative, with unique responsibilities and challenges. He does just as the angel commanded (vv. 24-25), naming the child Jesus and thereby placing him squarely in his lineage, the lineage of David. He nurtures him, loves him, and adopts him fully.

Bringing the Text to Life

1. Matthew always links God's new covenant through Jesus Christ with God's covenant with the Israelites. He bridges the two through the genealogy that immediately precedes this passage (vv. 1-17). This genealogy extends from Abraham to Jesus, and Joseph's adoption of Jesus puts him in this lineage. Take a moment and read through the lineage. Do you see anything odd? It mentions five women! Tamar, Rahab, the wife of Uriah (Bathsheba), Ruth, and Mary.

If you'll recall, Tamar dressed as a prostitute to trick her father-in-law, Judah, and become pregnant with his child, in order to receive the place in his family that he had unfairly denied her (Gen 38). Rahab the prostitute hid the Israelite scouts and helped them take the promised land (Josh 2, 6). Ruth, an alien from Moab, "meets" Boaz on the threshing room floor (Ruth 3). The wife of Uriah, Bathsheba, enters the lineage by committing adultery with David. And Mary is pregnant, but not by her betrothed.[2]

What do these women have in common? They are outsiders, threatened with disgrace, and unlikely participants in God's story! They experience God with them through gracious inclusion. God gives them a place in the lineage of Jesus even though many would have rejected them as worthy ancestors. What possibilities are opened to us when we experience God with us?

2. What does it mean to be fully adopted? Does Joseph's full adoption of Mary and Jesus bear witness to how God fully adopts us? Shouldn't we be comforted and overjoyed by the notion of God with us? Joseph wanted what was best for Mary and

Jesus. Do we fully conceive that God wants only what is best for us? Can we imagine the extent of that love?

3. Often following God is an adventure in which we don't fully comprehend what we are being asked to do. Are we willing, like Joseph, to take that leap of faith? Or is our obedience conditioned upon our own security and our own limited understanding of what lies before us?

4. What do we do when we sense that God is calling us to live beyond the letter of the law? Does God's direction displace the rules that we feel we are obligated to follow? What if the law isn't fair or loving? Even civil law tempers the rule of law with equity, which permits a judge to depart from the letter of the law if it is unfair or unjust in its application. How do we discern when God is offering us another way? What if others vehemently disagree with us in that discernment?

5. Is grace a more effective agent of transformation than law? Consider Bishop Welcome *("Bienvenu")* and Jean Valjean in Victor Hugo's *Les Miserables*. Recently I saw the musical yet again, and watched as Jean Valjean, recently released from jail and desperate to find employment as an ex-convict, accepts Bishop Welcome's kind invitation to spend the night at his episcopal residence. During the night, Valjean steals the bishop's only valuable possessions, some silver dishes. The next morning the townspeople bring the police to arrest Valjean. Before they can say anything, Bishop Welcome warmly greets Jean Valjean and tells him he forgot the two silver candlesticks the bishop had given him. The bishop goes into the house and brings the candlesticks out to Valjean. Bishop Welcome then blesses Valjean and tells him to use the silver to become an honest man.

This scene in this production was exceptionally well done, and there was a collective gasp from the audience as they witnessed such a profound enactment of grace. It should still be breathtaking. God doesn't give any of us what we deserve under the law. God pardons us and blesses us through Jesus Christ. Throughout Jesus's ministry we witness him extending grace to so many who were excluded under the law. This Advent let's let out a gasp at how Emmanuel, God with us, brings mercy, compassion, peace, and joy instead of contempt, bondage, ridicule, and moralistic superiority. Good news comes in the form of a God who brings grace even in our disgrace.

6. Are we imitating Christ by being agents of grace to those who are disgraced? Or do we find ways to feel morally and spiritually superior and lord it over others? Are we predisposed to be like the townspeople or Bishop Welcome? Take some time this week to read the first chapters of *Les Miserables*. Ponder what the world would be like if the world had more Bishop Welcomes.

7. The director of a prayer house in Cambridge came to know Christ through friends who "loved him into wholeness." That phrase has stuck with me. Are we known for loving others into wholeness?

December 24-25, 2022–
Nativity of the Lord

Isaiah 9:2-7; Psalm 96; Titus 2:11-14; **Luke 2:1-14** *(15-20)*

Sue Haupert-Johnson

Preacher to Preacher Prayer

We rejoice, O God, that you are so ready to be born in us. Help us, O God, to be as eager to receive you as you are to come. In Jesus's name. Amen.

Commentary

If you want, the virgin will come. Preaching on Christmas Eve (and on Christmas Day) is uniquely difficult. Many are there for one of the few obligatory events of the year, often not so much as a spiritual practice but as a nod to family tradition that is nonnegotiable. Often the best preaching in their estimation is that which takes the fewest minutes! Further, travel for the holiday creates a fruit basket turnover of attendance—we often look out upon a sea of strange faces, knowing that most of the familiar faces have traveled elsewhere to be with family and listen to preachers unknown to them. When you factor in the excitement of the children, who have reached a Christmas frenzy and are eager to get on to the more exciting festivities, the poor preacher has a Herculean challenge!

Despite the challenge, it is the most holy evening of the year. We have the rare and wonderful opportunity to open the hearts and minds of all sorts of people to the power of the Holy Spirit and a God who desperately wants to reach them. So desperately that God came to earth to live among them, full of grace and truth.

How do we best bear witness to the wonder of the incarnation? Some try to counter the familiarity of the story by taking some very creative approaches to the sermon. Most of these ventures, in my estimation, fall flat. Worse yet, some simply read the story and leave it at that. If so, the preacher fails to help the listeners appropriate the story into their own lives. The preacher leaves them with a shallow, Ricky Bobby (if you've never seen Ricky Bobby pray to the baby Jesus in *Talladega Nights: The Ballad of Ricky Bobby*, Google it or watch it on YouTube) treatment of the nativity and they go home having heard a nice story.

Yes, the story is important, but why is it important? What is *the story* that this story introduces? On Christmas Eve we must examine the meaning of the incarnation rather than just read the birth narrative of Jesus. *As I ponder the incarnation, this year I land on the importance of emphasizing that we must bear and give birth to Jesus Christ in our own lives.* We are, like Mary, Christ bearers. I have long loved Phillips Brooks's third verse of "O Little Town of Bethlehem":

How silently, how silently, the wondrous gift is giv'n!
So God imparts to human hearts the blessings of his heav'n.
No ear may hear his coming, but in this world of sin
Where meek souls will receive him still
The dear Christ enters in.

Bringing the Text to Life

1. The manger in Bethlehem becomes the birthplace for all humans! As Christ is born in each of us, we are changed and, as a result, the world will be changed. It's an epic story still unfolding, and I am a part of it. Sanctification plays a big part in my Methodist faith tradition and needs to reclaim a premier place in our preaching. It reminds us that the goal in life is to think Christ's thoughts, follow Christ's direction, and value what Christ would value. We are called to open every aspect of our lives to his power and influence, with the goal of letting him make us perfect in love. And, if we join forces with others seeking to grow up into Christ, we become a transformative force of love that changes homes, workplaces, communities, and the world. God's love remakes us and, ultimately, all of creation. Our work continues until Christ comes again in final victory and takes full charge over all things.

2. Every Christmas Eve is a time to reevaluate Christ's birth in our lives. Are we more like him than we were a year ago? Is the process of becoming more like him continuing, or has it stalled out amid the distractions and chaos of our daily lives? Are we daily setting aside time and space to pray, read scripture, and allow God to occupy our minds and hearts? Are we fully surrendering? Are we "meek souls" willing to receive Christ? Or are there parts of ourselves that we are withholding, parts of our lives of which we refuse to let go, parts of our being to which we stubbornly hold on? Are we afraid of how God could use us if we let down our guards? Are we shutting Jesus out just as effectively as he was shut out of places to stay in Bethlehem? The world still avoids God.

3. As you ponder the incarnation, reflect on a profound idea found in a poem, loosely attributed to St. John of the Cross (1542–1591, translated by Daniel Ladinsky), that emphasizes how we, like Mary, bear Christ: *"For each of us is the midwife of God, each of us."*

The Working Gospel and the Bridge Paradigm

Excerpt from Frank Thomas,
Surviving a Dangerous Sermon

Definition of Working Gospel

Every preacher has a constellation of culture, a family of origin, and ecclesiastical systems that influence, raise, and develop us from the earliest stages of life. Such systems include categories of gender, ethnicity, social and economic locations of neighborhood and class, as well as conditions of physical and mental health. Most preachers are heavily influenced by these systems as they shape both their theology and the sermon that flows out of that theology. In an article titled "Do You See This Woman? A Little Exercise in Homiletical Theology," André Resner clarifies that every preacher has an in-process "synopsis of the faith, an encapsulation of the whole point of Christianity, Christian community, of what difference God makes in and for the world."[1] Resner labels this "a working understanding of the gospel": "the preacher's 'working understanding of the gospel' is the imaginative theological and hermeneutical force that drives the way the preacher conceives, plots, and delivers sermons, structures worship services in which those sermons live, move, and have their being."[2] Though we do not have time to explore it, David Jacobsen has tremendous synergy with Resner and agrees with the fact that preachers have different working understandings of the gospel:

> In practice, preaching requires preachers to have a *habitus*, some theological core wisdom about gospel that helps them to do their task. . . . Preachers fret rightly about getting from the text to sermon, but underlying this concern is their commission to go preach the *gospel*. In doing so, I start the process of theological worth with a provisional confession of the gospel, i.e. what I call confessional homiletical theology. Confessional homiletical theologians think about preaching as a theological enterprise beginning provisionally with gospel and brought into critical dialogue with texts, contexts, and situations. André Resner has given this provisional confessional move a name: "working gospel."[3]

Not only based upon Resner and Jacobsen, but even with a cursory perusal of historical and contemporary theological debates, it is clear that preachers can read the same Bible and texts yet witness to different working gospels. This complexity then raises a monumental question begging for clarification in the theology of every preacher: What is the relationship between the Bible and the gospel? How does the Bible function in the preaching of the gospel? Or, how does the bridge paradigm work in our working gospel? Let's look closely at preaching the Bible and preaching the gospel.

Preaching the Bible and Preaching the Gospel

Resner identifies reflections by professor of homiletics Ed Farley as the initial catalyst for his thinking about the concept of working gospel.[4] Farley challenges the prevailing paradigm of preaching that uncritically assumes that every passage from scripture, whether by means of the lectionary or preacher's choice, contains a preachable "X" that results in a preaching "theme" or "claim." Farley argues that the preacher who seeks the preachable truth of God in a delineated passage of the Bible faces an impossible task. The impossible task is that, for several reasons (stated in the footnote below), there may be nothing preachable in the text and the preacher that must find a way from the text to the sermon—that is, the preacher must invent the "X," the preachable element.[5] The preacher determines the preachable "X" of the text that is to be preached, such as a word, phrase, image, action, or the text as narrative. This preachable "X" is then made into a lesson for life and preached. On strict exegetical grounds, passages are not developed for lessons for life, and therefore the preacher must wring the preachable "X" out of the exegeted passage. The result is that the passage is not so much preached as it becomes something that provides the jumping-off point for the sermon. To discover the lesson for life, the preacher must abandon exegesis and move to "interpretation"—that is, to apply the preachable "X" to the life situation of the congregation. I will make a clarifying demonstration of Farley's thinking in the later section titled "Your Haters Are Your Elevators."

Altering a phrase from the Vietnam War, Farley says the preacher must kill the passage in order to preach on it:

> Thus the preacher is not really starting with the text but with the lesson for life she knows is pertinent to the congregation. Rhetorically, the sermon may sound like it marches from the passage to the situation. Actually, the route is the reverse, from the situation, the in-the-light-of problem, to a constructed X of the text. The passage or its preachable X is not really that-which-is-reached, but the rhetorical occasion that jump-starts the sermon. Interpreting the passage is a modification of the exegeted content so that the passage's lesson for life can be applied.[6]

The construction of the preachable "X" is what Farley calls "the bridge paradigm," and its failure is built in from the beginning, by virtue of its abandonment of the text. The preacher's task is to build a bridge from that which is preached (the truth of the specific passage) to the situation of the congregation.[7] The construction of the bridge is not necessarily based in exegesis. That which is preached is not the content of the passage of scripture or the gospel but the preacher's preachable "X." Farley argues that if we are not careful, we will preach passages of the Bible and not the gospel.

As distinct from the paradigm of the early church, for us in this contemporary moment, preaching is a weekly liturgical event. Jesus and the early church preachers were itinerant preachers proclaiming the impending reign of God and were not the preachers of scheduled weekly liturgical services. Farley says, "Primitive Christian preaching as we find it on the pages of the New Testament was an itinerant tradition proclaiming the good news of salvation in Jesus Christ. It is somewhat anachronistic to compare what we now call preaching with the *kerisso* of Paul and other evangelists."[8] The fact that preaching is a weekly liturgical event can be a strong catalyst to preach the content of the passage as a weekly life lesson for hearers rather than as a gospel event through which we are saved.

Farley even questions the dissection of the Bible into chapter headings and verses as interpretation that helps to move the preacher from the big picture of the gospel to looking in these weekly divisions for a small lesson for life. The preacher looks at a partitioned text and then seeks to find a weekly lesson for living life, often disregarding the meaning of the whole message. Farley suggests this division and portioning is problematic:

> It is clear that to divide the Bible into necessarily true passages is only one way among many ways of thinking about the Bible, of being "biblical," of placing oneself under the power and influence of Scripture. Surely we can be moved and influenced by the *Iliad, King Lear,* or *The Color Purple* without dividing these great works into pericopes and assuming a necessary truth to each one. Why must this be done to Jeremiah or Paul?[9]

This atomistic approach to scripture and thinking of scripture as a collection of small units and segments helps the passage to become a jumping-off place for the sermon, and the gospel can be easily abandoned. Again, to discover the lesson for life, the preacher abandons exegesis and moves to "interpretation" in order to cross the bridge from passage to people.

Farley's argument is important because it leads to the struggle to clarify what one means by "gospel" as inclusive of distinct parts of the Bible and exclusive of others. Christian preachers all use the term *gospel* but do not all mean the same thing. Resner identifies an often unmentioned truth existing in the field of homiletics:

> One of the dirty little secrets about homiletics, the discipline that studies, writes about, and teaches preaching—that there is no consensus on what preachers and homileticians mean by the word *gospel*, and there is very little discussion about how a preacher's construal of gospel functions hermeneutically as the preacher engages the Bible with a view to its use in preaching.[10]

David Jacobsen, whom we quoted earlier, responds to both Farley and Resner and takes up the challenge of defining how the Bible functions in preaching. Jacobsen and others define the function of the Homiletical Theology Project as: "to place the theological task more squarely in the middle of the practice of preaching and in the field of homiletics."[11] Defining the relationship between the Bible and the gospel is a theological task that all preachers must engage in on at least a weekly basis. Jacobsen reminds us that all preachers are "residential theologians of the gospel wherever they are" and "all sermon preparation is actually theology."[12]

As promised, let me give a brief example to hopefully make Farley's bridge paradigm clear by discussion of a popular sermonic form of trope: "your haters are your elevators."

Your Haters Are Your Elevators

First, let's look closely at the text in 1 Corinthians 1:18-25 (NRSV) for an example of how we find the preachable "X":

> For the message about the cross is foolishness to those who are perishing, but to us who are being saved it is the power of God. . . . Has not God made foolish the wisdom of the world? For since, in the wisdom of God, the world did not know God through wisdom, God decided, through the foolishness of our proclamation, to save those who believe. For Jews demand signs and Greeks desire wisdom, but we proclaim Christ crucified, a stumbling block to Jews and foolishness to Gentiles, but to those who are the called, both Jews and Greeks, Christ the power of God and the wisdom of God. For God's foolishness is wiser than human wisdom, and God's weakness is stronger than human strength.

Exegesis on this text suggests that the proclamation of a crucified man as the Lord of glory was a stumbling block to Jews and Gentiles. Paul's preaching was considered pure foolishness, and he and other proclaimers were treated as stupid, ridiculous, and absurd. Exegesis helps us catch the flavor of the absolute outrage and indignation at the proclamation of the Lord of glory as a crucified criminal. It would be similar to a person in our time, condemned to death in the electric chair for a capital crime, and a small band of believers claiming that the deceased was raised and is the Lord of glory. Paul said Jews were looking for a sign and Greeks were looking for wisdom, but a crucified savior was offensive and a stumbling block. In the reality of the Greco-Roman culture to which Paul preached, a crucified Lord of glory was scandalous, embarrassing, humiliating, and shameful.

The preacher looking for the preachable "X" will transition from this exegesis to the interpretation of a life lesson from the text. One lesson would be to focus on "haters" in the contemporary context. Haters, in common vernacular, are people who dislike, disrespect, and disregard the value and work of a person and make it known by casting dispersion or disdain. The preacher would extrapolate that Paul and Christians had "haters" and then would call to mind that contemporary listeners have haters. The life lesson that the preacher brings forth is summed up as "your haters are your elevators," and this is the thematic focal point of the sermon. Your haters elevate you to your divine destiny.

My problem is that with all of the exegetical gospel texture that is available in this text, the preacher dismisses it or reduces it down and makes the point of how you can overcome your haters, given the fact that they raise you to your "destiny and purpose." This is to minimize the gospel to a weekly life lesson. It is to reduce the opposition and venom that Paul faced in preaching a crucified Lord of glory to a few people on your job who are jealous because you got a raise. It is not possible to give moral equivalence to haters on your job and haters of Paul and the gospel, but when we are looking for a life lesson applicable to the life situation of our hearers, we make such concessions.

Paul even goes so far as to say later, in 1 Corinthians 4:9-13 (NRSV), speaking to the rich about the factional struggles in the Corinthian church, that because of preaching a crucified Lord of glory, the apostles were the refuse and trash of the world:

> For I think that God has exhibited us apostles as last of all, as though sentenced to death, because we have become a spectacle to the world, to angels and to mortals. We are fools for the sake of Christ, but you are wise in Christ. We are weak, but you are strong. You are held in honor, but we in disrepute. To the present hour we are hungry and thirsty, we are poorly clothed and beaten and homeless, and we grow weary from the work of our own hands. When reviled, we bless; when persecuted, we endure; when slandered, we speak kindly. We have become like *the rubbish of the world, the dregs of all things, to this very day.* (italics mine)

We choose "haters are your elevators" because who really wants to hear the gospel of a God who has exhibited Christians as last of all in the parade of a defeated army—last and condemned to die. Who really wants to hear that we suffer for the gospel and are considered as spectacles and the trash, refuse, and garbage of the world? It is difficult to preach this part of the gospel of Christ, and so we settle for a lessening and a cheapening of truth, rather than the unsettling and challenging message of mystery of the gospel.

In this example, the preacher is not really emphasizing the text, but the life lesson of encouragement that she or he believes is pertinent to the congregation. Encouragement is a legitimate concern, and absolutely every one of us needs encouragement; but, in this case, to produce encouragement, looking for the preachable "X," the preacher minimizes Paul and the early church's suffering in the text. This gives the illusion that preachers are preaching the text, but the needs of the people and experience of the preacher are the jumping-off place for the sermon. So, in Farley's terms, preachers preach not the gospel but the Bible, the life lesson of a selected passage. This is a difficult and prophetic challenge to every preacher: just because the preacher is preaching a passage from the Bible does not mean that the gospel is being preached.

For those of us of the African American preaching tradition, I want to add this: just because we "go by the cross" at the close of the sermon every week does not mean that we are preaching the gospel. Going by the cross is the belief that regardless of what text one preaches, one must conclude the sermon with the death, burial, and resurrection of Jesus. Typically, the preacher would detail the events of crucifixion-resurrection narrative, starting with the crucifixion on Friday, the tomb on Friday night, and Jesus in the tomb all night Saturday, and closing with some form of emphasis on the resurrection such as, "Early, bright early, on Sunday morning, Jesus was resurrected with all power in his hands." There are many preachers who think that if another preacher does not "go by the cross," regardless of what that preacher has said, then that preacher has not preached. It is best to ensure that one has the gospel in one's preaching. In its popular form, going by the cross can be formalism, legalism, and—I dare even say—entertainment. Going by the cross must mean presenting the Christ-event in such a way that this past event opens up a new and liberative future in the present. I will say more later in the chapter, but we must preach the Christ-event, and not a trope that reduces automatic responses to clichés to induce emotional effect from the audience.

We Preach the Gospel

Excerpt from George Buttrick,
George Buttrick's Guide to Preaching the Gospel
(edited by Charles N. Davidson Jr.)

To the question, "What do we preach?," the average preacher would answer without hesitation, "The Gospel." But do we understand? Are we a-tiptoe with joy? The word *Gospel* (good spiel) means glad tidings! Now any good news is by nature an event, not what has been merely thought but a happening. So somebody coming into your home might exclaim, "The most wonderful thing has happened!" Glad tidings provoke exclamation. What has happened? God, the uncreated, unimaginable in purpose and power, "for us and for our salvation came down and became truly human."[1] That happening boggles the preacher's mind, shakes her heart, and taxes all wonder. She proclaims that Event: Christ living, dying, raised from the dead, and present in Spirit.

We now note the strangeness of any event. If it occurs in the order of nature, an earthquake or a spring flower, it can be gathered into a sequence the scientist too hastily calls "cause and effect," blotting out its particularity under an abstraction named "universal law," as in, "All earthquakes are due to the cooling of earth's interior fires." But an observation regarding nature does not apply in history. What happens to us as human beings, including an earthquake, has another face. For us a happening is invasive. It "takes place": our place. It is disruptive. It "comes to pass": our door. It is ecstatic in that word's original meaning: it requires us to stand outside ourselves to ask, "What now shall I do?" Any event is thus crucial. The Christ Event, God's visitation in the flesh, is the crux of history, the happening that rules all happenings.

I

We pause to say what preaching is not, for negative statements, despite a book named *Positive Thinking*,[2] have an initial bite while positive statements are ill-defined. The Decalogue is for witness. So preaching is not a moralism. Preaching leads on to an ethic, for the Event of Christ eventuates in a certain style of life, but preaching doesn't tell people what to do, still less what not to do. Many a preacher falls into this moralistic trap, as in a notice recently seen outside a certain church: "Don't procrastinate: the early bird gets the first worm." That preacher was peddling advice, but hardly on the level even of Aesop's Fables. Why not instead quote George Bernard Shaw: "They killed Him on a stick, but he seems to have gotten hold of the right end of it"?[3] Then the very notice board would have proclaimed the Gospel.

Again, preaching is not selling peace of mind. The Gospel is the only comfort, but it is not passport to money-making or to what is now called "an attractive personality." Perhaps Christ himself had no so-called peace of mind.[4] People such as us were too brutal toward him. But he had the peace of God. He bequeathed it to us in his last will and testament: "My peace I give [bequeath] to you."[5] Peace in the New Testament meaning is first the mending of the vertical line between God and humanity by the grace of God, and only then it becomes the fastening on that upright of the horizontal line between persons and persons.

Once again, preaching is not the discussion of religion. That vague word opens the door to any religion. Karl Barth proposed that our faith is the death of all religion. He meant that religion as popularly understood is the human attempt to reach God—by laws kept, rituals fulfilled, disciplines obeyed, or ethical regimens fulfilled. But no one on her own can reach God. So, William Blake shows a man at the foot of a ladder that disappears in the sky. If the man tries to climb he will fall soon from dizziness, so he stands there crying, "I want! I want!"[6]

But he does not need to climb because God "for us and for our salvation came down and became truly human." So preaching is not a discussion of some religion. There are other caveats: it is not argument or an excursion into rationality. But these negatives are enough to serve our present purpose.

II

Next we note that the Event is a fourfold Event, a many-splendored thing.[7] The preacher proclaims the life of Christ not as biography but as newly understood in resurrection light. We need not try to dodge problems raised by honest biblical scholarship, such as those uncovered by form criticism or by the fact of redaction, or by what is now called "demythologizing." Here is my own conviction: these overlays can themselves be an opening for the Holy Spirit and themselves point to a hard core of actuality. There is a staunch record that we here call the life of Christ. Mark's Gospel gives a rough-and-ready chronology. Note some facets of the picture.

We see Christ sharing and bearing our humanness. To speak thus is not to deny deeps in him that go far deeper than our glib word *divine*, but it is to maintain that if he were not genuinely human he would have nothing to say to us. He was not an angel come slumming. He was not a marionet let down from the sky. The proposal sometimes heard that he knew all along that he was the Son of God makes his temptation a mock encounter and turns even his cross into phony dramatics. He hungered for food. He hungered for friendship. When he cut his finger the blood was like our blood. The Apostle's Creed blazons that fact: "was crucified, dead, and buried." He was "in all things tempted as we are,"[8] yet with no break in his obedience to the will of God.

He confronted our choices. He did not lead a pastoral life in a simple culture, despite many a pulpit. He spoke Aramaic, knew some colloquial Greek (spoken then from Spain to northern India), probably learned Hebrew in the synagogue school, and picked up tags of Latin from the Roman garrison. There were Greek academies and Greek gymnasia in Galilee, with instances even in Jerusalem. Just over the Nazareth hill he saw caravans moving from Damascus to Tyre and Sidon. He was cosmopolitan. He lived in our crisscross of decision. Should he join the Zealot underground or collaborate with Rome along with the Sadducees or go monastic with the Essenes or parade a disciplined piety with the Pharisees? These groups have their present-day successors. He refused all these roads. The cosmopolitan Christ! So what becomes of our uptight proposal that "he taught spiritual truths to individuals"? He was not a little holy man peddling platitudes to hermits. He lived our human life.

Yet he is our judgment, for his human words strike to the marrow of our bones. He does more than quicken our conscience, for our conscience of itself can't be trusted: it is like a ship's compass thrown out of "true" by the ship's cargo. Christ "cleanses us from an evil conscience,"[9] and thus and then confronts us. He says, "Be pure in thought and deed"[10]—as if we could of ourselves! He says, "Love your enemies"[11]—though we rush to hate and kill them. He says, "Do good by stealth"[12] though we want to get credit for the little good we do. We speak of his sinlessness: who are we to know? What we mean is that in every crux of our life he is our judgment. He was so searching in word and act that his friends begged him to leave them, "for I am a sinful man,"[13] yet knew that if he did leave them they would have neither sun by day nor moon by night.

But judgment was held in a deeper love. Otherwise the judgment would leave us naked and lost. A story tells of a sculptor who fashioned in clay the perfect statue, and then feared that the night frost might break the clay. So he wrapped his bedclothes round the statue, and in the morning was himself found dead from cold.[14] We are anything but perfect, but Christ wrapped his life round us, and so died. The New Testament has a new word for this passionate goodwill—not eros, the fine fire of sexual love, for eros without this new love becomes erotic; and not philia, the solace of home love and friendship love, for philia without this new love becomes philistine; but agape, an abstract mold word at first, but now by Christ himself a very wellspring.

So, the preacher preaches the life of Christ, yet not as stated biography. Had that been all, Christ might have dwindled to a paragraph in some ancient history book. We are moved not by love alone but by love willing to suffer and die, rather than be anything else but love. Besides, there would be little promise or power in signalizing a past event. So, we turn to the next item in the Gospel, the death of Christ.

III

One chord in a symphony may haunt the memory. A friend says of one such chord in the Beethoven "Fourth,"[15] "Since that is so, everything is all right." Such a chord in the Gospel symphony is an agony of discord, the cross. The New Testament links it again and again with pain and evil, with sin and death. Now why? This stress is the preacher's burden because our culture thinks it is overcoming evil and blinks at the word *death*. What is sin? Not a breach of the moral code, though that breach is usually involved. Bad people break the code from below it, while good people break the law from above it (in the name of a higher law), as Jesus broke the Sabbath code, which (incidentally) was bastioned deeper than the statutes of our common law. In any event, guilt doesn't run between a person and a code but between a person and God. Sin is the human attempt to be one's own god. Our world is populated with atomized "godlets." If they join forces in a greedy corporation or a national power structure, there is still infighting for personal control. Any newspaper provides evidence. In some instances, the newspaper is itself evidence, its headlines a "come-on" and its ads defying decency. Who can measure the havoc of our sins? Reinhold Niebuhr has somewhere said that if there were no sin, the burden of pain and evil might be a tolerable load.

Thus it was sin that raised the cross. The word *sin* is nowadays a nonconductor, but the fact remains. All kinds of sin converged on Calvary: the avarice of storekeepers, the trampling of empire, the pride of ecclesiastics, the treachery of friends, and the bloody unconcern of the crowd. Say rather that sinful people there converged. Add what we call "natural evil": the flies stung, and the sun struck like swords. Add pain: cramps overtook him as the blood ebbed. Add death: on a gallows on a city dump. This is the discord of all human music. Yet it is the dissonant chord, the "rest chord" before the Great Amen.[16]

How and why? Before that question the preacher stammers, but the stammer stumbles on truth. How could any person be brash and confident before the cross? One fact is starkly clear: we can't save ourselves. How would we even begin? We can't go back to erase even one small lie. History moves forward; there is no return ticket. If we could go back, we have no eraser. That lie is not now ours alone: it is in the stream of history, and not a million chemists could extract it. If we could go back, we would take ourselves with us! Nothing is shallower than our modern doctrines of self-help. What price "progress"? Evolution and "the stream of history" can't save us, despite the nobility of de Jardin.[17] He has not grappled with the enormity of our transgression. Slums, racism, and southeast Asia[18] are hardly exhibit A of an evolving saintliness. Only God can save us. Only God who created life can recreate it. But how? The preacher still stumbles, but she is on the highroad.

God's redemption of our life can't be distant, it can't be by "wave of hand" or "turn of eye" from some remote paradise.[19] God can't say to the angels, "I've always had trouble with that unruly little planet, but write off their debt in the celestial ledgers." No, for we are not angels, and cannot read the angelic records. We are earth-born, and we have turned the earth into bloody shambles. If we are to be saved, we must be saved here in the midst of history.

God must take our flesh, walk our streets, knock at our door, and be victim of our cruel pride. Is that statement a presumption? Yes, but how else can we see it, and what else can we say? God must knock at our door and say in our speech, "Your sins are forgiven." How else could we understand? How else could we accept pardon? How else could we respond in joy, saying, "This I believe"? "See the Christ stand!"[20]

God's redemption can't be trivial. Our sin in Vietnam, in any comfortable suburb or any uncomfortable ghetto, is not trivial. If God shrugged off our lifelong pride or the red swath of war with an, "Oh, forget it," God would not be God and we would not be persons. Our concern would be nobler than God's unconcern. How to phrase this mystery? There must be trouble in the abyss, vast trouble, if we are to be saved. The New Testament word translated in the older versions, "He is the propitiation of our sins," is a mistranslation: the word is *expiation*. But that is no trivial word: in its Hebrew antecedent it goes back to the Old Testament "mercy seat" with all its agonies and cleansings. Doctrines of "propitiation" (the word is not there) that show God bartering Christ to the devil or Christ buying off God's justice (against God's love) are wrong, but they appeal to me more than some hopeless doctrine of self-help, or one that belittles Christ as mere "example." Sin and death are a fatal urgency. God is not trivial. There is a "Lamb slain from the foundation of the world."[21]

Again: God's redemption can't be local in either time or space, else it would be prisoner of the first century. Suppose Christ had blessed only that time: we would have been bereft, for sin comes down from generation to generation. In that sense and in a deeper sense it is "original sin." Freud bridles at such realism, and then unwittingly repeats it, for he tells us (what the Good Book told us long ago) that the sins of the fathers are "visited on their children."[22] How far back? All the way back. "As in Adam all die"![23] Suppose Christ had blessed only that land: again we would have been bereft. No national bounds can imprison human guilt. "Total depravity" does not mean that any of us is totally depraved. If we were, we wouldn't know it. It means that the whole area of human life in every land is disfigured by mortal pride. Every corporate structure is pockmarked—the National Association of Manufacturers, the Teamsters' Union, the city government in every city, the science that in the pretense of neutral mind consents to the wicked prostitution of science, yes, and the church itself. Redemption can't be local: "He is the expiation for our sins, and not for ours only but also for the sins of the whole world."[24]

We now stand before the cross. It is not trivial: "My God, my God, why have you forsaken me?"[25] The cry of dereliction is a midnight of midnight: even rats forsake a derelict ship. The cross is not distant. It is set up outside every city wall. The Northwestern University Chapel has planted it eastward outside the chancel window, in the common earth, where the traffic moves unheeding. Amazingly a gallows has crossed an ocean, and while we weren't looking became the monstrous, wonderful focus of our worship. Nay, it has chosen to stand above our graves, and that is the final nasty anachronism (a gallows over the grave of someone you love?) unless, unless—the cross is not of one land or one generation. You can buy Christmas cards in the Orient, though there the babe has tiny upraised slits for eyes. You can find pictures of the cross in every generation. Thus, the preacher's Gospel: God has visited our planet and taken on his heart the drear midnight of our sins.

IV

The cross is not the final term in our faith. It is an essential term, for without it there is no redemption of "the fatal flaw" that disfigures human life. But had the cross been the whole story, history would have been tragic. We would have had to say what some in our age of violence do say: "The best is at the mercy of the worst."[26] After Calvary, Easter! Yet the resurrection would have been a hollow triumph without the cross. Our clichés propose that only through "sacrifice" are we cleansed. Yes, but whose sacrifice? The sacrifice of a gangster daring death brings small cleansing. The sacrifice of the average church member, meaning you and me, is no huge asset. Only God's self-giving, in sharing of our life, can cleanse the whole family of humankind, provided that is not the end of the Story.

So the life and death of Christ give content and purchase to his resurrection, as the resurrection validates his life and death: "This is my beloved Son: hear him."[27] We must add that the resurrection would have been "locked in history" without his presence. The Holy Spirit gives the total Event its contemporary thrust. The Event is fourfold, yet indivisibly one Event. A friend wrote a book entitled *The Crucifixion in Our Street*.[28] It showed clotheslines strung from tenement to tenement across the road on New York's east side, the clothes props transecting the lines in a hundred signs of the cross. That friend knew the Gospel, so there was a sequel entitled *The Resurrection in Our Street*.[29] Both books came alive through the Holy Spirit of the present Lord. The Event is ongoing, dynamic, and instant. A sermon has those same marks. "Dynamic": the New Testament word is *dunamin*, dynamite! The explosive power of true preaching! But we anticipate. Our next glad task is to speak to the third and fourth terms in the one Event.

Christ: *Deus Dixit*

Excerpt from Will Willimon,
Preachers Dare

Though we don't know all we would like to know of God, this we know: the God of Israel and the church is a big talker. Relentlessly, resourcefully revealing, refusing heavenly obscurity, not content to rule without telling us all about it.

That's why Barth begins his *Church Dogmatics* with the longest exposition of the Trinity in five centuries. Before we speak of God, God must speak. Good news: The Trinity reveals God to be lovingly loquacious.[1] The one God is triune—Father, Son, and Holy Spirit—which not only names the complexity and unity of the One in whom we live and move and have our being (Acts 17) but also points to God's life as self-communicative. Jesus the Son in constant communication with the Father, the Father in eternal interaction and revelation with the Son, and the Holy Spirit incessantly empowering, moving amongst Father and Son, as One. Barth says an arcane, esoteric, silent God "would not be God at all,"[2] at least not the God who greets us as Christ.

Preaching, as oral communication, is the uniquely suitable mode of discourse for so exceptionally dynamic and extroverted a God. And distinctively difficult.

The modern misunderstanding, Barth believed, was to suppose that a personal encounter with God was somehow given in the structure of human nature. The preacher need only uncover a connection within the listener's self and build a bridge to that innate point of contact.[3]

Gods to be had by human yearning are idols. Barth says this not because of his pessimism about human nature but rather because of his great optimism about the self-revelatory capacity of the Trinity. Finding a point of contact between God and humanity is God's problem, not ours. The Word "completes its work in the world in spite of the world."[4]

A trinitarian God who speaks, who shows up, who intervenes, was too much God for the modern world's illusions of human control. So beginning in the eighteenth century, God was made mute and divine revelation problematic. We're at last free to run the world as we please, with God safely tucked into the confines of human interiority. When this happened, Barth argued, two things occurred: First, Jesus Christ ceased to be understood unequivocally as the Lord; and second, we usurped the center that rightfully belongs to him. (I am virtually paraphrasing the first thesis of Barth's 1934 armen Declaration.[5]) Rather than understanding ourselves from God, we concoct God from ourselves. Christ—God's unique, binding revelation—is fashioned as a postulate of our experience—"as an ideal case or an idea of our possibility and our reality."[6] Any God who can be accessed solely through human consciousness can never be the Lord.[7]

With our natural laws, predictable processes, explicable humanity, and demystified cosmos in service to our Promethean aspirations, we neither expect nor want trinitarian address outside our subjectivity.[8] God deactivated, rendered interior and intuitive, silenced, is no God at all.[9]

Immanuel Kant's once courageous *sapere aude*,[10] dare to think for yourself, to demand evidence, to think rationally—that is, autonomously, godlessly—eventually became a means of merging into the herd. The modern state found that we are more easily managed if we think that we are sovereign individuals answerable only to ourselves. By naming forms of past servitude with relish, we're loath to admit our own bondage. The murders of George Floyd or Aumaud Arbery are not aberration; they are apocalyptic revelation of who we are as a people. Two million Americans are incarcerated, millions more opting for slow suicide by opioids, a nation in thrall to a virus; we strut about, bragging of our freedom and liberation, even as we are tightly tethered to the market state, the great supermarket of desire, the USA Inc. Capitalism promises unrestrained freedom to choose what our lives mean—except the freedom to choose not to be servants of the market.

"I'm not listening to anybody standing up in a pulpit and telling me how I ought to live my life," explained a Duke student as his rationale for refusing to listen to my sermons. While free to resist my preaching, he was not free to make less than 1400 on the SAT, spend four of the best years of his life and thousands of dollars at Duke, marry someone of his race and economic level, or assume a half-million-dollar mortgage in Scarsdale where he could spend the rest of his days worrying about the wrong sort moving into the neighborhood.

Our most enduring American cliché is Ben Franklin's myth of shrewd self-invention. America is where you get to make up yourself, then keep remaking to give yourself the illusion that you are in control of your life.[11] As Stanley Hauerwas says, modernity tells us that we can choose whatever story we want (liberals call it "freedom")—except to choose a story other than the story that tells you that you must choose your story.[12] Our listeners think they are sitting through a sermon because they want to. Fancying themselves as controlling communication, they think that they can filter, unplug, and hit delete anytime they like. If you can decide who will be your Savior, that savior can't save you.

One of the characters in Marilynne Robinson's *Lila* says, "If there is no Lord, then things are just as they look to us."[13] It takes daring to address people who don't want an exterior word that changes what we see. Truth must be democratically available to all regardless of the nature of the knower. "Why?" or "Wherefore?" are answered through the exercise of our marvelously omnipotent, critical, innate rationality. What lies in front of us—in plain sight if we concoct the appropriate methodology to uncover it—is all we need to make sense of ourselves and the world. What you see is what you've got. This is it. Listen for no other. "God says . . ." is shushed by "In my experience . . ."

Our contemporary context makes outrageous the Barthian assertion upon which faithful preaching is based: *Deus dixit*. God has spoken (Scripture), God will have the last word (the eschaton), and—surprise—God speaks *hic et nunc*, here and now. *Deus dixit*. How? Primarily through preachers. . . .

> The Word of God is first an address in which God and God alone is speaker [Christ, the *Logos ensarkos*], in a second address in the Word of a specific group of people (the prophets and apostles) [Scripture], and in a third address of a limited number of its human agents of proclamation [preachers].[15]

The first form of God's address: The Word has become a Jew who speaks. We asked for the truth about God. God addressed us, saying, "Jesus Christ":[16]

> The Word became flesh and made his home among us.
> We have seen his glory, glory like that of a father's only son,
> full of grace and truth.
>
> John testified about him, crying out, "This is the one of whom I said, 'He who comes after me is greater than me because he existed before me.'"
>
> From his fullness we have all received grace upon grace;
> as the Law was given through Moses,
> so grace and truth came into being through Jesus Christ.
>
> No one has ever seen God.
>
> God the only Son,
> who is at the Father's side,
> has made God known. (John 1:14-18)[17]

John says, "No one has ever seen God" (John 1:18), a statement that held true until we saw Jesus preach in Nazareth (Luke 4:16-30). Jesus reads from the Isaiah scroll. Things went well until he preached. His sermon transformed an otherwise sweet congregation into would-be murderers. It's not only a picture of our reaction to the truth about God; it's a vignette of Barth's three modes of divine unveiling: (1) Christ speaking; (2) Scripture speaking through reading and hearing; and, most surprising and daunting of all, (3) a preacher speaking and hearers responding.[18]

Trinitarian faith says that the one who preached at Nazareth is none other than the whole truth about God, repetition of God the Father and God the Holy Spirit as God the preaching Son.[19] "When [Jesus] came, he announced the good news of peace to you who were far away from God and to those who were near [echoing Isa 57:19]. We both have access to the Father through Christ by the one Spirit" (Eph 2:17-18). Jesus, as much of God as we hope to see. No mere prophet talking about God or messenger from God, he is a brown-skinned Jew on whose body "the fullness of God was pleased to live, . . . and he reconciled all things to himself through him—whether things on earth or in the heavens. He brought peace through the blood of his cross" (Col 1:19-20).

The Father is Revealer, the Son the Revelation, the Spirit the Revealedness (revelation received); the one God is triune revealing agent, revealed content, and effect of revelation. Barth even says that we can substitute for the three forms of revelation—Christ, Scripture, and proclamation—the names of the divine persons, Father, Son, and Holy spirit "and *vice versa*."[20] Revelation—God face-to-face with us.[21]

> Look! God's dwelling is here with humankind. He will dwell with them, and they will be his peoples. God himself will be with them as their God. (Rev 21:3)

We ask God to show up; God does so as the Incarnate Word, God with a name, a face, God speaking.[22] As Paul says, we have been given "the light of the knowledge of God's glory in the face of Jesus Christ" (2 Cor 4:6). First John 1, echoing John 1, reverberating from Genesis 1, is declaration of the possibility and necessity of Christian preaching:

> We announce to you what existed from the beginning, what we have heard, what we have seen with our eyes, what we have seen and our hands handled, about the word of life. The life was revealed, and we have seen, and we testify and announce to you the eternal life that was with the Father and was revealed to us. What we have seen and heard, we also announce it to you so that you can have fellowship with us. Our fellowship is with the Father and with his Son, Jesus Christ. We are writing these things so that our joy can be complete. This is the message that we have heard from him and announce to you. (1 John 1:1-5)

"What we have heard," that which is revealed, compels preachers to "testify" that God is uniquely present in human space and time—Jesus, revealed, revealer, revelation.[23] Having been revealed to us, we now "announce to you what we have seen and handled." The goal of the declaration called preaching? "Fellowship," human camaraderie with "the Father and with his Son."

"I am the way, and the truth, and the life. No one comes to the Father except through me. If you have really known me, you will also know the Father. From now on you know him and have seen him" (John 14:6-7). Jesus hasn't come to tell us the truth or point us toward the truth: "*I* am the truth." Truth is not an idea; truth is personal, a crucified Jew from Nazareth who returned to resume the conversation. God doesn't wait for us to discover truth; God comes as the truth who speaks, who calls us to follow. Preaching is Jesus—Truth speaking for himself.

My own denomination is splitting apart in a debate between "traditionalists" (who claim to stand upon "biblical authority," asserting that Scripture gives fixed and final sanction to their views on marriage and sexual orientation) and "progressives" (who claim that their individual consciences trump Scripture and tradition). Jesus never said, "All authority in heaven and earth is given to the Bible," nor did he say, "Just follow your conscience." The conflicting parties approach Scripture (and Jesus, Lord of Scripture) with minds made up in advance, unwilling to hear a word that destabilizes their preconceived positions. Let's all beware.

"Lord, show us who you are, what you are up to." God said: *Jesus Christ.* If the Word has not become flesh and moved in with us, then we preachers have nothing to say that the world can't hear as well elsewhere. Jesus Christ is the only thing that preachers know that everyone else doesn't. The word that the church speaks in the face of the world's injustice, struggles, needs, fears, and church fights, the word that the world cannot say to itself? *Jesus.*

When prominent evangelicals like Albert Mohler, Eric Metaxas, or *First Things'* Rusty Reno attempt to defend Trumpism, equating Christianity with Republicans, never, ever do they refer to Jesus.[24]

Good call.

Spread the News

Barth contended that the only difference between Christian and non-Christian is "noetic," a matter of having been given knowledge of God. A Christian is no better morally or intellectually. A Christian's modest claim is to have received news of who God is and thereby now knows how it stands between us and God. Revelation, given to and received by empty-handed, undeserving recipients makes a Christian, Christian.

The gospel is neither *photismos* (enlightenment), *musterion* (mystery),[25] *gnosis* (knowledge), nor *nomos* (law). Gospel is *euangellion*—Good News.[26] The gospel is news that stays news, a happening that demands to be shared, information that is not self-generated but demands to be self-delivered.[27] Announcers of the news don't spend much effort worrying about how to spread the news; broadcasters urgently buttonhole the first person they meet. News begs delivery. The nature of the gospel as news explains why preaching is the primary activity of the church (that community convened by the news for the purpose of giving out the news), God's main means of getting out the word that God is not against us (Rom 8:31).

We don't know why God has given us this news, but we know wherefore, to give away what we have received. Thus missionary preacher Paul says that faith is not only hearing but also passing on news:

> All who call on the Lord's name will be saved. So how can they call on someone they don't have faith in? And how can they have faith in someone they haven't heard of? And how can they hear without a preacher? . . . So, faith comes from listening, but it's listening by means of Christ's message. (Rom 10:13-14, 17)

The substance of the good news? Paul repeats it as he heard it:

> Brothers and sisters, I want to call your attention to the good news that I preached to you, which you also received and in which you stand. You are being saved through it if you hold on to the message I preached to you, unless somehow you believed it for nothing. I passed on to you as most important what I also received: Christ died for our sins in line with the scriptures, he

was buried, and he rose on the third day in line with the scriptures. He appeared to Cephas, then to the Twelve, and then he appeared to more than five hundred brothers and sisters at once—most of them are still alive to this day, though some have died. Then he appeared to James, then to all the apostles, and last of all he appeared to me, as if I were born at the wrong time. . . . So then, whether you heard the message from me or them, this is what we preach and this is what you have believed. (1 Cor 15:1-8, 11)

There you have it. The good news of a Jew named Jesus ("God saves") who "died for our sins in line with the Scriptures, . . . was buried, . . . was raised on the third day, . . . appeared to Cephas, then to the twelve, . . . to more than five hundred brothers and sisters, . . . then . . . to James, then to all the apostles. Last of all, . . . he appeared to me"; so I announced, so you believed.

Gospel is not a set of ideas, a precious something tucked into our hearts, a decision we made, much less a feeling we experienced, nor is gospel a procedure for getting right with God. Gospel is news of what God has done and (because of resurrection) is now doing. Gospel is not how we wind up at an optimum ultimate destination, nor is it an exhortation to industriously work justice to make the world more habitable for victims of our injustice. Gospel—who God is, what God is up to, and how we are part of it—is a sermon that Paul did not come up with on his own, an announcement "which you in turn received, in which also you stand, through which also you are being saved," this story "that I proclaimed to you." Christians—saved by a true story of how Christ enfolds us into God's story.[28]

Most preachers learn that vagueness, abstraction, and generalization are the death of interesting preaching. Barth says that evasion of the concrete, particular, God-with-a-body-speaking personification of God leads to atheism:[29]

> The question can't be: What is God? The question must be: Who is God? And the answer can't be the description of an It; but must be the characterization of a person. This is the first and definitive depiction of God's identity that arises out of the fact that God is knowable to us through God's Word. What Christian preaching calls God's revelation is God's speaking, lightning that rends the darkness (what a lame comparison!), an unnatural occurence, the Logos, the free divine Spirit who makes God's true self known. . . . The miracle or paradox of revelation is that God personally speaks to us this Word and that we can hear this Word as an address, person to person. . . . God is a person, Christian revelation is trinitarian revelation.

> This decisively rules out any possibility of seeing God behind, above, or apart from God's personality. This is an axiom of Christian proclamation—God exists as a person, Father, Son, and Spirit from eternity to eternity. Once we abstract or conceptualize God as detached from the speaking person who addresses us, once we dissolve God into a general truth or idea that is no longer a person, we are no longer thinking about God.[30]

Paul's "Gospel of God" or "God's good news" (Rom 1:2-4 NRSV, CEB) tells us more about who Christ is than what he says or does. Paul describes Christ's post-Easter epiphanies as "appearances," not "Risen-Christ sightings." Christ's presence is gift, not our discovery, God coming to us rather than from inside us, speaking words we cannot say to ourselves.

A prominent preacher launched a series, "Learn How to Recognize God's Voice." In the first sermon, he promised to take the mystery out of revelation with "seven ways to test in order to know with absolute certainty you are hearing the voice of God." "You can't have a relationship with God if you can't hear God, if God never speaks to you." Still, "How do you know if your thought about God came from God or the Devil or a bad burrito you ate last night?"[31] His first example of hearing direct, unmistakable revelation? "Render unto Caesar." "If you're thinking of not paying taxes, it's a refusal to listen to God," says the preacher, guffawing.

Announcement of a New World

Barth's theological revolution began in 1918 through a close, creative reading of Paul's Letter to the Romans—and after a frustrating decade of attempting to preach. That which Barth received from Romans, leading to his bombshell of a book, was, "We have found in the Bible a new world, God. God's sovereignty, God's glory, God's incomprehensible love. Not the history of [humanity], but the history of God!"[32]

In a sermon on 1 Kings 17, Fleming Rutledge asks, "Why are the mainline churches having so much trouble?" She answers that mainline preaching is

> not about a God who judges and redeems, who causes great movements to come to pass, who puts down the mighty from their seats and exalts the humble and meek. Instead, the messages are about human activity. They are about human potential, human hopes, human wishes, human programs and agendas. . . . The living God of Elijah does not seem to be in view.[33]

Mainline, liberal preachers in my part of the world preach mostly from the Gospels, rather than the earlier letters of Paul. Is that because the Gospels, replete with Jesus's words and deeds, couching Christology within narrative, appear to encourage human agency? Christ, the great exemplar of goodness, hanging out with the good country folk of Galilee, giving them a gentle nudge to love their neighbor as themselves; Christ, the beloved teacher who told stories that brought out the best in us; Christ, of use in our projects of the moment.

Maybe Christ as exemplar of good behavior is a First World problem. Paul, at work in 1 Corinthians 15, is strikingly disinterested in details of Jesus's birth, life, and death, as if the sheer, luminous identity of Christ overshadows his deeds and words, as if in his resurrection, Christ—bodily presence of God's eternal benevolence—needs no bolstering.[34] God raised *crucified* Jesus. God raised crucified Jesus. God raised crucified Jesus. This, the sermon Paul was dying to preach, is news that propelled Paul all over Asia Minor, planting churches where nobody knew they needed a church. Is Paul's "Gospel of God" (Rom 1:2-4) too hot for accommodated, well-adjusted-to-decline-and-death, self-help, bourgeois, progressive Christianity to handle?[35]

Years ago, the errant Jesus Seminar caused a stir by attempting to isolate and identify the few "authentic" words of Jesus, only to be surprised that Christians don't worship the words of Jesus; we worship the Word. While it's fair for preaching sometimes to offer helpful hints for persons in pain, therapeutic advice for the wounded, a reason to get out of bed in the morning, a spiritual boost for the sad, or a call to arms for social activists, human helpfulness can never be preaching's main intent because such concerns are of little concern to Jesus.[36] Besides, why get up, get dressed, and come to church at an inconvenient hour of the week to hear what is otherwise readily available anywhere else. At least Rotary serves lunch.

Christ's identity makes preaching in his name dangerous in its consequences and cosmic in its intentions. . . .

On the Sunday after the 2016 presidential election debacle I preached in a United Methodist church in the suburbs of Washington, DC. The pastor expected to lose as many as thirty families—Obama political appointees sure to be purged. My text was the assigned epistle, Romans 5, "Christ died for the ungodly." I reminded the faithful that gracious Jesus died for sinners, only sinners, and that Jesus liked nothing better than to party with tax collectors and whores.

My sermon concluded with, "OK, good for us. We have elected a lying, adulterous, draft-evading, bankruptcy-declaring, misogynistic, racist riverboat gambler with tacky gold plumbing fixtures. He is a national disgrace *and* [pause for effect] *one whom Jesus Christ loves, saves, and for whom he gave his life.* [Leaning over the pulpit, looking into the whites of their eyes.] *Are you sure that you want to worship that Savior?*"

I preached not as I pleased that Sunday and let Paul do the talking.

There have been times—such as the moments before a funeral for a toddler in our congregation—when I sat in my study and groused to the Lord, "I'm not going out there and making some lame excuse for your behavior," only to have the Lord shove me on stage and insist that Paul feed me the lines. Though at that moment I wasn't convinced, it was encouraging to hear Paul say, "Nothing can separate us from God's love in Christ Jesus our Lord: not death or life, not angels or rulers, not present things or future things, not powers or height or depth, or any other thing that is created" (Rom 8:38-39).

Notes

January

1. Jaime L. Waters, *Threshing Floors in Ancient Israel: Their Ritual and Symbolic Significance* (Philadelphia: Fortress, 2015), 2.

2. Waters, *Threshing Floors in Ancient Israel*, 3.

3. Fred B. Craddock, *Craddock Stories*, ed. Mike Graves and Richard F. Ward (St. Louis: Chalice, 2001), 33.

4. Charles Dickens, *A Tale of Two Cities*, 1859 ed. (New York: Black and White Classics, 2014), 3.

5. Frederick Buechner, *Wishful Thinking: A Theological ABC* (New York: HarperCollins, 1993).

6. John Ortberg, *If You Want to Walk on Water You've Got to Get Out of the Boat* (Grand Rapids: Zondervan, 2001), 118.

7. Jimmy Carter, *Sources of Strength: Meditations on Scripture for a Living Faith* (New York: Times Books, 1997), 71–72.

February

1. "A Service of Word and Table I," *The United Methodist Hymnal: Book of United Methodist Worship* (Nashville: United Methodist Publishing House, 1989).

2. "Service of Word and Table I."

3. David L. Bartlett and Barbara Brown Taylor, eds., *Feasting on the Word: Year C, Volume 1, Advent through Transfiguration* (Louisville, KY: Westminster John Knox, 2009), 357.

4. Bartlett and Taylor, eds., *Feasting on the Word*, 357.

5. Nadia Bolz-Weber, "Blessed Are the Agnostics," The Corners by Nadia Bolz-Weber, entry posted on January 13, 2020, https://nadiabolzweber.substack.com/p/blessed-are-the-agnostics.

6. Joseph Shapiro, "Amish Forgive School Shooter, Struggle with Grief," National Public Radio, *All Things Considered*, posted October 2, 2007, https://www.npr.org/templates/story/story.php?storyId=14900930.

7. Terry Gross, "How Twitter Helped Change the Mind of a Westboro Baptist Church Member," National Public Radio, *Fresh Air*, posted October 10, 2019, https://www.npr.org/2019/10/10/768894901/how-twitter-helped -change-the-mind-of-a-westboro-baptist-church-member.

8. Olu Brown, *Leadership Directions from Moses: On the Way to a Promised Land* (Nashville: Abingdon Press, 2017), 26–27.

9. Walter Brueggemann, "The Book of Exodus," in the *New Interpreter's Bible*, ed. Leander E. Keck, vol. 1 (Nashville: Abingdon Press, 1996).

March

1. J. Clinton McCann Jr., "The Book of Psalms," in the *New Interpreter's Bible Commentary*, ed. Leander E. Keck, vol. 4 (Nashville: Abingdon Press, 1994), 885.

2. McCann, "The Book of Psalms," 887.

3. "The LORD regretted making human beings on the earth, and he was heartbroken" (Gen 6:6).

4. Lin-Manuel Miranda, *Hamilton: An American Musical*, 2015.

5. "A Service of Death and Resurrection," *The United Methodist Book of Worship*, https://www.umcdiscipleship.org/book-of-worship/a-service-of-death-and -resurrection.

6. All references to *A Christmas Carol* come from https://www.gutenberg .org/files/46/46-h/46-h.htm, public domain.

7. "David Foster Wallace on Life and Work," *The Wall Street Journal*, September 19, 2008.

8. Marcus Borg and John Dominic Crossan, *The First Paul: Reclaiming the Radical Visionary behind the Church's Conservative Icon* (New York: HarperCollins, 2009), 186.

9. "Turmoil and Triumph," Booknotes, C-SPAN, April 29, 1993. https:// www.c-span.org/video/?44051-1/turmoil-triumph.

April

1. Pope Francis, *Encountering Truth: Meeting God in the Everyday* (New York: Crown Publishing Group, 2015), 72–73.

2. J. Strong, *Strong's Expanded Exhaustive Concordance of the Bible* (Nashville: Hendrickson, 1890), #5614.

3. Alan Rudnick, "Lessons from a Donkey," Alan Rudnick (blog), March 26, 2010, http://www.alanrudnick.org/2010/03/26/lessons-from-a-donkey/.

4. Gail R. O'Day, "The Gospel of John," in *The New Interpreter's Bible Commentary*, ed. Leander E. Keck, vol. 9 (Nashville: Abingdon Press, 1995).

5. Luke Timothy Johnson, *The Gospel of Luke*, Sacra Pagina (Collegeville, MN: Liturgical Press, 1991), 387.

6. Fred B. Craddock, *Luke*, Interpretation (Louisville, KY: Westminster John Knox, 1990), 283.

7. James Luther Mays, *Psalms*, Interpretation (Louisville, KY: Westminster John Knox, 1994), 374–77.

8. Mays, *Psalms*, 377.

May

1. Fred Craddock, *Craddock Stories* (St. Louis: Chalice Press, 2001), 84.

2. This is an adaptation of the LovingKindness exercise in "On Healing," in Jon Kabat-Zinn, *Full Catastrophe Living: Using the Wisdom of Your Body and Mind to Face Stress, Pain, and Illness* (New York: Bantam Books, 2013).

3. *The United Methodist Hymnal: Book of United Methodist Worship* (Nashville: United Methodist Publishing House, 1989), 35.

4. Scott Cairns, "Adventures in New Testament Greek: Metanoia," in *Slow Pilgrims: The Collected Poems of Scott Cairns* (Brewster, MA: Paraclete, 2015), 173.

June

1. See "The Determination of Jesus" in Peter Wallace, *Heart and Soul: The Emotions of Jesus* (Edinburgh: T&T Clark, 1915), for more on this.

2. Emily C. Heath, "Plowing Ahead," June 15, 2016, UCC Still Speaking Daily Devotional, https://www.ucc.org/daily_devotional_plowing_ahead.

July

1. Richard A. Swenson, *Margin: Restoring Emotional, Physical, Financial, and Time Reserves to Overloaded Lives* (Colorado Springs, CO: Navpress, 2004), 15.

2. Swenson, *Margin*, 42.

3. Swenson, *Margin*, 69.

4. Swenson, *Margin*, 13.

5. Swenson, *Margin*, 51, 50.

6. Max Lucado, *And the Angels Were Silent: The Final Week of Jesus* (Nashville: Thomas Nelson, 2013), 91–92.

7. Steve Garnass-Holmes, "Prodigal Father," *Unfolding Light* (blog), https://www.unfoldinglight.net/reflections/1782.

August

1. Henri J. M. Nouwen, *Behold the Beauty of the Lord: Praying with Icons*, rev. ed. (Notre Dame, IN: Ave Maria Press, 2007), 30.

2. Thomas G. Long, *Westminster Bible Companion: Matthew* (Louisville, KY: Westminster John Knox, 1997), 48.

September

1. Walter Brueggemann, *A Commentary on Jeremiah: Exile and Homecoming* (Grand Rapids: Eerdmans, 1998), 61.

October

1. Fred Craddock, *Luke*, Interpretation: A Bible Commentary for Teaching and Preaching (Louisville, KY: Westminster John Knox, 1990), 202–3.

2. Craddock, *Luke*, 202–3.

3. Chris Arnade, *Dignity: Seeking Respect in Back Row America* (New York: Sentinel Publishing, 2019), 122.

4. Brett Dennen, "Ain't No Reason," *So Much More*, track 1, Dualtone Records, 2006.

November

1. Susan J. White, *Foundations of Christian Worship* (Louisville, KY: Westminster John Knox, 2006), 20.

2. Tom Long, *The Witness of Preaching*, 3rd ed. (Louisville, KY: Westminster John Knox, 2016), 85.

3. Rob Bell, "Noise," *Nooma Video Series*, episode 5, Flannel, Grandville, MI, 2005.

4. The NAS Old Testamen Hebrew Lexicon, s.v. "halal," https://www.biblestudytools.com/lexicons/hebrew/nas/halal.html.

5. Marjorie Suchocki, *In God's Presence: Theological Reflections on Prayer*, Kindle edition (St. Louis: Chalice, 1996), loc. 1281.

6. C. S. Lewis, "Is Theology Poetry?" in *The Weight of Glory and Other Addresses* (New York: HarperOne, 1949), 140.

December

1. Kenny Loggins, "Celebrate Me Home," *Celebrate Me Home*, track 8, lyrics by Kenny Loggins and Bob James, New York, Warner Bros., 1977.

2. Amy-Jill Levine, "Matthew," in *The Women's Bible Commentary*, ed. Carole A. Newsom and Sharon H. Ringe (Louisville, KY: Westminster John Knox), 1992.

Essay: "The Working Gospel and the Bridge Paradigm"

1. André Resner, "Do You See This Woman? A Little Exercise in Homiletical Theology," in *Theologies of the Gospel in Context: The Crux of Homiletical Theology*, ed. David Schnasa Jacobsen (Eugene, OR: Cascade, 2017), 19–24.

2. Resner, "Do You See This Woman?" 18.

3. See David Schnasa Jacobsen, "The Practice of Homiletical Theology in a Confessional Mode: An Interim Report on the Homiletical Theology Project," North American Academy of Homiletics meeting in Dallas, Texas (December 9, 2017), http://www.bu.edu/homiletical-theology-project," 31–32.

4. See Edward Farley, "Preaching the Bible and Preaching the Gospel," *Theology Today* 51, no. 1 (April 1994): 90–103, also in *Practicing Gospel: Unconventional Thoughts on the Practice of Ministry* (Louisville, KY: Westminster John Knox, 2003), 71–82. Two other articles on prevailing assumptions about the relationship of the Bible to preaching are conveniently gathered in *Practicing Gospel* as well: "Toward a New Paradigm of Preaching" (pp. 83–92) and "Sacred Rhetoric: A Practical Theology of Preaching" (pp. 93–103).

5. For Farley those reasons would include (a) the passage is a delimited piece in a larger writing, (b) there is no guaranteed inerrancy about the writing at any level, (c) there may be no X (preachable truth) in the passage, (d) the content of the passage would be something that must be preached against, and (e) the passage may have a moralizable content, something that lends itself to a lesson for life rather than the gospel. See Farley, "Preaching the Bible and Preaching the Gospel," 96.

6. Farley, "Preaching the Bible and Preaching the Gospel," 97.

7. Farley, "Preaching the Bible and Preaching the Gospel," 93.

8. Farley, "Preaching the Bible and Preaching the Gospel," 93

9. Farley, "Preaching the Bible and Preaching the Gospel," 95

10. Resner, "Do You See This Woman?" 20.

11. Jacobsen, "The Practice of Homiletical Theology in a Confessional Mode," 31.

12. Jacobsen, "The Practice of Homiletical Theology in a Confessional Mode," 35.

Essay: "We Preach the Gospel"

1. From the contemporary version of the Nicene Creed, formulated after the time of Buttrick's writing.

2. Norman Vincent Peale, *The Power of Positive Thinking* (New York: Prentice-Hall, Inc., 1952).

3. "We have always had a curious feeling that though we crucified Christ on a stick, he somehow managed to get hold of the right end of it, and that if we were better men we might try his plan." George Bernard Shaw, "Preface on the Prospects of Christianity," in *Androcles and the Lion* (New York: Brentano's, 1916), xiii.

4. Buttrick consistently criticized the "peace of mind" and "positive thinking" nostrums of Dale Carnegie (*How to Win Friends and Influence People,* 1936) and Norman Vincent Peale (*Power of Positive Thinking*). Buttrick wrote, "Another impressive form of sidestepping is seen in our modern cult of 'peace of mind.' It would have us believe that there is no evil that we ourselves cannot overcome by a prayer-formula and 'confidence.' 'Positive thinking' can guarantee both an attractive personality and business success. This world is a world in which we can always 'win friends and influence people,' if only we keep telling ourselves that 'every day in every way we are getting better and better.' When we set Jesus alongside this cheap evasion it dwindles into selfishness." George A. Buttrick, *God, Pain, and Evil* (Nashville: Abingdon Press, 1966), 137–38.

5. John 14:27 (RSV).

6. William Blake, "I Want! I Want!" engraving, The Fitzwilliam Museum, Cambridge, UK, May 17, 1793 https://www.fitzwilliamprints.com /image/1094684/blake-william-iwant-i-want-by-william-blake.

7. The fourfold Event: chapter 1, the life of Christ, the death of Christ; chapter 2, the resurrection of Christ, the living (Holy Spirit) of Christ.

8. Heb 4:15 (GAB). Buttrick's initials (GAB) following a biblical citation indicate that the English translation from the Greek or Hebrew text is Buttrick's.

9. Heb 10:22 (GAB).

10. Paraphrase in consequence of the Sermon on the Mount and Beatitudes: "You, therefore, must be perfect, as your heavenly Father is perfect" (Matt 5:48, RSV).

11. Luke 6:27 (KJV).

12. Alexander Pope's paraphrase of Matt 6:3-4, "When you give alms, do not let your left hand know what your right hand is doing, so that your alms may be in secret" (RSV). Thus, Pope: "Do good by stealth, and blush to find it Fame," in "Epilogue to the Satires in Two Dialogues (1738), Dialogue I," in *Alexander Pope: Selected Poetry & Prose*, ed. William K. Wimsatt, 2nd ed. (New York: Holt, Rinehart, and Winston, 1951), 363, l. 136.

13. Luke 5:8 (RSV), spoken by Peter to Jesus.

14. The story of French artist Gabriel Briand's sculpture of the god "Mercury drawing a thorn out of his heel," for which Briand received posthumously the Medal of Honor from the Paris Salon in 1868. "One night the cold was so bitter that he heaped upon his bed all the clothes he possessed. He suddenly remembered his masterpiece, which he had just finished, and dreading lest the damp clay should be frozen, he stripped himself and put all his clothing and best 'covering around the figure.' The next day, the sculptor was found lying on his bed frozen to death." W. H. Crossland, "XXXIII: The Royal Holloway College," *Transactions*, vol. 3, New Series (London: The Royal Institute of British Architects, 1887), 146.

15. Ludwig van Beethoven's Fourth Symphony in Bb major, Op. 60, 1806. The "dissonant" F-chord that "may haunt the memory" occurs at circa 3:15 in the first movement, as striking contrast to the allegro vivace that follows. Thus, the cross as "an agony of discord" contrasted with what follows, the Easter resurrection.

16. See n15.

17. Pierre Teilhard de Chardin (1881–1955), French Jesuit and evolutionist, author of The Phenomenon of Man and The Divine Milieu, who espoused the eventual consummation of all cosmic life in the "omega point" of divine, christological unity.

18. The Vietnam War, 1955–1975, waged in North and South Vietnam, Cambodia, and Laos by French and American colonial powers and their South Korean, Australian, Thai, and other allies, against communist North Vietnamese adversaries and their Russian, Chinese, and North Korean allies.

19. "It is by no breath, Turn of eye, wave of hand, that salvation joins issue with death!" from Robert's Browning's "Saul," XVIII, *The Complete Works of Robert Browning*, Cambridge edition (Boston: Houghton Mifflin Company, 1895), 184.

20. "O Saul, it shall be A Face like my face that receives thee: a Man like to me, Thou shalt love and be loved by, forever: a Hand like this hand Shall throw

open the gates of new life to thee! See the Christ stand!" Browning, "Saul," 184, last line. See also Acts 7:55-56.

21. Rev 13:8 (KJV).

22. Exod 34:7; Num 14:18.

23. 1 Cor 15:22 (KJV).

24. 1 John 2:2 (RSV).

25. Ps 22:1 (GAB [NRSV]).

26. "See how much the estates, liberties, and lives, even of the best men, lie at the mercy of the worst, against whose false oaths, innocency itself is no fence," Matthew Henry, late minister of the Gospel in Chester, *An Exposition of the Old Testament in Four Volumes*, vol. 3 (Edinburgh: C. Wright & Co., for the Publisher J. Wood, 1758), 205.

27. Mark 9:7 (KJV).

28. George Stewart, *The Crucifixion in Our Street* (New York: George H. Doran Co., 1927).

29. George Stewart, *The Resurrection in Our Street* (Garden City, NY: Doubleday, Doran & Co., 1928).

Essay: "Christ: *Deus Dixit*"

1. Nicholas Wolterstorff complains that Barth takes "an idea that plays a minor role in Scripture itself, namely, the idea of God revealing Godself and makes it the major theme of his theology." Nicholas Wolterstorff, *The God We Worship: An Exploration of Liturgical Theology* (Grand Rapids: Eerdmans, 2015).

2. Karl Barth, *Church Dogmatics*, vol. II, part 2, ed. G. W. Bromiley and T. F. Torrance (Edinburgh: T & T Clark, 1975), 121. Hereafter, *Church Dogmatics* referred to as *CD*.

3. Reginald Fuller said that preachers "are concerned with two poles—the text and the contemporary situation. . . . [Preachers] build a bridge between these poles." *The Use of the Bible in Preaching* (Philadelphia: Fortress, 1981), 41. This is the nineteenth-century text-to-sermon bifurcation that Barth deplores.

4. Karl Barth, *Witness to the Word: A Commentary on John I*, ed. Walther Fürst, trans. Geoffrey W. Bromiley (Grand Rapids: Eerdmans, 1986), 66.

5. Nothing can be allowed to supplant the free word of God. Barmen is political protest as a declaration of the freedom of preaching. Barth thought that the German Christians were a bigger threat to the gospel than Hitler. See Karl Barth, *Community, State, and the Church*, trans. G. Ronald Howe (Garden City,

NY: Anchor, 1960). Also William H. Willimon, *How Odd of God: Chosen for the Curious Vocation of Preaching* (Louisville, KY: Westminster John Knox, 2015), 90–91.

6. Barth, *CD*, II/1, 150.

7. "The paucity of systematic theological attention to divine speaking is surprising in light of its biblical prominence, especially in light of Scriptures' contrast between speaking God of Israel and the dumb pagan idols. . . . False gods tell no tales. But Yahweh talks!" Kevin J. Vanhoozer, "Triune Discourse," in *Trinitarian Theology for the Church: Scripture, Community, Worship*, ed. Daniel J. Treier and David Lauber (Downers Grove, IL: InterVarsity, 2009), 52.

8. "How can theology make [God's] revelation in Jesus intelligible, and validate its true claim, in an age when all talk about God is reduced to subjectivity?" Wolfhart Pannenberg, *Systematic Theology*, vol. 1, trans. G. W. Bromiley (Edinburgh: T & T Clark, 1991), 128.

9. My theory: Preachers are ridiculed in modern fiction because preachers insist on talking about matters that the modern world wants to keep quiet. See Douglas Alan Walrath, *Displacing the Divine: The Minister in the Mirror of American Fiction* (New York: Columbia University Press, 1993).

10. Immanuel Kant, "What Is Enlightenment?" [1784] in *The Enlightenment: A Comprehensive Anthology*, ed. Peter Gay (New York: Simon and Schuster, 1973), 384–89.

11. William Giraldi, *American Audacity: In Defense of Literary Daring* (New York: Norton, 2018), xix.

12. Stanley Hauerwas, with Robert J. Dean, *Minding the Web: Making Theological Connections* (Eugene, OR: Cascade, 2018), 102.

13. Marilynne Robinson, *Lila* (New York: Picador, 2014), 44.

14. Ludwig Feuerbach, *The Essence of Christianity*, trans. George Eliot (New York: Harper & Row, 1957), 63.

15. Barth, *GD*, 14, my translation. Chris Currie says that "the threefold Word of God is a crucial element in Karl Barth's vision of the church and . . . for the whole of his theological project. Disregarded by the field of Barth studies and rejected by modern ecclesiologists." Currie's work is the best we've got on preaching as God's word in Barth and is an impetus for *Preachers Dare*. Thomas Christian Currie, *The Only Sacrament Left to Us: The Threefold Word of God in the Theology and Ecclesiology of Karl Barth* (Eugene, OR: Pickwick, 2015), ix.

16. Barth, in Romans, following Luther and Calvin, showed that the Bible is first and last, the word, "Jesus Christ." Barth looked upon the Old Testament as

"the name Jesus Christ, concealed under the name Israel in the Old Testament, revealed under his own name in the New Testament." *CD*, I/2, 720.

17. John doesn't refer again to Christ as "The Logos." Doesn't have to. The Word is a barrage of words such as the long, rich "Farewell Discourse" in John 14.

18. Later, in *Church Dogmatics*, Barth discusses "The Word of God in its Threefold Form," beginning not with the speaking of the Incarnate Christ but rather with proclamation, "The Word of God Preached" (CD, I/1, 88), thus highlighting the Word of God in the present. This move is remarkable, though no ranking or subordination is implied in the way the forms are listed. Barth says, "We can substitute for revelation, Scripture and proclamation the names of the divine persons Father, Son and Holy Spirit and vice versa, that in the one case as in the other we shall encounter the same basic determinations and mutual relationship" (*CD*, I/1, 121).

19. Early in his lectures, Barth unfolds the threefold Word of God through Chalcedonian terminology to describe revelation's unity in differentiation, "neither to be confused or separated," and differentiated while being "trinity in unity, unity in trinity"—one God in three ways. *GD*, 14–15. Helpful on Chalcedon is Christopher A. Beeley, *The Unity of Christ: Continuity and Conflict in Patristic Tradition* (New Haven, CT: Yale University Press, 2013).

20. Barth, *CD*, I/2, part 1. Italics in original.

21. "Revelation is no more and no less than the life of God . . . turned to us. . . ." Barth, *CD*, I/2, 483.

22. The Bible is the word of the living God that says, "Jesus Christ." Even in the Old Testament we have "the name Jesus Christ, concealed under the name Israel in the Old Testament, revealed under his own name in the New Testament." Barth, *CD*, I/2, 720.

23. "The Bible is about Jesus. . . . Jesus was God's plan all along." Sam Wells, *Speaking the Truth: Preaching in a Pluralistic Culture* (Nashville: Abingdon Press, 2008), 40.

24. Will Willimon, "Evangelicals Get Real," April 2020, "Peculiar Prophet," https://willwillimon.com/2020/04/27/evangelicals-get-real/.

25. Except in the sense of Colossians 1:27 and 2:2.

26. Never did anybody suggest concilium (church-sanctioned teaching), or magisterium (ecclesiastical pronouncements).

27. Barth says, "The word 'announcement' [*Ankündigung*] has the advantage over 'proclamation' [*Verkündigung*]" that in it God is the one "who speaks, and not we, who simply have the role of announcing what God . . . wants to say." Karl

Barth, *Homiletics*, trans. Geoffrey W. Bromley and Donald E. Daniels (Louisville, KY: Westminster John Knox, 1991), 46.

28. My teacher Hans Frei said that when Christian interpreters shoehorned the biblical story into the stories dominated by secular philosophy, rather than enfolding the world's account of itself into the biblical story, the battle was lost. Hans W. Frei, *The Eclipse of Biblical Narrative: A Study in 18th and 19th Century Hermeneutics* (New Haven, CT: Yale University Press, 1974), 130.

29. Michael Buckley shows how modern atheism arose out of Christian apologists' depersonalization of God. Michael J. Buckley, *At the Origins of Modern Atheism* (New Haven, CT: Yale University Press, 1987).

30. Barth, *GD*, 368–69, my translation. Schweitzer's famous last paragraph of The Quest of the Historical Jesus says. "He comes to us as One unknown, without a name, as of old, by the lakeside, He came to those men who knew Him not. He speaks to us the same words: 'Follow thou me!' . . . And to those who obey Him, whether they be wise or simple, He will reveal himself, . . . as an ineffable mystery, they shall learn in their own experience Who He is." Albert Schweitzer, *The Quest of the Historical Jesus*, trans. W. Montgomery (London: A & C Black, 1911). Unfortunately, Schweitzer's failed prophet, apocalyptic Jesus, revealed in our "own experience" is a depersonalized "ineffable mystery" who can't offer true "fellowship."

31. Rick Warren, "Learn How to Recognize God's Voice," October 7, 2014, https://www.youtube.com/watch?v=kglsnPp-foU. See also Priscilla Shirer, *Discerning the Voice of God: How to Recognize When God Is Speaking* (Chicago: Moody, 2012).

32. Barth quoted by Gary Dorrien, *The Barthian Revolt in Modern Theology* (Louisville, KY: Westminster John Knox, 2000), 51. Karl Barth, *The Epistle to the Romans*, trans. Edwyn C. Hoskyns, 6th ed. (London: Oxford University Press, 1975 [1933]).

33. Fleming Rutledge, *And God Spoke to Abraham: Preaching from the Old Testament* (Grand Rapids: Eerdmans, 2011), 144.

34. Christ "did not rise to be a disembodied wraith flitting through time; he rose to be a speaking body." Robert W. Jenson, *Visible Words: The Interpretation and Practice of Christian Sacraments* (Philadelphia: Fortress, 1978).

35. In his Beecher Lectures, Brian Blount waxed apocalyptic, celebrating the "reckless implausibility" of the resurrection. Brian K. Blount, *Invasion of the Dead: Preaching Resurrection* (Louisville, KY: Westminster John Knox, 2014), xv.

36. The Roman Empire didn't trouble itself over the Gnostics because the "Gnostic Gospels" aren't good news of an event; they are instructions on how to organize life in accord with a fixed, unredeemed world. No government is made nervous by gnostic spirituality.

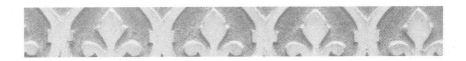

Contributors

Sermon Helps

Olu Brown is founding pastor of Impact Church in Atlanta, Georgia.
Transfiguration Sunday and Last Sunday before Lent—February 27, 2022; Ash Wednesday —March 2, 2022; First Sunday in Lent—March 6, 2022

Robert W. Clark is pastor at Isle of Faith United Methodist Church in Jacksonville, Florida
Fifth Sunday in Lent—April 3, 2022; Palm Sunday, Sixth Sunday in Lent—April 10, 2022; Holy Thursday/Maundy Thursday—April 14, 2022

Lisa Degrenia is senior pastor at Trinity United Methodist Church in Sarasota, Florida.
Seventh Sunday after Pentecost—July 24, 2022; Eighth Sunday after Pentecost—July 31, 2022; Ninth Sunday after Pentecost—August 7, 2020

Magrey R. DeVega is senior pastor of Hyde Park United Methodist Church in Tampa, Florida.
Fourth Sunday of Lent—March 27, 2022; Twenty-Fourth Sunday after Pentecost, Reign of Christ—November 20, 2022; Thanksgiving Day—November 24, 2022

Sue Haupert-Johnson is Resident Bishop at North Georgia Conference of The United Methodist Church.
Third Sunday of Advent—December 11, 2022; Fourth Sunday of Advent—December 18, 2022; Nativity of the Lord—December 24–25, 2022

Juan Carlos Huertas is pastor at Houma First United Methodist Church in Houma, Louisiana.
Tenth Sunday after Pentecost—August 14, 2022; Eleventh Sunday after Pentecost— August 21, 2022; Twelfth Sunday after Pentecost—August 28, 2022

Allen Johnson is associate pastor at Johns Creek United Methodist Church in Johns Creek, Georgia.
Holy Friday/Good Friday—April 15, 2022; Easter Sunday, Resurrection of the Lord— April 17, 2022; Second Sunday of Easter—April 24, 2022

Chris Jones is senior pastor at Asbury United Methodist Church in Maitland, Florida.
Epiphany—January 16, 2022; Epiphany—January 23, 2022; Epiphany—January 30, 2022

Sky McCraken is senior pastor at Jackson First United Methodist Church in Jackson, Tennessee.
Sixteenth Sunday after Pentecost—September 25, 2022; Seventeenth Sunday after Pentecost —October 2nd, 2022; Eighteenth Sunday after Pentecost—October 9, 2022

Cyndi McDonald is pastor at Barnesville United Methodist Church in Barnesville, Georgia.
Third Sunday of Easter—May 1, 2022; Fourth Sunday of Easter and Mother's Day— May 8, 2022; Fifth Sunday of Easter—May 15, 2022

Mandy Sloan McDow is senior minister at Los Angeles First United Methodist Church in Los Angeles, California.
Second Sunday in Lent—March 13, 2022; Thirteenth Sunday after Pentecost— September 4, 2022; Fourteenth Sunday after Pentecost—September 11, 2022; Fifteenth Sunday after Pentecost—September 18, 2022

Jason Micheli is senior pastor at Annandale United Methodist Church in Annandale, Virginia.
Nineteenth Sunday after Pentecost—October 16, 2022; Twentieth Sunday after Pentecost —October 23, 2022; Twenty-First Sunday after Pentecost—October 30, 2022

Lori Osborn is associate pastor at Johns Creek United Methodist Church in Johns Creek, Georgia.
Fifth Sunday after Epiphany—February 6, 2022; Sixth Sunday after Epiphany— February 13, 2022; Seventh Sunday after Epiphany—February 20, 2022

Charley Reeb, editor, is senior pastor at Johns Creek United Methodist Church in Johns Creek, Georgia.
Third Sunday in Lent—March 20, 2022; First Sunday of Advent—November 27, 2022; Second Sunday of Advent—December 4, 2022

Alex Shanks is assistant to the bishop of the Florida Annual Conference of The United Methodist Church.
Fourth Sunday after Pentecost—July 3, 2022; Fifth Sunday after Pentecost—July 10, 2022; Sixth Sunday after Pentecost—July 17, 2022

Peter Wallace is an Episcopal priest and president, executive producer, and host of the Day1 radio program at Alliance of Christian Media.
Trinity Sunday—June 12, 2022; Second Sunday after Pentecost—June 19, 2022; Third Sunday after Pentecost—June 26, 2022

Cynthia D. Weems is superintendent of the South East District of the Florida Annual Conference of The United Methodist Church.
Sixth Sunday of Easter—May 22, 2022; Seventh Sunday of Easter/Ascension—May 29, 2022; Day of Pentecost—June 5, 2022

Jennifer Stiles Williams is senior pastor at St. Luke's United Methodist Church in Windermere, Florida.
All Saints Day—November 1, 2022; Twenty-Second Sunday after Pentecost—November 6, 2022; Twenty-Third Sunday after Pentecost—November 13, 2022

Will Wold is associate pastor at Mandarin United Methodist Church in Jacksonville, Florida.
Second Sunday after Christmas Day—January 2, 2022; Baptism of the Lord—January 9, 2022

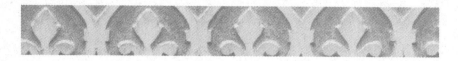

Contributors

Essays for Skill-Building

Frank Thomas is the Nettie Sweeney and Hugh Th. Miller Professor of Homiletics and the director of the PhD in African American Preaching and Sacred Rhetoric Program at Christian Thological Seminary in Indianapolis, Indiana. He is the author of Abingdon Press titles *Introduction to the Practice of African American Preaching, How to Preach a Dangerous Sermon,* and *Surviving a Dangerous Sermon.*

George Buttrick (March 23, 1892 – January 23, 1980) became one of the most influential preachers in the United States and England. He was the famed pastor of the Madison Avenue Presbyterian Church in New York City, and professor of preaching at Harvard, Garrett, Vanderbilt, and Louisville's Presbyterian and Southern Baptist seminaries. Buttrick was the author of thirteen books about parables, prayer, evil, and other topics. The exerpt included here is from *George Buttrick's Guide to Preaching the Gospel,* edited by Charles N. Davidson Jr.

Will Willimon is Professor of the Practice of Christian Ministry at Duke University Divinity School in Durham, North Carolina, and a retired bishop of The United Methodist Church. Willimon has published widely, including his preaching subscription service on MinistryMatters.com, *Pulpit Resource, Fear of the Other: No Fear in Love,* and *Prachers Dare.*

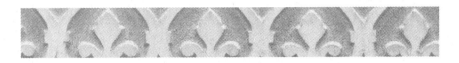

Scripture Index

Thematic Index

Online Edition

The Abingdon Preaching Annual 2022 **online edition is available by subscription at www.ministrymatters.com.**

Abingdon Press is pleased to make available an online edition of *The Abingdon Preaching Annual 2022* as part of our Ministry Matters online community and resources.

Subscribers to our online edition will also have access to preaching content from prior years.

Visit www.ministrymatters.com and click on SUBSCRIBE NOW. From that menu, select "Abingdon Preaching Annual" and follow the prompt to set up an account.

If you have logged into an existing Ministry Matters account, you can subscribe to any of our online resources by simply clicking on MORE SUBSCRIPTIONS and following the prompts.

Please note, your subscription to *The Abingdon Preaching Annual* will be renewed automatically, unless you contact MinistryMatters.com to request a change.